The
Ministry Playbook

# The
# Ministry Playbook

*Strategic Planning for Effective Churches*

## Henry Klopp

Baker Books
A Division of Baker Book House Co
Grand Rapids, Michigan 49516

© 2002 by Henry Klopp

Published by Baker Books
a division of Baker Book House Company
P.O. Box 6287, Grand Rapids, MI 49516-6287

Printed in the United States of America

**Library of Congress Cataloging-in-Publication Data**

Klopp, Henry.
    The ministry playbook : strategic planning for effective churches / Henry Klopp.
        p.    cm.
    Includes bibliographical references.
    ISBN 0-8010-9149-7 (pbk.)
    1. Church management.  I. Title.
    BV652 .K57 2002
    254—dc21
                                                        2002008642

For current information about all releases from Baker Book House, visit our web site:
http://www.bakerbooks.com

# Contents

# Acknowledgments

As I was putting together this book I was forced to reminisce about my life as a Christian and all the people who taught and mentored me along the way. I truly have been blessed in my time as a Christian. I have had the opportunity to be around some phenomenal Christian leaders who were willing to help train and equip me for ministry.

There were five men that significantly influenced me during my training years. Dr. Donald McGavran of Fuller Seminary and Dr. H. B. London of the California Graduate School of Ministry became personal models for me of what dedication and commitment to Christ can mean in terms of lifelong ministry. I was also fortunate to be trained by Carl George, John Wimber, and Peter Wagner. Each of these men challenged me not only to grow spiritually, but to learn to serve the church in a consulting capacity. My seminary training as well as my consultant training gave me the practical tools necessary to work across denominational lines and minister in a wide variety of settings.

During my years as a pastor, I learned a great deal about the local church, particularly about churches that were really trying to impact their communities in the area of evangelism. My years working with pastors Doug Murren and Mike Meeks at Eastside Foursquare Church in Kirkland, Washington, were invaluable in helping me understand the real issues pastors face every day. I treasure my friendship with both of these men today.

I worked together with several mentors and friends in developing consulting services for churches. The first was the Church Consultants Group where I worked with Jon Huegli, Dan Reeves, Gary Reinecke, and Craig VanGelder. The second was Nehemiah Ministries where I worked with Doug Anderson and Kent Myers. I am deeply indebted to each of them as together we shaped many of the ideas that appear in this book.

I was blessed to work with a number of outstanding pastors and churches during my years as a consultant. Each pastor and church was very unique and helped me to understand the rich diversity we can have in local church ministry. I would love to mention them all, as I was influenced and shaped by each of them. Because of space constraints, let me mention a few, who became not only clients but friends and mentors: Pastor Paul Berube, Grace Fellowship Church, Nashua, New Hampshire; Pastor Craig Bishop, Branch Community Church, Harleysville, Pennsylvania; Pastor Brent Cantelon, Christian Life Assembly, Langley, British Columbia; Pastor Tom Ellsworth, Sherwood Oaks Christian Church, Bloomington, Indiana; Reverend Michael W. Foss, Prince of Peace Lutheran Church ELCA, Burnsville, Minnesota; Pastor John Piper, Bethlehem Baptist Church BGC, Minneapolis, Minnesota; Pastor Steve Sjogren, Cincinnati Vineyard Church, Cincinnati, Ohio; Pastor Mark Slomka, Mount Soledad Presbyterian Church, La Jolla, California; Pastor John Wagner, Christ the Rock Community Church, Ft. Lauderdale, Florida; and Rector John Yates, The Falls Church Episcopal, Falls Church, Virginia.

In the International Graduate School of Ministry we have a board of directors who are not only good friends, but also very creative minds who have helped shape the initial direction of the school. Together we have wrestled with how to make practical concepts and principles such as those found in this book available to more pastors and leaders. A huge thanks to Larry Abbott, David Curry, Lance Klopp, Mike McCorkle, Kim Wilson, and Joe Woodruff. Their commitment first to Christ and then to IGSM and pastoral training has been inspiring.

I also have three personal friends who have had a great influence on my life. The first is Larry Shelton who served with me in pastoral ministry and has served several seminaries as a teacher, scholar, and leader. The second is Pastor Lee Bennett of Northwest Community Church. I have benefited very much from his wisdom and personal friendship. The third is my present pastor, Greg Wingard, of Redwood Hills Community Church. It has truly been exciting for my wife and me to be involved in an exciting church plant that is reaching many unchurched people in their twenties and thirties. Greg is a wonderful communicator and leader, and Bev and I treasure his friendship.

Last but not least is my wife Bev. She not only helped lead me to Christ, but constantly inspires me by demonstrating what a life totally committed to Christ can accomplish. She started her own ministry, Gateway Ministries International, in 1988 and has been involved in training, equipping, intercession, spiritual warfare, and evangelism around the world. Because we were married for twelve years before we became Christians, and no one in either of our families was Christian, we have grown and learned together how to submit our lives and our marriage to Christ. Today we see the fruit of those years in the members of our families who have come to Christ including our own son and daughter, Lance and Raundi, as well as our grandchildren. God is truly amazing.

# Introduction

Can the data be any more clear and compelling? Fewer than 1 out of 10 non-Christians stated that the Protestant church in America is very sensitive to their needs. For three-quarters of the people groups studied non-Christians were less than half as convinced that the Protestant churches are very sensitive to the needs of people in those groups. Given these perceptions, how attractive can the Church be to these non-believers?[1]

George Barna

For the last sixteen years I've been consulting with churches across the country. In that time I've observed the church from a number of perspectives, including multiple denominations and a variety of locations (rural, suburban, and urban). I've tried to keep up with popular trends within the church by reading relevant books and publications. In addition, I've visited a number of churches that are recognized as innovative or exceptionally effective.

Because of my work and research, I'm often asked, "What are you seeing?" "What are the trends?" "What are your impressions of how the church is doing?" "What is the overall picture?" While it can be dangerous to generalize, especially about the church, I have learned some things from working almost every day with different churches. I've noticed things that occur over and over, regardless of geography, denomination, or location.

For some aspects of church life, the picture is clear, easy to describe, and relatively easy to understand. For other aspects, the picture is more complicated and more difficult to describe. Hopefully what I have written will contribute to the views of others who are trying to describe the church from their own perspectives.

## Purposes and Assumptions

The purpose of this book is to add fuel to the revitalization of the church in the United States. It is driven by several assumptions that come from my consulting work, as follows:

- The church in the United States is facing increasing challenges from both inside and outside. Many churches are unaware of, or ignoring, these challenges.
- The typical church culture is not strong enough, nor adaptable enough to meet today's ministry needs.
- Most churches are unaware of the difficulty of change and are using inappropriate change strategies.
- Many churches have an unrealistic picture of who they are and how they are doing.
- Few churches have a compelling vision for their future. Most churches are trying to do too much with too few resources, both in terms of volunteers and finances.
- Few churches have clearly defined plans for ministry including clear standards for measuring progress.
- The organizational design of most churches is at best limiting its effectiveness. Churches have too much micromanagement and not enough players on the playing field.
- Few churches have done the necessary financial and facility planning that will be necessary for maximum effectiveness in the future. The result is crisis planning and funding, which

means carrying more debt than necessary and not having the facilities when they are needed.

- Any church that has the desire and commitment can engage in strategic planning that will increase its health and effectiveness.
- Unless churches in the U.S. become more focused, intentional, and proactive, they will become increasingly irrelevant in today's world.

This book will provide not only the foundation for ministry planning, but also a detailed step-by-step outline that any church can use to develop its own unique game plan. As we move forward, let's remember the words of Rick Warren, founder of the fastest-growing Baptist church in American history: "Our job as church leaders, like experienced surfers, is to recognize a wave of God's Spirit and ride it. It is not our responsibility to make waves but to recognize how God is working in the world and join him in the endeavor. . . . The task of church leadership is to discover and remove growth-restricting diseases and barriers so that natural, normal growth can occur."[2]

## Personal Background

First, let me give you some background information about me to help you understand the perspective from which I write. Relative to the lives of most Christians, my background is a bit unusual. When my wife and I came to the Lord in 1974 and 1975, no one in our immediate or extended family was Christian. During the first twelve years of our marriage, we were never invited to a church or a Bible study, and no one ever attempted to share the gospel with us. We attended church only twice during this time.

Obviously, the church did not have a great effect on our lives. However, through a series of wonderful events we both did become Christians. Interestingly, both of our conversions took place outside the church. We both prayed to receive Christ by ourselves, and very few people played a significant part in our conversions. As is often the case in families today, my wife became a

Christian first and I followed some time later as a result of her prayers and those of several of her Christian friends.

Judging from our conversion story, you might think we were living in Siberia or that we were hardcore atheists or agnostics who were resisting God and the church with all of our strength. Neither speculation is true. We lived in a suburb of Seattle, Washington, and were very involved in community activities, as well as the activities of our children. I was teaching and coaching in a public high school and attempting, like most others, to make sense of my world.

The point of my testimony is that as far as Bev and I were concerned, the church was a nonentity. It did not reach out to us in any way or through anyone. We did not seek the church because it did not seem relevant to our needs. God bridged the gap, however, and we will be forever grateful for that.

I have often wondered why no one took the time to reach out to us. We had some friends who were Christians, but they kept their faith to themselves and never tried to involve us in any way. When I asked them why, they said they thought we might be offended, we didn't seem like the type, or they just didn't know how.

I'm convinced our experience is much more common in the U.S. today than most Christians would like to admit. While other people may not be as unchurched as we were, it is amazing how blind the average congregation is to those in its community who are outside the body of Christ. It's as if non-Christians don't exist. As my wife and I have reached out to all kinds of people since our conversions, we have found very few who were antagonistic toward the gospel message or us. Certainly we have had to learn how to share more sensitively than we did in the beginning (when we had more zeal than sense), but we see a spiritual hunger wherever we go and an openness to the Good News of Jesus Christ that the church has to offer.

Over the last twenty years I have experienced the church from the inside as a participant and a pastor, and from the outside as a consultant. I think I understand how the church works as well as the problems it faces. And I continue to believe that there must be significant revitalization of the American church if it is going to have the impact for which it was created.

## Lessons from My Coaching Experience

I have coached on every age level from nine years old to high school in three different sports (football, basketball, and track). Even while I was pastoring, I helped coach football at a local high school. I did this for two reasons. One was to stay on the cutting edge of evangelism. Ninety percent of the athletes did not know Christ, and coaching gave me an excellent opportunity to share Christ and participate in an environment that challenged my life and my beliefs as a Christian. The second is that I love both coaching and young people. Coaching this football team resulted in one of the most powerful experiences of my life. It always amazes me how close athletes get to their coaches. Years later, many of these same athletes come up to me and reminisce about the good old days. I saw the effect a coach can have on the lives of his players. So, when I became a pastor and consultant, I began to ponder what I learned from the coaching profession and how the experience was applicable to my work with churches.

My conclusion was that coaching is a good metaphor for what we are trying to do as leaders in our churches today. Throughout this book you will find applications from coaching that I believe will help us become more effective pastors and church leaders.

## The Role of Paradigms and Paradigm Shifts

A paradigm, in a sense, tells you that there is a game, what the game is, and how to play it successfully. The idea of a game is a very appropriate metaphor for paradigms because it reflects the need for borders and directions on how to perform correctly. A paradigm tells you how to play the game according to the rules. A paradigm shift, then, is a change to a new game, a new set of rules. . . . It is my belief that changes in paradigms are behind much of society's turbulence during the last thirty years. We had sets of rules we knew well, then someone changed the rules. We understood the old boundaries, then we had to learn new boundaries. And those changes dramatically upset our world.[3]

Joel Barker

Initially popularized by Joel Barker in his books and videos, the terms "paradigm" and "paradigm shift" have become household words. While they have been somewhat overused in the last few years, they help us understand the dynamics of change and particularly why change is so difficult for both people and organizations.

In this sense a paradigm is simply a view of the world and how it operates—a mental filter through which we interpret everything we see. Every person operates from these paradigms, or assumptions, or biases, or whatever you choose to call them. In order to make sense of the world, we develop certain rules about how things are and how things operate. These rules guide us even when we are not aware of them. They operate at both the conscious and subconscious levels of our minds. They help order our lives and categorize many things we see and do.

To the degree that our paradigms are accurate pictures of the world of today, as well as the world of tomorrow, they help us to make sense of what is going on around us. However, when we have faulty paradigms, or paradigms that are no longer accurate, they prevent us from seeing reality and from making the changes necessary to deal successfully with a changing environment.

In working with churches as a consultant, it is important for me to try to understand what the paradigms are for people who attend the church, rather than to impose my own. I need to understand how they think, how they view the world, and particularly how they view ministry. Often I find their fundamental beliefs significantly different from mine and it usually surprises me.

### Personal Paradigms

Although everyone would like to believe he or she is objective, most people realize their background experiences color the way they see things. I realize that as a result of my personal background and spiritual heritage, my paradigm of the church has certain distinct features:

- I view the church, even today, more through the eyes of an unchurched person than as a churched person. I easily see the unintended barriers and roadblocks most churches put up to unchurched people. I understand the frustration that many unchurched people feel when they begin to explore the option of a relationship with Christ. I find developing relationships with non-Christians an exciting and rewarding challenge, and therefore I probably spend as much time with non-Christians as I do with Christians.

- I view the church with a specific passion for outreach. Both churches in which I served focused aggressively on reaching unchurched people, and this is the model in which I was raised. It fits well with my own background, so it is comfortable for me. Although I understand there are other commands besides the Great Commission in Scripture, I have difficulty understanding how churches think they are having an impact for God's kingdom without evangelism.

- I view churches as agents of change in their communities. The role of the church is not just to exist, but to make a significant difference in its area of local ministry. I don't see the church as a fortress, protecting itself from the world, but as a force going forth to transform its world. I see Sunday as important, but the real battlegrounds occur Monday through Saturday.

- I view the church as adaptable and flexible; the church can contextualize its ministry to every cultural setting. I am excited about the many different models of ministry I see, and feel no compulsion to get back to the good old days or to define a single biblical or New Testament model for church life. I view change as a positive and energizing facet of church life.

- I view the church as a body of believers whose primary agenda is to lead lives that honor Jesus Christ, not to debate or fight over nonessential issues such as how many hymns to sing on a Sunday morning. I am comfortable with a variety of worship and ministry styles and find this variety encouraging to my faith rather than threatening to it.

- I do not believe the primary purpose of the church staff is to meet people's needs. The staff will never be able to meet all the needs of its members. Instead, I see the church as a place where laypeople should be challenged and equipped to meet their own needs and the needs of others. I believe it is the responsibility of every Christian, not just the paid staff, to pray, serve, give, evangelize, disciple, study, worship, counsel and comfort others, and so on. Christians who are not doing these things on a regular basis are unhealthy spiritually and need to be aware of it.

All of these features of my paradigm seem valid to me. However, it did not take a long time in the consulting field for me to discover that few churches operate from assumptions similar to my own.

### The Vital Role Paradigms Play in the Life of the Church

Christ's Spirit is moving in the world, but the success of this commission depends on His best effort and ours. He told us the what, but depends on us to provide the how . . . God could do it alone, but apparently He won't. This is not too surprising, however, for He has usually chosen to share His purposes with those who believe in Him to share in such a way that He and they share in the successes and failures of the effort. God has chosen us as His co-workers. And it is almost a truism that, having established a relationship with us, He leaves us at liberty to plan and organize our work according to our best judgments.[4]

Alvin Lindgren and Norman Shawchuck

Most of us falsely assume that others view the world through the same lens as we do. However, any of us who have developed close relationships with others soon find out this is not the case. Furthermore, because the church operates from a common set of guidelines (the Bible), churchgoers often assume all churches operate from the same perspective. While it's true that we have some basic doctrinal truths and some guiding principles given to us in Scripture, it is also true that we have a lot to work out for ourselves. The whole issue of contextualization requires us to be continually interacting between biblical principles and the world we live in.

My personal contention is that no institution in America should be more flexible, dynamic, innovative, dramatic, or fulfilling than the church. As we attempt to comprehend the very nature of God, the work of the Holy Spirit, and even the history of the church, we come to the realization that God is indeed flexible, dynamic, innovative, dramatic, and fulfilling. We the church, as his body, should reflect these vital characteristics. The reality, however, is we often don't, and the interesting question is, why? Nothing seems to have fossilized faster than the church. Historically, the church has always needed a major shakeup, reform movement, revival, or even persecution to shake it out of its malaise.

Don't get me wrong. The church will survive. We have that promise from one end of Scripture to the other. However, can and should the church be more vibrant, alive, powerful, and transforming tomorrow than it is today? The answer is a resounding yes. While we can all point to a few churches that show evidence of vitality, most church leaders feel there could and should be more. Many pastors, writers, and speakers have sensed the lack of direction and focus that seems so pervasive in the church across the country. People are asking why this loss of vitality exists and how to develop it. This book will attempt to address these critical issues.

# ONE

# Preparation

## *The Necessity of Proper Planning*

We may be many, but we ain't much.[1]

Vance Havner

African parable—Every morning in Africa, a gazelle wakes up. It knows that is must run faster than the fastest lion or it will be killed. Every morning a lion wakes up. It knows that it must outrun the slowest gazelle or it will starve to death. It doesn't matter whether you are a lion or a gazelle: When the sun comes up you had better be running.[2]

John Maxwell

Suppose you were asked to invest a large amount of money in an existing business. When you receive the prospectus showing the company's past and present performance, you note the following:

- The company has increased its sales for the last few years at the rate of only 3/4 of a percent per year!
- The company has seen its market share drop approximately 10 percent in the last thirty years!
- The company has seen its personnel and facilities costs increase almost 20 percent in the last ten years to consume over 60 percent of all expenses leaving less than 40 percent for all overhead and operational expenses!
- The company has seen its income drop approximately 10 percent in the last ten years!
- The company has seen many of its competitors growing at rapid rates at the same time it has experienced a net decline!
- The company has had to make severe cuts to its international investment because of a lack of resources and is predicting more serious cuts in the next three to five years.

How likely is it that you would want to invest your dollars in this company? Probably not very likely! And yet, this company is a picture of the average church in the United States. Is it any wonder why some people are questioning the effectiveness of churches today?

## Why Planning Is a Critical Issue for the Church Today

What needs to be done to increase the health and effectiveness of the American church today? The source of some of the problems are spiritual issues that will need to be addressed on a case-by-case basis. However, there are other factors that limit the overall effectiveness of our churches.

### *Most Pastors Are Unprepared for Dealing with Organizational and Planning Issues*

A pastor of a large church received a very unusual call. The caller identified himself as a new pastor who had just assumed his position in a small church in the area. It was his first week and his first pastorate. As this new pastor sat staring at his empty desk, an interesting and challenging question came to him. *"What am I supposed to do now?"*

All of his praying and training did not prepare him for how to begin. All of his theology did not tell him what to do. His love of the Lord and his desire to be found faithful did not automatically translate into an action plan for the day or the week. In his frustration, he was reaching out to an experienced pastor for help.

While this may be an extreme example, it is not too far from the truth for a lot of pastors. Many are frustrated and feel ill prepared for the work of ministry. The incidence of clergy stress and burnout is high, and the average career length for ministers is steadily decreasing. Why is the ministry such a difficult profession?

### The Difficulty of Leading a Church in a Post-Christian Era

Today religion does not have the hallowed place in our culture that it once enjoyed. For more people, no religion is now as good a condition as a little religion used to be.[3]

John and Sylvia Ronsvalle

The post-Christian culture is a culture of "many gods" that rejects absolutes. . . . Our culture is not agnostic. It is "ignostic." They are ignorant when it comes to recognition of biblical ideas and Christian language.[4]

Michael Slaughter

Many Christian writers have pointed out that we have entered a *post-Christian* era in the U.S. Basic Christian beliefs, assumptions, and values are no longer held by a majority of the people across the country. In the past, although most Americans were little more than nominal Christians, nevertheless they accepted the basic tenets of Christianity as reasonable and valid. A simple look at our Constitution or Declaration of Independence demonstrates this.

Today, however, while the vast majority of Americans still say they believe in God, their acceptance of fundamental Christian principles is no longer automatic. The values and assumptions of the church are no longer commonplace in our society. This requires a whole new set of rules and assumptions for the local church as it attempts to have an impact on its culture.

- How should the church respond to this changing culture?
- How can the church maintain its core values and yet minister effectively in a post-Christian era?
- What changes will have to take place for the church to remain relevant in the prevailing culture?

### The Difficulty of Leading a Church in an Era of Unprecedented Change

To compound the problem, the church is faced with a world that is changing at an ever increasing pace. The level and degree of change that has taken place in the last twenty years is unparalleled in the history of the world. Everyone is trying to figure out how to deal with this new and changing environment. Old systems and methodologies no longer work. New methods of thinking are required to cope with our new environment.

- What does this mean for the church?
- What are the implications of this changing context for the ministry style and practices of the church?

### The Frustration Most Pastors and Church Leaders Feel in Dealing with the Corporate Aspects of Church Life

. . . The non-profit institutions themselves know that they need management all the more because they do not have a conventional bottom line. They know that they need to learn how to use management as their tool lest they be overwhelmed by it. Indeed, there is a management boom going on among the non-profit institutions, large and small.[5]

Peter Drucker

The role of the practical aspects of running a church are less clear, to the degree that there appears to be a prejudice against practical aspects of ministry at the seminary level . . . the message is, "theology is real, and practical pastoring is not."[6]

John and Sylvia Ronsvalle

Jim Dethmer, former teaching pastor at Willow Creek Community Church in Chicago, has pointed out succinctly that there appear to be three major areas of church life. The first is *community* or relationships. The second is *cause* or what some would call vision. The third is *corporation.* The corporate aspect of church life deals with the necessary organization and planning issues that every church faces.

In Dethmer's estimation, virtually every pastor has a major strength in one of these three areas, a moderate strength in another, and a real weakness in the third. He points out that for most pastors, the weakest area is the corporate side of church life. The second weakest area is that of cause or vision. Many other writers and consultants have come to a similar conclusion as they have studied the American church.

When asked what areas of ministry most frustrate them, pastors will invariably say organizational, administrative issues, or lack of a compelling vision. Why is that?

Few pastors and church leaders have an understanding of the planning and visioning aspects of church life. In most cases their training did not prepare them for dealing with these issues and yet they must face them every day. Most of what they have learned has been the result of on-the-job training and much of that has come too late to help them.

However, we should not be overly critical of training institutions. While it is true that seminaries and Bible colleges could do a better job of preparing pastors for church life, it would be difficult if not impossible to train pastors for all the situations they will face in their ministries. For the most part, training institutions can provide only a theoretical framework, which many of them do very well. Actually, it makes more sense for churches to provide the bulk of practical training for pastors. And because few churches have a clear grasp of their own issues, few are able to pass on the necessary training and skills to seminarians and other church leaders in training.

Churches are both organizations comprised of a number of people and institutions that are intended to stand for something, so it is imperative that pastors and church leaders come to grips with the realities of planning and vision. While it is not necessary for pastors and church leaders to be management or visioning experts, it is necessary for them to understand the fundamental principles and concepts that are relevant to the planning and visioning of their local churches.

When I come in to do consulting work, pastors and church leaders often ask many of the same questions.

- To what degree does our church compare with the national data and trends?
- To what degree is leadership, or lack of leadership, responsible for the health and effectiveness of our church?
- Is it possible to reverse some of the negative trends? If so, how?
- What is a healthy and effective church? What are the real indicators of church health and effectiveness? What is a biblical definition of success? How is the church affected by its geographical and sociological contexts?
- What does it mean to take care of "the flock"? What is the pastor's role and responsibility, particularly as it relates to organizational and planning issues?
- What principles and practices in the organizational and visioning aspects are necessary to ensure health and effectiveness for the local church?

All of these questions are important and demand an answer.

Recently there has been a resurgence of interest in church health, effectiveness, and revitalization. I use the term *effectiveness* because it doesn't carry the theological or secular baggage as do terms such as "missional" or "successful." Effectiveness does not happen automatically but requires both thought and action. It is the product of a lot of hard work on the part of pastors, staff, and church leaders alike as they carry out their God-given responsibilities.

## Some Dark Clouds on the Horizon

After nearly two decades of studying Christian churches in America, I'm convinced that the typical church as we know it today has a rapidly expiring shelf life.[7]

George Barna

The church wouldn't even make a good museum any more. Museums are more fun.[8]

Leonard Sweet

Every day people are straying away from the church and going back to God.[9]

Lenny Bruce

Many researchers who have analyzed various measures of church life and effectiveness in the U.S. have come to the startling conclusion that the American church as we know it is in serious trouble. Multiple sources of information lead to this conclusion. While many churches and church leaders are failing to recognize the trends, those who do the research are starting to sound the alarm.

An example of these trends is a district analysis I did for an evangelical denomination. While the district's church-planting efforts resulted in twelve new churches during a period of ten years, eighteen churches closed during the same timeframe for a net loss of six churches. Unfortunately, this is a common trend, and I'm not talking about the decline of so-called liberal mainline denominations.

The question is whether churches, districts, and denominations are willing to see what's going on and make an effort to reverse the trends.

## Arguments for and against Strategic Planning

It would be unfair to go into the specifics of strategic planning for churches without addressing the criticisms that strategic planning has received from both inside and outside the church. While there is a lot of talk about planning, few churches actually undertake planning with a strategic approach. Even those churches that plan often wonder if they are doing the right thing.

## Arguments against Strategic Planning from Inside the Church

In working with churches for the last fifteen years as a consultant, I've been surprised by the amount of resistance to strategic planning. It comes from all sizes of churches and all theological persuasions. Before starting any serious planning effort in the church, it is important to recognize the bias against planning and to help people understand how strategic planning fits within the framework of Scripture and the ministry of the church.

### ARGUMENT 1: PLANNING IS A SECULAR TOOL

Many fundamentalist evangelical churches see planning, organization, and visioning as *secular* while the ministry of the church is *spiritual*. In fact, many churches make a distinction between the *spiritual* affairs of the church and the *business* affairs. But biblically there is no such distinction between the two. Jesus' use of agrarian parables and illustrations shows the importance of viewing everything we have and everything we do as spiritual.

### ARGUMENT 2: PLANNING ELIMINATES OR REDUCES THE ROLE AND LEADING OF THE HOLY SPIRIT

Wanting to be flexible and open to the leading of the Holy Spirit is not an excuse for failing to plan. Many charismatic and Pentecostal churches see planning as usurping or at least limiting the role of the Holy Spirit. They believe planning connotes manipulation or circumvention of the Holy Spirit's role in the church. I am not proposing a choice between planning or following the Spirit's leading. Obviously we need to look to the Holy Spirit for guidance in all we do, including planning, but the importance of seeking God's leading does not negate our responsibility to plan ahead. Scriptural examples of Holy Spirit-led planning are numerous; I'll refer to some a little later.

### ARGUMENT 3: THE TYRANNY OF THE URGENT

The typical church is an activity trap. Having lost sight of the higher purpose for which it was originated, it now attempts to make up for this loss by an increased range of activities. Too often, activity is confused with effectiveness.[10]

A. Lindgren and N. Shawchuck

Most pastors and church leaders are facing an incredible time crunch. In an effort to meet all the demands of their jobs, many leaders confuse the urgent with the essential. They are like the logger who is so busy he doesn't take time to sharpen his saw. He works hard, but not smart. He works long hours, but gets little done. If you asked most church boards to list their expectations for the senior pastor and to assign time equivalents for each, it would be clear that one person could not meet all their expectations even if he or she could work twenty-four hours a day.

### ARGUMENT 4: LACK OF EXPERTISE ON THE PART OF STAFF AND LAITY

Many churches that attempt to do strategic planning find it overwhelming for their staff and laity. There are many models available, and some of them do depend on a great deal of expertise and training. However, it is not necessary to do that level of planning in the church. We don't need to throw out all planning efforts simply because we don't have the time or expertise to do the kind of planning NASA does.

If the church truly feels it cannot do this type of planning by itself, consultants are available who can help guide the church through the process.

## Arguments against Strategic Planning from Outside the Church

Resistance to strategic planning does not come solely from those in the church. Many people outside the church environment have serious concerns about the usefulness of strategic planning.

### ARGUMENT 1: PLANNING ASSUMES A PREDICTABLE ENVIRONMENT

Formal planning, and the associated forces that encourage it, may discourage the very mental state required to conceive new strategies.[11]

Henry Mintzberg

Because the world is becoming more and more complex, some question the validity of extensive planning. Planning in an unstable environment is much more difficult than in a stable one. However, equally strong is the argument that because of the complexity and instability of today's world, strategic planning is more necessary than ever. Good planning takes into account all possible variables and produces a clear plan demonstrating how best to chart a course during difficult times.

### ARGUMENT 2: PLANNING TENDS TO BE DONE IN ISOLATION WHICH DIMINISHES ITS EFFECTIVENESS

Specialists who are not on the front lines where the action really takes place are often the ones who do the planning. However, information from the front lines is critical to making good decisions. Specialists usually prefer information that is easy to collect and quantify over softer kinds of data (attitudes, beliefs, and opinions), which is really the most important for successful planning. On this basis people argue that planning is futile, but this isn't an argument against planning as much as it is an argument against top-heavy, out-of-touch planning. We shouldn't throw the baby out with the bathwater.

### ARGUMENT 3: PLANNING CANNOT BE FORMALIZED INTO A SYSTEM

Many planning efforts consist of an assembly line of steps that need to be followed rigorously to complete the planning effort. This sort of planning usually comes from an emphasis on analysis at the expense of intuition and higher levels of thinking. Most planning efforts rely too heavily on the former, because people who like to plan tend to be very analytical. Good planning certainly should include a component of analysis, but it also should allow people to "go with their gut" when analysis is unwieldy or unhelpful.

### ARGUMENT 4: PLANNING TAKES TOO LONG

Many planning efforts take so long and are so complex that by the time any actual plans are implemented, they are too late to do any good, or the situation has changed so drastically that they are no longer valid. The kind of planning I will propose in this book is efficient and can be quickly implemented.

## *Arguments for Strategic Planning in Today's Church*

Strategic thinking and behavior are hallmarks of godly leaders. The Bible is filled with examples of leaders going to great lengths to devise strategic responses to their circumstances, involving God in the process through prayer, fasting, and consulting with spiritual scholars or prophets.[12]

George Barna

Careful planning puts you ahead in the long run; hurry and scurry puts you further behind.

Proverbs 21:5 THE MESSAGE

To be prepared is half the victory.

Miguel Cervantes

For all the entrepreneurial approaches many churches demonstrate, Gary McIntosh of the American Society for Church Growth points out that market-savvy approaches to swelling the flocks remain more the exception than the rule. By his estimate, only 20 percent of America's 367,000 congregations actively pursue strategic planning.[13]

Marc Spiegler

What are the most convincing arguments for why a church should consider a strategic planning process?

### ARGUMENT 1: BECAUSE WE ARE STEWARDS

Now it is required that those who have been given a trust must prove faithful.

1 Corinthians. 4:2

We believe that the problem isn't with "strategy," but with the particular notion of strategy that predominates in most companies.[14]

Gary Hamel and C. K. Prahalid

From everyone who has been given much, much will be demanded; and from the one who has been entrusted with much, much more will be asked.

Luke 12:48

The biblical ideas that are equivalent to effectiveness as I am using the term include faithfulness, fruitfulness, and stewardship. Jesus taught these principles over and over in the New Testament (see Matt. 25:14–30; Luke 12:42–48; 16:1–12; and 19:12–27). The basic concept that underlies Jesus' message is that when God entrusts something to us, he expects us to manage it properly to promote fruitfulness. We are held accountable not merely to maintain what we have, but to increase these resources. Therefore it is not enough to say our intentions are good. Faithfulness implies more than intentions, it implies results.

While we are not solely responsible for the outcomes, we are expected to be totally involved and committed to the process. One of the primary teachings regarding biblical stewardship is that to whom much is given, much is required.

### ARGUMENT 2: BECAUSE WE ARE DEALING WITH LIMITED RESOURCES

No one would disagree that if the church had unlimited resources in terms of people, time, and dollars, the need for overall planning would not be as great. We could simply try a lot of things until we discovered what worked. However, research shows that the church has a declining resource base. The net result is that every decision we make tends to make another decision impossible or extremely difficult. Under those conditions, decisions need to be made about where to place the best people, how to use people's time, and how to spend the dollars. A shotgun approach simply will not work. Most churches find that as a result of a good planning effort, they need to do less, rather than more, to increase their effectiveness. It's a matter of priorities.

### ARGUMENT 3: BECAUSE FAILING TO PLAN IS PLANNING TO FAIL

Your system is perfectly designed to produce the result you are getting.[15]

Dallas Willard

The church by its basic design is intended to be focused and intentional. We are not in the business of making a profit or improving the bottom line. We are, however, in the business of bringing people to Christ and helping them to mature into fully devoted followers of him. If we are not focused and intentional, these results are not likely to occur. For example, many churches assume that if they simply teach the principles of Scripture, people will automatically become soul winners. This has proven to be false time and time again. Many churches assume that Christians will automatically become givers or grow into spiritual maturity. This is not true. Only to the extent that churches plan and hold themselves accountable will these things happen.

### ARUGMENT 4: BECAUSE OF THE COMPETING AGENDAS WE FACE

Most Christians think they are objective and do not have major agendas. However, if you ask most pastors and church leaders, they will verify the fact that people do have significant agendas. Particularly today, when we have so many Christians transferring from one church to another, the issue is magnified. The problem is that people assume that their agendas are the same as everyone else's. If the church fails to plan, these agendas begin to compete and can become extremely destructive.

Take the typical budget-setting process. Few budgets are vision based. Instead, they are lobbying efforts that more closely resemble the U.S. Congress than a peaceful meeting of the Lord's faithful. It may be as important for the church to decide what it is *not* going to do as for it to decide what it *is* going to do. An effective planning effort will bring competing agendas to the surface and address them openly and honestly.

### ARGUMENT 5: BECAUSE OF THE NEED TO CLARIFY ASSUMPTIONS

One reason few churches do a serious job of evaluating the success of their ministries is because of a pervasive assumption that evaluation is impossible. The fine-sounding purposes set forth for a ministry are almost immediately discarded once the ministry has begun, and these purposes are seldom brought up again. Only by means of a strategic planning effort can church leaders and laypeople clarify these assumptions and bring them to the surface.

### ARGUMENT 6: BECAUSE IT FORCES CHURCHES TO DEAL WITH THE ISSUE OF CHANGE

As mentioned previously, the church, for whatever reasons, is generally very resistant to change. As you will see later, getting an organization to change when it doesn't want to change is a difficult process. It takes some serious intervention techniques to force the church to look at itself and decide where it is going and why. Certain steps and actions improve the chances of change taking place, and strategic planning is one of the best tools to make this happen.

## Biblical Examples of Planning

### The Apostle Paul

The apostle Paul is an outstanding example of someone who definitely was led by the Holy Spirit, but who also was an outstanding planner and strategist. If you study Paul's missionary strategy in the Book of Acts, you'll see the depth of planning and organization that he used to accomplish his vision.

- *Paul had a definite plan for where he wanted to go and why.* He chose to go to areas where the gospel had not already been preached, and he strategized his itinerary accordingly.
- *Paul never traveled alone.* He always took one or more individuals along with him (e.g., Barnabas and John Mark on his first journey; Silas, Timothy, and Luke on his second journey). His purpose was to mentor, disciple, and train others to fulfill the Great Commission, so that his work could be multiplied.
- *Paul had a strategy for evangelizing cities.* Even though Paul had been commissioned as a messenger to the Gentiles, he always went first to the local synagogues. While he did not shrink from testifying to the Jews assembled in those syna-

gogues, his real target audience was the God-fearing Gentiles who had attached themselves to the synagogue. The reason he did this was to maximize his effectiveness. He could have preached on any corner of town. But instead, he went where he knew he would find people who were most open to the gospel message.

Usually within a short period of time Paul was forced out of these synagogues. He then would begin to meet with the new believers and their network of friends and relatives in one of their homes. These networks became early churches.

- *Paul had a follow-up program.* Paul regularly sent designated helpers to early Christian churches to see how they were doing and to encourage and exhort them in their faith. He also wrote letters to many of the churches giving them instructions and answering their questions.

Notice that while Paul had a definite strategy and specific plan in mind, he was flexible enough to change his plans when prompted by the Holy Spirit, delayed by Satan, or when ministering in a different cultural context. This is the essence of good planning. We must keep our eyes on our mission and vision but adjust our methods and strategies as necessary along the way. Paul's strategy and methodology clearly reflected the unique combination of his call, his training, and his context.

### Nehemiah

Jumping back to the Old Testament, Nehemiah not only grieved over and prayed about the reports he had received about the condition of Jerusalem, he also *planned*. And he continued to demonstrate this affinity for planning as well as his leadership skills when he arrived in Jerusalem to lead the rebuilding of the walls. We can learn several practical lessons from Nehemiah's planning efforts:

- Nehemiah began his planning in prayer.
- Nehemiah organized his own thoughts and plans before presenting them to others. Good leaders lead. They recognize their gifts and calling and accept the responsibilities that

come with them. It may take them some time to come to the point of decision (think of Moses, Gideon, Jeremiah, and Esther), but once they grasp their role, they move forward.

- Nehemiah held firm to his vision despite the inevitable opposition from the outside. He faced severe opposition from powerful people, but he did not shrink from his task.
- Nehemiah held firm to his vision and task despite concerns from within. He listened to the concerns and dealt with them, but he did not let these concerns stop his work.
- Nehemiah kept his focus on what needed to be done and did not allow himself to be distracted. He had to spend his time on the essentials. Regardless of all that was going on around him, he kept doing the things that would accomplish his mission and vision.
- Nehemiah divided the project into manageable pieces that others could understand and accomplish. You can look at the division of labor in chapter 3.

Nehemiah's efforts were not effective because of chance. He had a strategy. He was able to visualize how a massive project could be subdivided into smaller segments. Through the efforts of many people accomplishing these smaller units of the overall job, the walls of Jerusalem were rebuilt in just fifty-two days. Good planners and organizers must be able to see the big picture, but they also need to see how to break it down into bite-sized pieces, so the work does not become overwhelming for those involved.

### Jesus

There was nothing haphazard about His life—no wasted energy, not an idle word. He was on business for God (Luke 2:49). He lived, He died, and He rose again according to schedule. Like a general plotting His course of battle, the Son of God calculated to win. He could not afford to take a chance. Weighing every alternative and variable factor in human experience, He conceived a plan that would not fail.[16]

Robert Coleman

The model of Jesus' own ministry is another example of organization and planning at its best. Jesus was certainly faced with a major dilemma. Knowing that his time on earth would be extremely short, knowing that he would need to leave behind a framework that would take Christianity throughout the world, and knowing the pressures and demands of the people, Jesus had to be very strategic with his time.

Robert Coleman very clearly defined Jesus' plan in his book, *The Master Plan of Evangelism.*

- *Jesus chose to focus and concentrate his ministry on a few.* Although Jesus had a large public teaching ministry, the majority of Jesus' ministry was spent training and equipping his twelve disciples. While the demands on his time were incredible, he made sure he spent the necessary time with those who would carry on his ministry after his ascension.
- *He had a specific training plan.* Jesus followed a very careful training format of

  1. Teaching the disciples the basic principles of ministry through parables, illustrations, and focused teaching
  2. Doing the ministry himself with the disciples watching
  3. Having the disciples do ministry while he coached them
  4. Releasing the disciples to do ministry on their own

Interestingly, most of the training was on the job.

- *Jesus taught the disciples how to evangelize and disciple others.* He showed them that what he was teaching and training them was not for them alone. He expected them to fulfill the Great Commission. While the concept was difficult for many to grasp, we do see the early church spreading the gospel into the entire world.

When you think about it, Jesus' strategy was risky. Leaving the church in the hands of twelve ordinary men could have been a disaster. But it was exactly what Christ had planned. And with the teaching and training Jesus gave them, these disciples proved faithful in advancing the kingdom.

We would do well to learn from Paul, Nehemiah, and Jesus the importance of proper planning as we minister.

God's plan for the world stands up, all his designs are made to last.

Psalm 33:11 THE MESSAGE

Put God in charge of your work, then what you've planned will take place.

Proverbs 16:3 THE MESSAGE

## Introduction to Strategic Planning

While it is not critical what name we use for this process, it is essential that each church have a clearly thought-out game plan for its ministry. While many churches assume this is automatic, it's not. By far the majority of churches do not have such a plan. What passes for a plan is usually a negotiated consensus, based on the power and personal views of the various leaders in the church. Much of what drives this plan is not carefully spelled out, which creates a lot of confusion as the church attempts to carry out its mission and vision.

There is no one right way to do strategic planning. If you read the literature about strategic planning, you'll find many common thoughts but a multiplicity of methods. What follows is a simplified version of the phases involved in strategic planning. This version has been used effectively with churches of all sizes and types. It is somewhat less complex than the methodologies found in other fields, but it is sufficient for most churches. There are six basic phases to the process.

### 1. Discovery Phase

The key questions during the discovery phase are, *"What is our ministry context?" "What are the strengths, needs, opportunities, and challenges of our present ministry?"* and, *"How are we doing at fulfilling our mission?"*

Unless the church thoroughly understands its present condition and its context, it will be unable to make adequate plans for its future. The discovery phase is the equivalent of a doctor's checkup. It establishes the baselines upon which the rest of the strategic planning is built. It establishes where the church is today, which is often referred to as "Point A."

### 2. Pre-Visioning Phase

The key questions during the pre-visioning phase are, *"What is God's plan for our future?"* and, *"What does he want us to look like and be like in the future?"*

This phase is where pastors, church leaders, and congregations spend a lot of time looking into the future, praying and asking God for his wisdom, and trying to capture the key thoughts and ideas that need to be part of the church's future.

### 3. Visioning Phase

The key question during the visioning phase is, *"What is God's clear and compelling picture for our future?"* It's essential that the congregation as well as the leadership of the church have a clear and compelling picture of where they want to be in the future. The clarity of this picture determines to a large degree the accuracy of their plans to get there. This phase takes the input generated in the pre-visioning phase and defines the proposed vision for the church in terms that are as clear as possible. Led by the senior pastor who must initiate the process, this phase establishes where the church is headed, or "Point B."

### 4. Planning Phase

Once we know where we are today as well as where we want to go in the future, the logical questions are, *"How will we get there?"* and, *"How will we know if we are on track?"* During the planning phase, the church defines intermediate targets for where it is going (objectives) and how it will know when it gets there (standards and benchmarks).

The last part of the planning phase addresses the question, *"What strategies are necessary to accomplish our objectives and meet our standards?"* Once the objectives, standards, and strategies are in place, many churches assume the job is done. But the real work has just begun. Turning the paper-and-pencil work into action is a difficult and challenging step. Allocating the necessary resources (time, dollars, and manpower) in the most strategic areas is particularly important if you want to see positive results.

### 5. Resourcing Phase

At the end of the planning phase a typical church will find that it simply does not have the necessary resources to carry out its plans. Therefore, the key questions during the resourcing phase are, *"What are the resources we need in order to carry out our plans, meet our objectives, and fulfill our vision?"* and, *"How are we going to acquire these resources?"* Normally churches need three key resources:

- Prayer
- Volunteer involvement
- Finances

### 6. Implementation Phase

The key questions during this final phase are, *"How well are we accomplishing what we set out to do?"* and, *"What changes do we need to make to continue on course and to fulfill our mission and vision?"* It's important for the church to stop and evaluate progress at regular intervals. Without periodic evaluation, it is impossible to stay on course. As the old saying goes, "You can only expect what you inspect." Adjustments are always necessary along the way because little goes exactly as planned. We must be willing to adjust our methodologies when necessary to fulfill our vision.

## Summary

A wise man thinks ahead; a fool doesn't.
                                    Proverbs 13:16 TLB

We should make plans counting on God to direct us.

Proverbs 16:9 TLB

Any enterprise that is built by wise planning, becomes strong through common sense, and profits wonderfully by keeping abreast of the facts.

Proverbs 24:3–4 TLB

But the noble man makes noble plans, and by noble deeds he stands.

Isaiah 32:8

If you always do what you've always done, then you will always get what you've always gotten.[17]

John Maxwell

Insanity is doing the same thing the same way, but expecting different results.

Anonymous

A church I consulted a while ago was going through a difficult time and had been for at least two years. One of the staff members fell into immorality, and the consequences were incredible. In one year the church lost over three hundred people.

The senior pastor had been at the church for many years but as a result of the problems and the criticism he received, he began to question his future with the church.

The initial meeting of our planning team was particularly interesting. After presenting a basic overview of the process, I took time to answer some questions. The first question was, "If we do not reach consensus as we go through this process, will we be allowed to produce minority reports for distribution to the congregation?" Needless to say, this was not an overly optimistic starting point for discussion. The second question was, "Will this planning team have the right to make decisions and institute policies and procedures without interference or changes from the elder board?" This was obviously an equally pessimistic question, which showed the level of distrust in the church at that time.

I was even more discouraged by a conversation I had with the senior pastor following the meeting. He asked me whether I believed a senior pastor had the right to initiate and lead a vision-seeking strategy for the church, and secondly, if the vision of the senior pastor was not in alignment with a significant number of people in the congregation, should the pastor leave the church or stay and press forward with the vision. I could tell we had a long way to go.

What a contrast it was when eight months later the planning team reached a 100 percent consensus on the pastor-led visioning process, and the elder board wholeheartedly endorsed the work of the planning team! Comments from members of the planning team included the following:

> I've never been as excited about anything as much as I am about what we are doing. I really feel we are listening to God and moving ahead together in unity.

> I can't sleep some nights because I am so excited to come to our next meeting and see what God is doing. I lay awake thinking and dreaming about how God wants to use us in the future.

What a turnaround in such a short period of time! Today this church is moving aggressively forward to fulfill its vision. A lot of prayer was instrumental in the change, but I believe the planning process allowed the church to get away from dwelling on the past to gaining its focus on the future. I believe God has the same kinds of dreams and plans for every church as he did for this one.

Planning is not an option; it is a basic biblical principle. In the New Testament Jesus used a parable to teach the importance of proper planning.

> "Suppose one of you wants to build a tower. Will he not first sit down and estimate the cost to see if he has enough money to complete it? For if he lays the foundation and is not able to finish it, everyone who sees it will ridicule him, saying, 'This fellow began to build and was not able to finish.'
>
> "Or suppose a king is about to go to war against another king. Will he not first sit down and consider whether he is able with ten thousand men to oppose the one coming against him with twenty thousand? If he is not able, he will send a delegation while the other is still a long way off and will ask for terms of peace."
>
> Luke 14:28–32

Churches in the United States are being forced to take a hard look at what they are doing and why. Much of the push and incentive comes from a decrease in resources. In the long run this may turn out to be a blessing, as it is requiring churches to think through their ministries much more carefully.

Paul put it this way:

> Do you not know that in a race all the runners run, but only one gets the prize? Run in such a way as to get the prize. Everyone who competes in the games goes into strict training. They do it to get a crown that will not last; but we do it to get a crown that will last forever. Therefore I do not run like a man running aimlessly; I do not fight like a man beating the air.
>
> 1 Corinthians 9:24–26

## Questions for Reflection

1. Generally, what is the strongest area for the senior pastor: cause, community, or corporation? What is the weakest?
2. How open are members of the leadership team in your church (staff, elected leaders, and key church leaders) toward strategic planning?
3. How would you characterize the planning efforts of your church over the last few years?
4. In the planning that has taken place, which phases (discovery, pre-visioning, visioning, planning, resourcing, or implementation) have been overlooked or executed poorly? Which ones have been executed well?
5. In the planning that has taken place, did your planning team proceed through the phases in the right sequence? If not, how important do you think it is to follow the sequence presented in this chapter?

# TWO

# The Playing Field

## Challenges Facing the Church

 Challenges from Outside the Church
 Challenges from Inside the Church
 Summary

Before addressing issues specifically related to planning, we need to understand the full extent of the challenges facing the United States church today.

The church must address two distinct types of challenges. The first set comes from outside the church and consists of societal changes that are affecting all institutions, including the church. The second set deals with challenges that have come from inside the church over the last twenty to thirty years.

## Challenges from Outside the Church

We cannot ignore the influence that society has on the church. The environment in which the church operates is bound to have an effect on the life and vitality of the church. As society changes,

45

it can make the ministry of the church easier or more difficult. For the church in the United States, the period from 1960 to the present has been an increasingly difficult environment.

### Decline in Public Perception of the Church

Americans often consider religion important in their own lives and relevant to the pressing problems of the day, but even many of the devout now feel that its influence on their country is declining. Currently, only about one person in four (27 percent) sees a rise in the influence of religion on American life. Disagreeing are 63 percent who feel religion's sway is declining . . . This is the lowest level of influence since the period of 1969–1970.[1]

Princeton Religious Research Center

A 1993 measurement of eight key religious beliefs and practices of the American public showed the lowest point ever recorded by the Princeton Religious Research Center Index. The PRRC considered factors such as belief in God, membership in a church or synagogue, confidence in clergy, and the importance of religion to provide an overall picture of the state of religion in America. A perfect score of 1,000 would indicate that every person in the country was committed to God and the church. A look at the PRRC Index for the past fifty years shows the public perception of the church has been in serious decline since the 1960s and shows only slight improvement in the last few years.

**Princeton Religion Index[2]**

| Year | Score |
|------|-------|
| 2000 | 673 |
| 1999 | 672 |
| 1993 | 650 |
| 1992 | 653 |
| 1983 | 660 |
| 1982 | 672 |
| 1973 | 680 |
| 1972 | 690 |
| 1963 | 740 |
| 1962 | 738 |
| 1953 | 760 |
| 1952 | 748 |
| 1942 | 731 |

## Isolation from One Another

One Gallup poll reported that four in ten Americans admit to frequent feelings of "intense loneliness."[3]

*Newsweek*

The plain fact is that for most modern people, community is either a rare experience or a distant, even mocking, ideal.[4]

Os Guinness

Although largely unnoticed, a number of indicators show people are becoming more and more isolated from one another in our society. Families no longer live in close proximity. Extended families living together are a rarity. The result is that people are more isolated from one another than they used to be. This is particularly true with urban and suburban living. If and when people do develop relationships, they often have little to do with where people live or family ties. Add to that the constant moving that people do from one place to another, and it is not surprising that one survey revealed seven out of every ten people do not know their neighbors.

This increasing individualism has had a significant effect on churches and their ministries. While there are many examples of certain ethnic or socioeconomic groups congregating together in this or that section of town, research indicates individuals in urban areas are more isolated than ever. The result for churches is that they are basically having to reach these people one by one. Less and less are people coming to church because of the encouragement or invitation of neighbors.

Most people have not developed relationships with their neighbors that are deep enough to attract them to a church service or the gospel message. Many churches try to form small groups based on geography even though no one in the church develops personal relationships this way.

## Segmentation and Fragmentation of Our Culture

The "generation gap" of the sixties and seventies will have nothing on what is to come. And the number of age-related sub-cultures is rising. As one writer notes, "The Boomers had the hippies, folkies, and yippies (politicized hippies). By my count, in emerging generations there are about a dozen major categories of subcultures, each with multiple "tribes."[5]

George Gallup Jr.

American culture is becoming increasingly heterogeneous as we divide ourselves into more and more groups. Some social historians are saying the degree of growing heterogeneity in just a five-year time span is the equivalent of differences that took a generation to occur a century ago.

Businesses must conduct demographic and psychographic research to identify and understand the differences between various groups in order to meet the needs of these groups. Smaller businesses in particular have realized that unless they are able to identify and reach specialized niche markets, they may not survive.

The issue of homogeneous versus heterogeneous churches is a serious one. The debate centers on the issue of whether churches were intended from the beginning to be more homogeneous, being made up of people of similar cultural or demographic backgrounds, or heterogeneous, being made up of people of multiple cultural or demographic backgrounds. Many contend churches that do not aggressively pursue the heterogeneous model are not being true to the gospel. However, it appears from early church history that homogeneous churches were the norm. In Jerusalem, for example, evidently there was a split between Hebrew- or Aramaic-speaking Jewish Christians and Greek-speaking Jewish Christians. We also see the existence of separate Jewish Christian congregations and Gentile Christian congregations. While everyone recognized they were indeed one church, churches developed along homogeneous lines.

The debate began in earnest during the early days of the Church Growth Movement, and the debate continues. The reality is that when we study where people live and where they attend church, demographics play a significant role. Churches that ignore this information and fail to address the implications are making a serious mistake.

The typical model of church life is still based on rural models of several generations ago. The false assumption of these models is that all churches are basically the same.

For churches, at least five different demographic types are based on geography. These include rural churches, suburban churches, urban churches, inner-city churches, and ethnic churches. Each of these requires somewhat a distinctive model of ministry. Any effort to impose a single model of church life on all these settings is doomed to failure. Yet, most churches continue to operate as if demographic types did not exist. For churches to minister as effectively as possible, they should grasp additional demographic factors, but as a minimum they need to understand the differences in these demographic contexts.

### Diversity of Family Forms

In 1958, the number of homes in America where the husband was the "breadwinner," the wife the "homemaker" and "child-rearer" was 72 percent. In 1990 it was 7 percent. Two incomes are now almost an economic necessity.[6]

Leonard Sweet

Since 1970, living alone has grown more common. By 2010, more than one in four households will be single-person homes.[7]

*Newsweek*

The traditional concept of family is rapidly disappearing. In most communities, particularly in urban settings, there are more single people than married people. The old-fashioned "Leave It to Beaver" family of mom, dad, and two kids represents less than 25 percent of the population. Society is now composed of a number of different kinds of family units that include fractured families, singles, blended families, and on and on.

Yet most churches have continued to minister primarily to the traditional family culture. Most pastors, if they examined their sermons and particularly their illustrations, would find almost a complete absence of awareness of other family types. The result is when people from these other types of families come to church, they feel out of place.

For most churches, the focus is on ministering to couples who have been married once and have children at home. While this used to be the dominant group in most communities, it isn't anymore. In fact, that type of family arrangement represents less than

25 percent of the total population for most areas. Thus, the church is unintentionally strategizing its ministry to ignore 75 percent of the population.

### Disparity of Wealth

The rich are getting richer and the poor are getting poorer. The middle class is no longer growing as it was, except in a few areas and among a few demographic groups. The ability to move from the poverty level to middle class has become increasingly difficult. Wealth is primarily in the hands of those fifty-five and older who represent Truman Generation values. While this group of people represents only 26 percent of the population, they own 80 percent of all the money in banks and savings and loan associations. They hold 77 percent of the nation's financial assets, and they buy 48 percent of all luxury cars.[8] As many of them move into retirement and face fixed incomes, there are likely to be major changes in the way non-profit organizations are funded.

A study of most types of Christian enterprises—Christian radio and TV, parachurch ministries, churches, and others—shows that most of these organizations are funded primarily by the over-fifty-five crowd. At this point it is unclear whether baby boomers or baby busters will pick up the baton when the older group does not have the resources to give. Churches attempting to reach boomers and busters, particularly unchurched boomers and busters, are already facing economic realities that are significantly different from those of preceding generations.

### Polarization over Moral, Social, and Political Issues

Leaders will increasingly be forced to take firm positions on matters they would rather not address. As those positions are taken, they and their organizations will pass the litmus test of acceptability for some and alienate and disenfranchise others. It will be increasingly difficult to keep many churches and para-church organizations mobilized by purpose and loyalty to Jesus Christ.[9]

Leith Anderson

Our society is more deeply divided than ever over moral and political issues. While many people try to explain why, the fact is that it is getting more and more difficult to gain consensus on virtually any social or political issue. The result is a growing militancy among many diverse groups, all feeling like their particular points of view are not being represented adequately or fairly in the society at large.

This polarization has definitely affected the church and its followers. The level of Christian political activism has increased dramatically in the last decade. While many see it as a much-needed and overdue response on the part of the church, it also has created a serious division of opinion between Christians and between the churched and unchurched. The view of the average unchurched person is that in order to be a Christian, you must be a right-wing, Republican, radical Christian activist.

Many congregation members are no longer asking whether or not their church should be involved in politics, they are demanding it. Where a church stands on certain political issues has become more important in many cases than where it stands on theological issues. The result of all this has been increasing pressure on pastors and churches to clarify their political stances. This is a very unfamiliar arena for most pastors and few are faring well.

### Differences in Learning Styles

Perhaps the most important impact of television was that it replaced the word with the image: Henceforth the dominant medium would be the fleeting, discontinuous flow of electromagnetic pictures. Instancy and intimacy would be the distinguishing features of this new medium; seeing, not reading, would become the basis for believing. The implications were staggering, far beyond anything we have yet grasped. And once again boomers could claim a first: the first generation to experience what amounts to a major transformation in mode of communication.[10]

Wade Clark Roof

Americans revere the Bible—but, by and large, they don't read it. And because they don't read it, they have become a nation of biblical illiterates.[11]

George Barna

Two major changes have taken place in the learning styles of people during the last generation. According to a study by the United States Department of Education, 54 percent of American adults are functionally or marginally illiterate. Almost half of all adults do not read one book during a typical year.[12]

This change in learning style is radically affecting churches. For example, half of today's adults cannot read or write at an eighth-grade level.[13] However, even the New International Version of the Bible is written at a level higher than that. This is one of the reasons why churches are failing to get people to read the Bible more, especially men.

Another major change is that learning is no longer viewed as a series of sequential events that take place only in the early years of our life. Learning is no longer a stage of life, but a lifelong process for most people. Again, the educational systems are struggling with trying to develop lifelong learners rather than just depositing a bunch of basic information into students' heads. People at all ages and all stages of life are getting involved in the learning process. And the demand for variety and quality of learning opportunities is increasing consistently.

A look at the typical church shows an education and training philosophy that is mired in the thinking of a generation ago. Very few churches are developing lifelong learners who can study the Bible for themselves and determine their own application. Most church classes are based on sit-and-listen rather than interactive styles of learning, relying heavily on reading and sequential curriculum. A simple walk-through of a typical children's Sunday school class along with a look at the curriculum reveals an approach to learning that is considerably out of date.

### Dependence on Networking Rather Than Institutions

We network. We initiate loose connections with people and groups on the basis of some common denominator. Networks are voluntary associations. As long as the network meets our needs, we continue the association, knowing that we are free to leave at any time. . . . People are choosing churches not denominations. They view local churches more as networks than formal organization.[14]

Leith Anderson

No matter how you measure it, the last three decades have seen a sharp decline in trust and belief in institutions. This includes schools, government, corporations, and churches. People prefer to network or to develop temporary relationships with people who have common interests, ideas, or needs. These are purely voluntary associations. People feel free to leave these relationships at any time, thus there are no long-term commitments required. While people still recognize institutions as a necessity, the loyalty of people to those institutions is minimal.

Few churches and denominations have understood the significance of this change. But economic realities are starting to drive the point home. Most people who join churches have little loyalty to the particular denomination to which it belongs. Furthermore, they do not feel obligated to support the denomination financially. The result has been severely declining resources at the denominational level. Most churches are finding it easier to raise funds to send out missionaries from their own congregations than to raise funds to support the denomination's missionaries. Denominational events are usually poorly attended.

Even at the local church level there is evidence of this institutional distrust, particularly among the baby boomers and baby busters. Few see official membership as necessary in the church. They are likely to put the issue this way: "If we give, serve, and attend on a regular basis, doesn't that make us members? Why do we have to attend a particular class, go through a membership ceremony, or get our name on some special list?"

More and more people attend more than one church at a time, or move from one church to another—a reflection of the rise of consumerism, even among churches.

### Transition of Power from the Truman Generation to the Baby Boomers

A 1985 Gallup Poll found that boomers were the least trusting of all age groups toward social and political institutions, even less so than for those younger than themselves. Alienation and estrangement born out of the period continue to express themselves as generalized distrust of government, of major institutions, and of leaders. . . . Compared with other generations, their distrust of institutions simply runs deeper.[15]

Wade Clark Roof

Without a doubt, the greatest societal change in the United States came from the emergence of the baby boomers (born between 1946 and 1964). Their emergence, along with their continuing conflicts with their parents' generation, often referred to as the Truman Generation, have caused a social and cultural shift in the United States that is unprecedented. Conservatism, family togetherness, cold-war ideology, conventional gender roles, anti-Communism sentiment, and confidence in free-enterprise capitalism were all challenged by the events of the 1960s.

One of the major differences facing the church in the United States as compared to the church around the world is the continuing rift between the boomers and the Truman Generation. Historians and sociologists will probably look back at the 1960s as one of the most incredible shifts ever to take place in our society. Those changes and the division between these two generations have continued unabated. While the debate about the differences between the two groups is not as violent or apparent as it was during the 1960s and 1970s, nevertheless it is still having a tremendous impact on our society and our churches.

The worldviews of these two groups are quite different from one another. In the church either group's view of God, the church, evangelism, discipleship, commitment, and so on are also quite different. Examples of topics about which boomers and the Truman Generation have differences include:

- What time you arrive at church
- How you dress
- Why you give
- What type of worship is expected
- Denominational loyalty
- Why you support or do not support world missions

The result of these and other differences is that very few churches are reaching both groups at the same time. These two generations view their differences not merely as differences of opinion but as deep spiritual and theological impasses. While some churches will say they are reaching both groups, if you look at the demographics of the church population, usually you will find that the social attitudes and beliefs are fairly homogenous. For example, more conservative members of the boomer generation attend churches dominated by Truman Generation values. However, generally the two groups do not coexist well in the same congregation. If you don't think these generational differences are serious, listen to the comments from a member of the Truman Generation. This comment represents the thoughts and feelings of a lot of people between the ages of fifty-five and seventy.

> We feel caught between the Builders who built and the Boomers who insist on rebuilding it. I notice among many within my generation an anger and a growing stubbornness. We are becoming blockers. Out of fear that the systems we have faithfully served will pass us by, we have begun digging in our heels and using our skills as processors, stopping forward progress. Ironically, we rode the system the longest and received the most from it. Now we are afraid the ride is over, and we don't know what to do. So we block. Change is the enemy. [16]

Many pastors recognize the attitude mentioned in this quote as dominating the leadership meetings in their churches.

### Cultural and Ethnic Shifts in Our Society

> For centuries, immigration to North America has been slow, individual, and primarily European. Leaders could assume a fundamental homogeneity of race and culture, and assimilate one individual at a time into the church. Now immigration is rapid, collective, and global. Radical diversity typifies every neighborhood, and displaced peoples are finding their place in the community. [17]
>
> William Easum and Thomas Bandy

Few people understand the cultural and ethnic shifts (maybe *earthquakes* is a better term) taking place in our country. The United States has become increasingly multinational. The old melting-pot theory has given way to the stew-pot. Most ethnic groups are choosing to maintain their cultural heritage while at the same time being fully American. This is particularly true of first-generation ethnics but is increasingly true among second- and third-generation ethnics also.

Our public schools and our welfare system are being overrun as they attempt to keep up with the changing ethnic realities. Almost every ethnic group is growing proportionately faster than Anglo-America. The fastest growing group, by far, are Hispanics.

Church leaders and churchgoers are probably the least pre-pared people in the United States for these cultural changes. Most evangelical denominations and churches are primarily Anglos. Few reach out in any significant way to ethnics and even fewer are training ethnics or helping to plant ethnic churches.

If these are the fastest growing segments in our society, why isn't the church responding? Many ethnics would blame our WASP (White Anglo-Saxon Protestant) mentality. Whatever the reason, only recently has the evangelical community begun to recognize the significant work being done among ethnics in our country.

## Challenges from Inside the Church

The church faces a whole set of additional challenges from inside. In many ways these challenges are more threatening than those coming from the outside, because they are closer to the heart of the institution. The church may be able to ignore or shut out society to some extent, but it cannot ignore what's going on inside its own walls.

### Debate Regarding Contemporary versus Traditional Ministry Styles

Debates over worship style are almost always sociological and per-sonality debates couched in theological terms.[18]

Rick Warren

There are thousands of churches steeped in tradition who want to change but are afraid of the traditionalists. There are traditional-ists who are afraid of the innovators, worrying that absolute core values will be forsaken. There are thousands of churches being polarized over the style of worship services—with no acceptable compromise.[19]

Leith Anderson

Unfortunately, in many churches the terms *contemporary* and *traditional* have become rally cries of warfare. In many cases, the combatants cannot define either term. To some, contemporary means anything they don't like or want.

In one church I worked with, an elder told me with tears in his eyes and anger in his voice that contemporary worship was tearing his church apart. When I asked him for his definition of the term, he replied, "Use of the overhead projector, use of the New International Version of the Bible, and laypeople being allowed to lead the congregation in prayer!"

Pastors are being forced to defend how many or how few hymns they sing versus how many choruses they sing. They have to debate what kind of instrumentation is used, who is allowed to be up front, the volume of the music, and on and on it goes.

Most of the debate centers on worship style. At one time a lot of the issues had to do with whether or not the church was charismatic or non-charismatic. However, that does not seem to be as big an issue today.

The groups that seem particularly upset and concerned about the move toward a more contemporary style are those fifty to sixty-five years old, and those who have been Christians for a number of years. The source of the concerns is difficult to pinpoint and appears to relate to a number of other issues covered in this chapter. But the net effect is a lot of difficult choices for pastors and church leaders.

### *Isolation of the Churched from the Unchurched Community*

The church leaders of Christendom . . . deliberately do not venture among the public, unless it is to represent the institution as its spokesperson. Sharing coffee with complete strangers in a bar, coffee shop, or sports arena is "time off" from their "true" work.[20]

William Easum and Thomas Bandy

Instead of reaching people in their cocoons, the church itself is
cocooning. Instead of making the church as comfortable as the
home, the church is itself constructing fragile fortresses. When the
church goes into a cocoon, there is no telling what sort of crea-
tures will emerge from it.[21]

Leonard Sweet

The charismatic movement, which had a significant impact
on the church, was primarily a shifting of Christians from one
church to another. It did not significantly impact the unchurched
community. Thus, for about the last thirty years, the church has
gradually lost its evangelistic fervor. Most of the growth has been
by transfer growth, not conversion growth. The longer this
remains true, the less the church is in touch with unchurched
people. More and more Christians are sensing the widening gap
between Christians and non-Christians and are retreating to the
safety of their Christian fortresses. These Christians purposely
separate themselves, feeling that if they involve themselves with
non-Christians, they will be compromised in some way. The result
has been a genuine fear and misunderstanding of the unchurched
in most churches.

Most churches who are experiencing growth, if they take a hard
look at that growth, will discover that the large majority is coming from transfer growth rather than conversion growth. In fact,
in the average church only 15 percent of those who are attending
were not active constituents of another church before coming to
their present church. While some of the transfer growth could still
be called conversion growth (if the church they previously attended
did not lead people to a personal commitment to Christ), the fact
is that conversion growth is steadily declining.

### Apathy and Denial

The establishment church is intellectually marginal, a theological
shambles. It has lost the capability to address the intellectual culture of the "p" (postmodern) world. And what is more frightening
of all options, it sees no need to.[22]

Leonard Sweet

Many denominational leaders have refused to admit they have a problem. The milder form of this denial is indifference, but the extreme form is the contention that church decline is a blessing of God.[23]

Peter Wagner

With all of the statistics that are out about the health and effectiveness of churches in the United States, you would think that the average church would be concerned. However, as I have worked with all sizes of churches in most areas of the United States, I have not found this to be the case. In fact, I find a general acceptance of the way things are. Church people either deny or ignore clearly evident problems.

Most pastors and church leaders assume that if they are tired at the end of the day or week, they must have been doing effective ministry. They are generally unwilling to monitor the results of their ministries and assess what the church is really accomplishing. Until there is a significant level of dissatisfaction with the condition of most churches, churches are unlikely to have enough energy or commitment to solve their problems.

### Demands to Meet Personal Needs and Agendas

We are now in a state of hedonism . . . where members think of themselves less as members (What contribution can I make?) than as consumers (What's in it for me?), buying services from the church.[24]

Leonard Sweet

A number of congregations might better be described as coalitions of special interest groups that have gathered out of mutual convenience around a single physical plant.[25]

John and Sylvia Ronsvalle

The pastor as servant is great if he or she is modeling servanthood. But in too many congregations, the pastor is servant and the congregants those served, period. . . . The whining and criticism is unending.[26]

Mike Regele

One of the worst things about the baby boomer generation is its demand that everyone else meet its needs. Many church leaders express this concern about the boomer generation when they try to reach boomers in their communities or disciple them in their churches. However, a similar attitude is prevalent among those older than the boomers. Many of these people are resisting change at every opportunity and evaluating the church on the basis of how it is meeting their needs.

An example of this self-serving attitude is in the area of worship. Many believe that the primary criteria for which type of worship music to use is which type appeals to their own tastes. People not only get upset with changes in the music style, they get angry and bitter.

The same is true for other aspects of church life. Many Christians believe the way to evaluate the health and effectiveness of the church is by figuring out the degree to which the life of the church meets their own individual needs. To those on the outside, this seems like an incredibly narrow way to evaluate and extremely self-centered. Something does not match up between these types of attitudes and the teachings of Scripture.

Unfortunately, too many Christians view the church this way. They do not see themselves as responsible for evangelism, discipling, caring for others, and so on. Those responsibilities, the laypeople think, lie with the pastoral staff. This is typical of the old chaplaincy model of ministry. Unfortunately, many pastors are spending the majority of their time trying to answer these demands, and in the process the rest of their ministries spin out of control.

### Resistance to Change

Since its inception, the Church remains one of the most resistant organizations in the world, when it comes to change. Our stubbornness, which amounts to a "hardening of the heart," is ironic because we follow a God who is continually doing new things.[27]

Michael Slaughter

In a world where everything is changing, and the pace of change is increasing, it is not unusual for people to resist change. People want to find some area of life where they can have stability and predictability.

Because the church is viewed as superseding culture and time, which is partially true, people attempt to create a safe haven that is both stable and predictable. Many have come to the conclusion that they are virtually powerless to influence the direction of the majority of institutions they are forced to deal with in their daily lives. However, churchgoers sense they can have a measure of control over the church because the church is by nature a volunteer institution. While many feel they have lost control over their government, their cities, their jobs, and even their families, they sense an opportunity to create a safe place for themselves in the church.

How can they do this? By resisting change at every opportunity. The degree to which this is conscious or subconscious varies from person to person, but the fact remains that these people tend to view the church as the last vestige of hope in an attempt to control their world. The result is chaos and stagnation in the church.

### *Declining Financial Resources*

Giving patterns in the United States indicate the church is losing market share among its own members. Even denominations that are growing in membership are receiving a smaller portion of their members' incomes.[28]

John and Sylvia Ronsvalle

In most congregations 20% of the people give 50–80% of the budget; there are indications that, in a number of congregations, one-third to one-half give no financial assistance to support their church.[29]

John and Sylvia Ronsvalle

When you study the financial numbers for churches in the United States, it is clear that giving is declining. Giving per capita as it relates to income has declined for eighteen out of the last twenty-two years. Operating budgets for most churches, when inflation is taken into account, are at least 10 percent less than they were ten years ago. And at the same time personnel and building and debt costs are increasing.

The net effect of this decline is churches are having to operate with a budget that is getting smaller and smaller.

Thus, those who are already giving are being asked to give more and more to maintain the present level of ministry. The result for many has been what is termed "compassion fatigue." Compassion fatigue sets in when people think that even if they gave everything they had, it wouldn't make much of a difference. Along with this is a growing frustration on the part of the givers toward the non-givers.

Many churches have to make the difficult choice of what to cut. The first choice of most has been missions. Because this least impacts the immediate ministry of the church, it is usually less objectionable to make cuts in this area. This has resulted in a decline of almost 50 percent in missions giving. The next area of cutback tends to be in either the personnel budget or ministry costs.

The effect a declining budget has on morale cannot be overlooked. Leadership meetings wherein discussion revolves around financial shortfalls and what cuts should be made are very demoralizing for church leaders. This carries over into other areas of church life also. A lack of funds can cause a church to spend more time talking about money on Sunday mornings, which again causes many people to leave and turns off newcomers in particular.

### Fragmented Approach to Ministry

It is often more comfortable for business owners to put out fires on a daily basis than to design their businesses to be less flammable.[30]

Caryn Spain and Ron Wishnoff

Because of the expectation levels of churchgoers, most churches try to provide a wide range of options in every area. While this may be done well in larger churches, it is very difficult for smaller churches. Regardless of size, trying to be all things to all people usually leads to burnout among the volunteers because there are simply more needs than volunteers to fill them. Given the lack of time most people have these days, this is an increasing problem for churches.

If the church does not have a clear picture of itself and what it is trying to accomplish, it tends to take on the agendas of those who speak the loudest in the congregation. Many of these agendas are in competition with one another. The result is fragmentation and lack of focus and intentionality. Not surprisingly, the net effect is a lack of church health and effectiveness.

When churches look beyond themselves for ministry ideas, they almost always look for programs that other churches are using. Yet this strategy has proven to be dangerous at best. The successful transfer of a program from one context to another is bound to be tenuous. Instead of looking for key principles or key questions which would allow churches to formulate their own unique, tailored programs, most churches tend to buy in to copying other programs already in existence. To compound the problem, curriculum designers, whether denominational or from parachurch ministries, continue to develop programs without clarifying what assumptions underlie those programs or what changes could and should be made for various demographic contexts.

As Bob Buford of the Leadership Network has stated, "It's more important we learn the right questions rather than buy into someone else's right answers." If we start with the right questions and answer them for ourselves, taking into account our contextual situation and the unique mission and vision of our church, then we have a chance for success.

This does not mean churches cannot or should not use programs developed outside the local church. But before adopting them, make sure they fit *you* and *your church*. In virtually every case, outside programs will need some revising to fit your unique needs.

## *Dysfunctional Nature of Many Pastors and Churches*

The leadership dilemma of Christendom at the close of the twentieth century is that it is trapped between a polarization of "dictators" and "enablers."[31]

William Easum and Thomas Bandy

If everybody loves you, you're probably not doing anything worthwhile. . . . In studying effective leaders, one of the things I've discovered is that they are willing to be misunderstood and disliked

by others as a result of their unshakable conviction in what they
are doing.[32]

George Barna

We are seeing more and more evidence of dysfunction among
pastors and churches; this comes from two sources.

One is the growing number of dysfunctional people in our culture. In many ways those who become pastors represent the same
trend we are seeing in our society. Many pastors are extremely
codependent in their behavior, which is unhealthy for them and
the churches they serve.

The other source of dysfunction is the growing expectations
placed on pastors. The definition of a pastor, and what they are
supposed to do, has become an issue of debate. Many of the expectations placed on pastors are unrealistic. Pastors are expected to
be visionary leaders, profound pastors, caring chaplains, spiritual giants, and so on. Part of this dilemma comes from the
increase of Christian media. Christian radio, Christian TV, and
high-profile Christian events have exposed the typical church
member to a wide variety of experiences. When these same people view their own church, they tend to compare the level of worship, preaching, training, and equipping to what they have seen,
heard, and experienced from other, multimedia sources. In many
ways this is an unreal and unfair comparison.

### Declining Loyalty to Home Church

For those who will become committed Christians, their commitment will be more to Jesus and less to church.[33]

Leonard Sweet

As a consumer mentality invades the religious domain, "brand loyalty" among churches is disappearing. More often than not, people
are asking what the church has to offer them, without much regard
for what they can invest in the church as a community of believers
called to be one body.[34]

George Barna

No matter how you measure it, the involvement and participation level of people with their churches is declining. The num-

ber one issue on people's minds is time or lack of it, which definitely has had an effect on the church.

People attend church less regularly, as other activities seem to take up their time. Their giving and serving is less regular also. What's the end result for churches? Conveying information to members, scheduling activities, and staffing volunteer positions is a nightmare.

The number of people who attend more than one church is growing. Many of these people view going to church much like going to a movie. This is particularly true for special events. Because most churches advertise these events, it is easy for Christians to know what is going on, when, and where. They go to these events, which take place at different churches in their area, and thus "participate" in several churches at one time. Interestingly, most people who regularly move from one church to another choose not to get significantly involved in giving or serving at any of the churches they attend.

### Low Priority of Prayer

Prayer, both corporate and individual, has become a low priority in churches across the country. This is particularly clear when you look at where prayer fits on the organizational chart of a typical church. Very few churches know where to put prayer, and only a few, even in the case of large churches, have a staff member who is responsible for prayer.

Churches that schedule prayer meetings find few people who are willing to attend on a regular basis. Few people can identify people in their congregation with the gift of intercession. Most people, when asked to rate their prayer life, say it is less than adequate. While we talk a good game about the necessity and priority of prayer, our actions or in this case our inaction speaks louder than our words.

### Failure to Evangelize

Jesus had a market-place theology. He met people where they lived. He walked where they walked. . . . His message didn't play very well in the temple or the academy.[35]

Michael Slaughter

The time for getting people to come to church is over. It is time
now to get people to come to Christ. . . . Replace centripetal evangelism that tries to draw outsiders in with centrifugal evangelism that
drives insiders out.[36]

Leonard Sweet

The typical church has forgotten what evangelism is. That the
average church is reaching such a small portion of the unchurched
in their community is evidence enough. But when you look at the
typical evangelism ministry in most churches, you realize just
how big a problem this is. These ministries are based on confrontational evangelism strategies or on reaching people who are
already coming to the services—I call it "corral strategy."

While research indicates 70 percent of those who become Christians do so by the time they are eighteen years old, most churches'
evangelism strategies are aimed solely at adults.

Our current evangelism strategies worked well when the
unchurched in our communities were still somewhat familiar
with what church is. Thirty years ago, when church-attendance
levels were not significantly higher than today, the average person understood what the church stood for and pretty well knew
what to expect if he or she attended a Sunday service. This is no
longer true, but churches are still behaving as if it is.

Numerous studies have shown that for at least twenty years the
main reason people come to church is because of the personal
invitation of a friend, relative, neighbor, or work associate. In fact,
the figure used to be something like 70 to 80 percent of those who
attend come by way of another's invitation. Today the typical
church assumes that the average person in its congregation is
developing significant relationships with non-Christians and invit-
ing these people regularly to church. This is simply not a valid
assumption. In fact, my latest surveys indicate that only about 50
percent of people are coming because of a personal invitation!
This means the number of people coming to church because of
an invitation has declined 33 percent in the last twenty years. The
number of people who are coming without an invitation is
approaching that of those who come with one!

Needless to say, the gulf between the churched and the
unchurched is widening. Very few churches approach their geo-

graphical area of ministry like a missionary would. Missionaries, or at least good missionaries, try to understand the people they are seeking to reach and create a culturally relevant ministry that incorporates points of contact between the people and the gospel. Contextualized ministry—ministry that has been adapted to the cultural norms of the ministry area—is the exception rather than the norm.

## Lost Definition of a Disciple

While religion is highly popular in America, it is to a large extent superficial; it does not change people's lives to the degree one would expect from the level of professed faith.[37]

George Gallup Jr.

True, you will find few scholars or leaders in Christian circles who deny that we are supposed to make disciples or apprentices to Jesus and teach them to do all things that Jesus said. . . . Jesus' instructions on this matter are, after all, starkly clear. We just don't do what he said. We don't seriously attempt it. And apparently we don't know how to do it.[38]

Dallas Willard

When our nation's four to five hundred thousand clergy address their congregations each week, they face people whose choices contradict their values. "The great disconnect," someone has called it.[39]

George Gallup Jr.

If we look back a generation ago, it is relatively clear that most churches had a somewhat common definition of what a true disciple is. While the criteria tended to be a long list of what people did not do, rather than what they should do, nevertheless there was agreement. Today this is not true.

In an attempt to get away from some of the legalism of the past, the church has lost a clear definition of what a fully devoted follower of Christ should look like. Discipleship strategies in most churches operate on the assumption that if you take a few basic classes, you will become a disciple. This has never proven true. Most churches are depending more and more on the Sunday message as their primary training vehicle for disciple making. It seems obvious that this is a defective plan. Church leaders should not expect learning that is based on a sit-and-soak approach, rather than an interactive one, to produce mature disciples.

Most churches are finding it increasingly difficult to move people from the input side of discipleship to the output side. The majority of Christians are stuck on the input side. They don't know how or why they should move to the output side, and the typical church has no plan to get them there.

Many researchers have pointed out the increasing divergence between what the Bible teaches and what the average Christian believes or how the average Christian lives. Churches are realizing that the discipleship process is much more difficult than it used to be. Many common assumptions have to be challenged and it is taking more and more time to develop mature Christians.

### Focus on Power and Control Rather Than Mission and Vision

While few leaders in the church will admit it, the reasons for most conflict in the church center on the issues of power and control. Change implies someone will get increased power and control and someone else will have less. Therefore, those in charge fight change because they don't want to lose their power and control. Most decision making is done consciously or unconsciously with these two issues as the guiding factors.

Instead of mission and vision, which should be the primary considerations, we allow control and power to dominate. In most leadership meetings discussion on how a particular decision is in alignment with the church's mission and vision is rare. Instead, the discussion centers on how people in the room personally feel about the issue, or who will be affected by the decision and how.

### Failure of Denominational Leadership

Without a clear understanding of the services provided by the denomination, the term "taxes" was sometimes used by pastors and lay congregational leaders alike to describe denominational financial requests.[40]

John and Sylvia Ronsvalle

Most pastors of denominational churches indicate they get very little in the way of assistance or support from their denominational office. Many question the value of the denomination, particularly in light of the resources they send to the national center. Many pastors feel if they kept those resources and used them in their churches, they would accomplish a lot more. Many churches have opted for affiliation in other networks of churches, either officially or unofficially, to get the help and support they need. In fact, we're hearing more and more about the rise of the *post-denominational* church.

### Increasing Levels of Conflict

There is so much anger in the church today. The older generations are angry at the younger for rejecting their life's work. The younger are angry because of the barriers the older have erected to ward off change. Anger is part of the process. But we must call it for what it is—an expression of our fears. It reflects the faces of uncertainty about our world and the mission of the church.[41]

Mike Regele

Consultants who work with churches across the country agree that the level of conflict has increased significantly over the past few years. Whether it be pastoral turnover or just the level of acrimonious debate in a typical meeting, most churches are experiencing a significant increase in conflict situations. Because most churches do not expect this conflict and are unprepared to deal with it, these conflicts have a very negative effect on the church. In many cases the level of dysfunction in church life has gone on for some time and is a familiar pattern but is becoming more apparent to members.

This conflict is consuming more and more of the time and energy of pastors and church leaders. Instead of focusing on the mission and vision of the church, they spend the majority of their time in fire-fighting efforts. In many cases, this effort proves totally ineffective and simply diverts the attention of the congregation from its real mission and vision.

### Difficulty of Adequate Communication

Electronic media is to the "Reformation" of the twenty-first century what Gutenberg's press was to the Reformation of the sixteenth and seventeenth centuries. . . .The effective congregation of the twenty-first century will be part of the Church that makes use of multimedia. The New Reformation will speak the language of the culture and employ the communication technology that shapes the culture.[42]

Michael Slaughter

A study of the communication process in most churches shows we are still dependent on bulletin or pulpit announcements. Both of these communication vehicles are having less and less impact on listeners. Even church members constantly say they don't know what is going on. A recent study on the mail that people receive from church revealed that 85 percent of it is never opened.

If you compare the communication process of a typical church with the way other groups in our society are communicating, churches are generally one to two generations behind. An example is the fact that most communication outside the church is visual, but the typical church is still operating primarily by speaking and writing. Also, the visual quality (graphics, layout, and so on) of the simplest business mailing is usually lacking in church communication pieces.

Similarly, most churches are far behind the rest of society in the area of technical sophistication. Most baby boomers have better sound systems in their homes than the church does in its worship facility. Very few support personnel in churches are computer trained, and few churches have computer systems that are above the elementary level. It is surprising to me the number of churches that do not have answering machines or fax machines. Many of the leaders in the church have these in their homes, offices, and even cars.

Basic modes of technology with which people in the rest of society work every day are unavailable in the church. This not only handicaps the church and keeps it from doing things that would increase its effectiveness, it also tells church workers in loud, clear terms that the church is old fashioned and behind the times.

## Organizational Structure Failure

Churches that are successfully reaching unchurched populations are redefining themselves by eliminating most of the committee-based organizational models. Jesus didn't give his life so people could come to an administrative meeting.[43]

Michael Slaughter

If you study the organizational structure of most churches, it is immediately apparent that church structure is seldom based on mission or vision, but on history and power. Committees that long ago were outdated and ineffective still continue to function. The number of layers in a typical organizational chart reflects a business model of thirty years ago. Very few churches have an organizational structure that will work as the church grows, so it continually has to be changed or adapted.

Change, as we already have noted, is unusually difficult for most churches and normally requires significant congregational input as well as some kind of vote. Thus, many churches are unable to change even though they recognize a real need for re-organization. Key church leaders quickly recognize that they have to work around the system or become political lobbyists in order to get simple things done. This represents a significant waste of time and loss of effectiveness.

## Ignorance of Spiritual Warfare

Many pastors and churches operate as if they were in a spiritual vacuum. When they encounter resistance or conflict, they immediately try to figure out what is wrong and apply their wisdom to solve the problems. Few recognize the reality that Paul talks about in Ephesians; there are real battles taking place in the heavenly realms with the powers of darkness that affect what we are doing here on earth.

Only recently have some pastors and church leaders begun to recognize the real enemy behind many of the problems they face. Rather than go into battle naively, with inadequate weapons, pastors have begun to gather together for serious warfare. These pastors and church leaders now understand that this is not just a *charis-*

*matic* issue. Other churches have chosen to ignore these realities and have been forced to fold as a result.

### Decline in Participation and Serving

The joy that ought to come from serving others in Christ's name is missing because so much of what we do for the church is done out of a spirit of obligation.[44]

Bob Buford

Volunteering time to a church has declined slightly since the onset of the nineties. . . .The decline was more prolific among Protestants (from 35 percent to 27 percent—a 23 percent decline) . . . during that time frame.[45]

George Barna

Ask anyone who has been involved in recruiting volunteers for several years, and they will tell you how difficult it has become to attract and keep volunteers. Not only that, but the term of commitment is also shrinking. While ten years ago it was possible to get most people to make an annual commitment to service in the church, now this is extremely difficult. Churches have to recruit volunteers who work anywhere from one Sunday a month to maybe as long as three months.

Interviews with volunteers indicate that many of them feel overworked and undervalued. When volunteers serve, it is not unusual for them to do so without training, objectives, standards, evaluation, or a mentoring process. We say we want the laity to serve, minister, and exercise their spiritual gifts, but in many cases the experience of the laity proves otherwise. Ministry leaders who work with these volunteers will attest that church constituents are attending less frequently and no-shows are increasing.

Many churches are frustrated in their efforts to get people involved in the life of the church. While there is a lot of talk about empowering the laity and getting the average person involved in ministry, fewer and fewer churches are doing so.

## Summary

We structure our churches and maintain them so as to shield us from God and to protect us from genuine religious experience.[46]

Clyde Reid

In summary, the old-line denominations are losing their market share of the American public, so to speak. The newer denominations, including the Pentecostals, have flattened out.[47]

Peter Wagner

I'm sure the list of challenges could be even longer. You can see that the church in the United States is definitely facing a radically changing context for its ministry. The sheer number of challenges should be an indicator of the difficult job pastors and church leaders face. This doesn't mean the task of being effective is impossible by any means, but effective churches are ones that are not caught off guard by the circumstances they encounter.

The typical church in the United States does not seem to have the adaptive culture necessary to provide effective ministry or to survive in this increasingly competitive and changing ministry environment. Thus, the typical church is facing an increasingly difficult challenge as it tries to minister successfully in its community.

Until the 1960s, there was enough stability in the world at large and the church in particular to allow churches with relatively nonadaptive cultures to survive and prosper. In the 1960s and 1970s the more liberal mainline denominations began to see an exodus of members. Many of the emerging charismatic churches saw significant increases as a result. Now many of these charismatic churches are seeing their own decline.

We have seen a similar situation with the so-called "return" of the baby boomers to church. While several national magazines were writing ten to fifteen years ago about a large return of baby boomers to church, recent research indicates an equally large exodus of those same people.

All the evidence indicates a growing instability in the church and a challenging future. And yet, it's also very important for church leaders to understand that every survey done in the United

States over the last few years that attempts to gauge people's interest in spiritual things indicates that people are still interested in spirituality. In fact, the number of people who say they believe in God and pray has stayed virtually the same for many years. During the previously mentioned period of decline many cult groups (most notably the Mormons) have seen astonishing increases. This suggests most people don't dislike or hate God but are antagonistic toward the church as they know it. Today, at least in the United States, appears to be a pivotal time in the church's history. The obvious question is, *"What is it going to take for the church to reverse the trends and fulfill its God-given mission?"*

## Questions for Reflection

1. What challenges from outside the church are most significantly affecting the health and vitality of your church? What are you doing to navigate or circumvent these challenges?
2. What challenges from within the church are most significantly affecting the health and vitality of your church? What are you doing to navigate or circumvent these challenges?
3. How many of your leaders are aware of these challenges?
4. How many of your long-term members understand the changing context in which the church has to operate?

# THREE

# Team Psychology

## *Understanding How Organizations Work*

Inherent in any desire to be more focused, intentional, and proactive (i.e., to do strategic planning) is the realization that change must take place. The church has often found itself unprepared or unwilling to change, so planning efforts have not always brought about the desired results.

Before a church seriously engages in any planning or change effort, it needs to understand the difficulties it can expect to face and why. Understanding three key areas will help leaders as they lead their churches through change.

- Organizational culture
- Organizational change
- Organizational leadership

## Organizational Culture

> Cultures result from the interaction of temperament and experi-
> ence. Over time, their dictates slip from consciousness into the
> realm of habit: People cling to once-useful beliefs and patterns of
> behavior as if no alternative existed.[1]
>
> Noel Tichy and Stratford Sherman

In order to understand the church and develop a theology of change, it is necessary to discuss organizational culture. At the deeper and less visible level, organizational culture refers to the assumptions and values of a group of people and tends to persist over time even when group membership changes. At this level culture can be extremely difficult to change, in part because group members are often unaware of the values that bind them together as a group.

At the more visible level, organizational culture represents the behavior patterns, style, and practices that veteran members automatically encourage new members to follow.

Although multiple groups exist in every organization, organizational culture usually refers to the values and practices that are shared among all the groups, particularly those within the leadership team.

Organizational cultures can be very stable over time, but they are never static. The introduction of new ideas, principles, or even new people introduces a certain element of change in any organizational culture. Some organizations try particularly hard to train people to understand the organizational culture so it can be maintained.

Organizational culture by itself is neither positive nor negative. It can be either and it can be both. It depends on the situation. Certain kinds of organizational cultures help, while others undermine, long-term effectiveness. Every organization needs to examine its culture to determine what aspects will help it to achieve its long-range mission and vision. Where the culture is dysfunctional or counterproductive, the organization needs to change. It takes specific intervention techniques to accomplish this change. Change will not happen just because someone recognizes the need or talks about it. Genuine change to an existing organizational culture requires long-term deliberate action.

Because of the high degree of pastoral turnover in our churches, most pastors find themselves leading churches with histories that extend long before they arrive. They need to understand the organizational culture before they try to change it. The degree of rigidity in the organizational culture determines to a large degree the opportunity for changing that culture. It is not surprising that most of the fastest growing churches in the country are churches where the senior pastor was the founding pastor. It is much easier to start a church where the desired organizational culture can be fostered from the beginning. Trying to change an existing culture is much more difficult.

Churches in which significant change takes place often suffer significant losses in both numbers and finances before they see revitalization. In many cases the change is so painful for some people, they have to leave the church rather than stay and work it through.

Most pastors and church leaders underestimate the difficulty of changing the existing organizational culture. They assume most churches want to change. It is true that during the interview process for selecting a new pastor, the church leaders are likely to express such a desire. But that is because the nature of the change is uncertain during the interview process. Everyone in the room has a totally different view of what sort of change should or might take place. When new pastors begin to implement any kind of major change, they are usually surprised by the level of resistance from the church.

One of the reasons behind this resistance is that many church members generalize their personal experiences and opinions, assuming that what is of value to them is equally important to others in the church. They forget that their personal experience, while indeed important to them, is not always applicable for the whole church.

## *How Organizational Culture Develops*

Disney requires every single employee—no matter what level or position—to attend new employee orientation (also known as "Disney Traditions") taught by the faculty of Disney University, the company's own internal socialization and training organization. Disney designed the course so that "new members of the Disney

team can be introduced to our traditions, philosophies, organization, and the way we do business."[2]

James Collins and Jerry Porras

People join organizations, particularly volunteer organizations such as the church, that are in basic agreement or alignment with their own values and ideas. People assess in a number of conscious and unconscious ways the organizational
culture and decide to what degree it aligns with their own ideas
and needs.

Most people associate with a church for some time before deciding whether or not they wish to be regular participants or members. During this period of time they are constantly evaluating.
This evaluation centers primarily on two issues:

- *To what degree are other people in the church like themselves?*
  While there is a great deal of debate in the church about the
  concept of demographic homogeneity, the fact is that most
  people prefer to worship and fellowship with people like
  themselves. While some people may be comfortable with a
  diverse demographic, the average person feels a lot more
  comfortable when they are around people they perceive to
  be demographically compatible. The characteristics people
  usually take into account include socioeconomic level, educational level, age, and dress.
- *To what degree does the church meet or satisfy their needs?*
  Visitors assess a church's values on a formal level by reading its literature and studying its theological foundations.
  But they also observe the church on a more informal level
  to discern how the church lives out its faith in word and
  deed. Often churches are unaware of the messages they send
  about what they really value.

Once people decide they want to be part of an organization,
normally the organization has some way of ensuring the new person understands and adopts the organizational culture. The operating styles and values most important to the organization are usually conveyed both officially and unofficially. People learn about
organizational culture from a variety of sources.

### STORY TELLING

These stories, or "ghost stories" as some call them, are power-ful vehicles for letting people know what is important, or what is expected from them. Such stories are not transmitted directly by the organization to its members, but are more often shared from person to person. You can learn a great deal about organizational culture by hearing the stories that make their way throughout an organization.

### THE EXAMPLES OF LEADERS

Whether they want to be or not, leaders are primary examples of the expected thinking and behavior patterns of any orga-nization. Because these leaders are usually quite visible, it is not difficult for people to discern what is or is not of value to them. People in organizations not only look to official pronouncements from these leaders, they also watch them in every type of setting to determine what leaders believe. It is often in these unofficial settings that people pick up their most important signals about the organizational culture. It is particularly frustrating and con-fusing to new people when the words of leaders do not match their actions. When in doubt, most people choose to read the actions of leaders as the most reliable source of information.

### RECOGNITION AND REWARD

By watching who is and who is not recognized and rewarded over a period of time, people learn what is highly valued in a cul-ture. In fact, one way an organization can emphasize its values is by purposely selecting and promoting people who reflect core val-ues of the organization. In many churches most of the elected leaders are male, married, older, and have been long-term mem-bers of the church. This conveys a powerful message to people who do not fit in this category.

### GENERATIONAL HERITAGE

Older members pass on organizational values to younger mem-bers in an official or unofficial mentoring process. Younger folks tend to observe older folks to identify key values and behaviors of the organization. This is probably more true in the church than it is in other types of organizations. Families comprise a larger percentage of church populations than they do of the rest of the population, and in these families both parents and the church convey to the children what the expected values are. While many of these children will go through a period when they ignore or reject these values, most will return to them.

## *Essential Elements of Organizational Culture*

Organizational cultures, like human beings, range from strong and healthy to weak and unhealthy. Healthy and effective organizational cultures have at least three major components.

### ORGANIZATIONAL STRENGTH

The visionary companies more thoroughly indoctrinate employees into a core ideology than the comparison companies, creating cultures so strong that they are almost cult-like around the ideology.[3]

James Collins and Jerry Porras

Organizational strength comes from a defined culture that is well understood by those in the organization. And the behavior of the members and leaders is consistent with this culture.

In the church, organizational strength comes from

- leaders who have communicated to the congregation the church's mission and vision;
- laypeople who have adopted this mission and vision; and
- leaders and laypeople who clearly communicate this mission and vision to the outside world in word and deed.

### STRATEGIC APPROPRIATENESS

A strategically appropriate organizational culture is one that is in alignment with the people it is trying to reach or influence. The better the fit, the better the performance; the poorer the fit, the poorer the performance. To foster a culture that is strategically appropriate, the leaders must fully understand their environment and develop a culture that is consistent with the values of that environment.

In the local church, a strategically appropriate organizational culture would fit the demographic context of the area the church has chosen to reach. While the church is to be transformational, nevertheless it must operate within cultural contexts. Debates over this issue took root in the early church between those with Jewish backgrounds and those with Gentile backgrounds. While the fundamental principles of the Word of God never change, the Bible does allow for a variety of cultural practices and experiences.

### ORGANIZATIONAL ADAPTABILITY

Organizational adaptability means that only cultures that anticipate and adapt to the environment will be healthy and effective over long periods of time. Adaptive culture reaps rewards for taking risks and implementing a proactive approach on both organizational and individual levels. To survive, every organization must be able to adapt to changes in environment.

In the local church, an organizational culture with adaptability is open to and welcomes change. Church programs are secondary to the mission or vision of the church. If a program does not produce the desired results, the church is not afraid to try another one. Mission and vision dictate the organizational structure, not the other way around.

## An Example of Organizational Culture in Action

Perhaps one of the best scriptural examples of effective organizational culture in action is found in Acts 6. Here we see the apostles facing the first major internal problem in the church. The issue was the care of widows, and the friction might have been the result of ideological differences between the Aramaic- and Greek-speaking Christians. The Grecian Jews did not speak Aramaic, the native tongue of Jews living in Israel, while the native Jews spoke primarily Aramaic. In the Jewish world, significant tensions existed between the Grecian Jews and the Aramaic-speaking Jews, and these strains were naturally reflected in the church.

Even though all of these believers came from Jewish backgrounds and Jewish culture, the organizational culture of Jews who came from Greek backgrounds was significantly different than those who were raised in the area around Jerusalem. This created tension and suspicions that carried over into the early Christian church.

Fortunately, the early church leaders recognized the real issues of organizational culture that were at work and addressed them directly.

The solution the apostles presented was to have seven men appointed to supervise the proper care for these widows. Significantly, all seven men had Greek names, implying they were Hellenists.

This solution pleased all the disciples and shows both how influential organizational culture can be as well as how important organizational culture is to an organization's health and effectiveness.

## Organizational Change

> Because society is dynamic, those churches that refuse to change their story will die. The only question is how long it will take.[4]
>
> Leith Anderson

The church should be the most flexible and change-oriented institution known to man. Why? Because it is to be ruled by Christ, not us; because we are called to be directed by the Holy Spirit, not by our own feelings or desires; because from its inception, the church has been designed to reach every culture.

However, the history of the church shows that it has been one of the least flexible institutions known to man. Reform movements have consistently been necessary to get the church back in touch with its mission and mission field. We see this demonstrated at several key points in church history. Perhaps the greatest example of this was the Protestant Reformation led initially by Martin Luther.

If the church is going to be everything it was designed to be, we need to develop and adopt a theology that allows for and adapts to change.

## Why People Resist Change

Change is avalanching upon our heads and most people are grotesquely unprepared to cope with it.[5]

Alvin Toffler

In order to promote an organizational culture that is open to change, we need to understand the basic reasons why people in every organization tend to resist it. Failure to understand these reasons and deal with them in an open way is a recipe for failure.

### THRESHOLD OF AWARENESS IS TOO HIGH

Most people fail to see the necessity of change until it's too late. They are not sensitive enough to their environment to recognize the early signs of trouble, and by the time they do, change is extremely difficult. This has been accurately described as the *boiled frog* phenomenon. If you try to put a frog in a pot of boiling water it will quickly leap out of the water to avoid being burned or scalded. However, if you put the frog in cool water and slowly, but gradually, increase the temperature of the water, the frog will be unaware of the temperature change until it is too late.

### FEAR

Change invokes simultaneous personal feelings of fear and hope, anxiety and relief, pressure and stimulation, threats to self-esteem and challenges to master new situations. The task of transformational leaders is to recognize these mixed feelings, act to help people move from negative to positive emotions, and mobilize the energy needed for individual renewal.[6]

Noel Tichy and Mary Anne Devanna

It is natural for people to value stability over innovation. We tend to prefer the known, even if it has significant problems, rather than risk changing to something that is unknown. While a small percentage of people are actually stimulated and motivated by change, this is not true for the vast majority. Most of us spend a great deal of time trying to keep things around us as stable as possible.

It is particularly interesting to study the development of the early church, keeping in mind the Great Commission given by Jesus. Even though the disciples had heard Jesus give them the command to go into all the world and make disciples, the reality is that this took a long time to sink in. In fact, as we read Acts 8 we discover that only through persecution from outside the church did the gospel spread outside of Jerusalem, and then primarily through others, not the disciples themselves.

### Unwillingness to Suffer Discomfort and Pain

We have made the absence of pain and suffering almost a constitutional right (or in the church, a spiritual right). We resist change because most people realize change, even if it is good, will cause some discomfort. If change is bad, the probability of pain and suffering is high. Because we cannot guarantee change will result in success, and in fact often encounter failure when we try to change, many try to protect themselves by limiting the amount of change in their lives.

Remember that in many cases you're more likely to experience the pain of failure if you don't change than if you do. There is no surefire way to protect ourselves from discomfort and pain. But this much is certain: trying to control one's environment and avoid change is a poor strategy for protecting oneself.

### Enchantment with the Past

Most people yearn for the good old days even if their memories are very selective. They would rather return to what they think is the security of the past. Change means the loss of organizational predictability. People naturally try to return to the predictability of the past. When people would rather behave in ways that are predictable, even if they are self-destructive, we categorize their behavior as dysfunctional. And yet this is the situation in many churches. Given the choice between making changes that would at least allow for the possibility of increased effectiveness, people choose to continue with church structures and strategies that show a continuing decline in effectiveness.

### Unwillingness to Deal with Past Failures

The difference between average people and achieving people is their perception of a response to failure.[7]

John Maxwell

Change implies we are willing to examine our unproductive behaviors and actions and make appropriate modifications, but most people would rather not face their failures.

Willingness to change is a critical step in the life of a disciple. If we believe the biblical idea that we are a people in process, it is essential that we not resist change but embrace it. How can we grow as disciples if we are unwilling to change? One of the greatest things we can do for ourselves and those around us is allow the Holy Spirit as well as the Scriptures to call our lives into question. As we see areas that need change or adjustment (and we all do), to make those changes is to grow spiritually. There is no such thing as a mature disciple who is not willing to change. Understand that fear of the unknown is natural, but this should not stop us from pursuing those changes which God has clearly shown us are in our best interests.

### Avoidance of Feeling Awkward

Most of us will do most anything to avoid looking or feeling awkward. We all can remember times when we were embarrassed because of something we did for the first time, and it was a very unpleasant experience. Yet awkwardness is always part of growing too.

There are many different opinions regarding how long it takes to break an old habit and establish a new one. All agree it takes a considerable amount of time. The first time a person relaxes or fails to monitor his actions carefully, he usually reverts to old behavioral patterns. It is only by repetition and effort that the change becomes a regular part of a person's or institution's behavioral pattern.

## The Process of Organizational Change

Not only must we recognize resistance to change, we must understand the process of change too. If we are going to overcome the natural opposition to change, we must help people accept change by taking them through a carefully planned process of change. In particular, churches need to go through three major stages in the process of change.

## *Recognizing the Need for Change*

If Christianity is going to survive, it must continually reinvent itself, adapting its message to the members of each generation, along with their culture and geographic setting.[8]

Donald Miller

One of the reasons we fail in our efforts to be change agents is that we forget most people will change only when they must. To try and effect change in a church without laying the proper foundation for why change is necessary is to plot disaster. Churches should do at least two things to create a receptivity to change.

### CREATE DISSATISFACTION WITH THE STATUS QUO

But there was method to the mayhem: This was the creative destruction that precedes renewal. It calls for decisive, unilateral action, and a willingness to engage in conflict. This is when a leader must eliminate whatever obstacles stand in the way.[9]

Noel Tichy and Stratford Sherman

Unless people are significantly dissatisfied with the way things are, they will not be motivated to change. How do we create this discomfort? One of the best ways for a church to create dissatisfaction is to analyze how the church is doing compared to how the church should be doing. Usually a very significant gap stands between the two scenarios. The information from the analysis can be used as evidence for the need to change.

Another way to create dissatisfaction is to compare the church with other effective churches in its community or to churches within its own denomination. Often this will take the form of actual trips by members of the leadership team to see what others are doing.

A third way to create a necessary dissatisfaction is to use natural crises that occur in the life of the church. Every church faces crises—inadequate income, key families leaving the church, and so on. Church leaders can often use these crisis events as a positive force to motivate the church to consider change.

### CELEBRATE THE PAST

Pastors and church leaders often miss the crucial step of celebrating the past on their way to incorporating change. Many people, particularly long-term church members, view change as a rejection of the past and therefore resist it. When people can see links with the past and celebrate accomplishments of the past, the change process will go much more smoothly, not to mention more quickly.

I remember working with a church that was considering relocating to another area of the city. The pastors and leaders were convinced of the need to relocate, but several long-term members of the church were not sure. A ninety-three-year-old wife of the first pastor of the church made the difference. She told the congregation the story of how and why the church moved to its present site and talked about the similarities between the circumstances of the previous relocation and those of the one they were facing. After her presentation, 97 percent of the church voted in favor of moving.

## Creating a New Future

> Innovators introduce new ideas into social networks. Those who first accept them are called "early adopters." Others come in as "middle adopters," still others as "late adopters," and those who never accept the innovation are "nonadopters."[10]
>
> Peter Wagner

Once a dissatisfaction with the past has set in, it will be possible to chart a new future. But what does the future look like and how do you get people to buy into the vision? Church leaders must create a picture of the future that is compelling and captivating. They must create in the hearts and minds of a core of the church an excitement about the proposed changes. Leaders should address at least three essentials during this phase.

### CASTING OR RECASTING THE MISSION AND VISION

Much more will be said later about the development or redevelopment of the church's vision. For now let it simply be said that until the leaders, led by the senior pastor, have a clear and compelling picture of the future, little change can take place.

### DEFINING SUCCESS

For a church to stay on target and focused in its ministry, it must define what it is trying to accomplish. This provides accountability for all involved and defines the assumptions, values, and expectations that must take root for the vision to become reality in the life of the church.

Leaders may use a variety of names to describe these measuring tools—objectives, goals, standards, benchmarks, key success indicators, critical success factors, and so on. The key is that these benchmarks are measurable and that they are tracked on a regular basis.

Once the vision is clearly defined, the next step is defining how the church will know if it is accomplishing the vision and how it will assess progress toward that vision.

### CONVINCING THE INNER CORE

It is especially frustrating to visit a church where the leader has God's vision for the church's ministry, but has simply overlooked a crucial step in the process: disseminating the vision so it can be owned and implemented.[11]

George Barna

Before any significant change can be implemented in the congregation, the inner core of the church must own the new vision. Every church has what is referred to in the consulting field as a *dominant coalition*. These are the key opinion makers in the congregation. They may or may not be in the formal leadership structure, but they are essential for the church's successful acceptance of new ideas.

One characteristic of these people is that they do not like to receive key information for the first time in a public setting. To them, this implies you do not trust them or do not value their opinions. The number of people will vary from church to church, but the basic concept remains the same. Until and unless the key decision makers in the congregation support the desired changes, implementation will be impossible.

Most churches assume that in order for significant change to take place, the proposed change must be adopted in advance by the majority of the congregation. This is not true. Even if the decisions need the approval of a congregational vote, if you win the confidence and support of most of the critical leaders in the church, you can begin to institute critical changes that will move you toward the new vision.

## Institutionalizing Change

Once the leadership is convinced of the need for change and is excited about the prospects for change, the job is still not over. The church must now sell the vision to the congregation as a whole, make the changes last, and integrate those changes into a new church culture. To make change a reality requires at least three action steps.

### DEVELOPING EFFECTIVE ACTION PLANS AND STRATEGIES

To turn the new assumptions, values, and vision into a reality, it will be necessary to develop specific action plans and strategies for implementation. People need to see the *flesh* put on the bones, not just concepts and outlines. The more people involved at this point, the greater the chance of success.

Perhaps the most difficult yet crucial part of this process is making sure the new plans match the new vision. Usually people have a difficult time understanding the implications and assumptions underlying the new vision unless they are clearly defined. No action plan or strategy should go forward that has not been measured against the values of the new vision.

### CONVINCING A CRITICAL MASS OF THE CHURCH TO ACCEPT AND EMBRACE THE DESIRED CHANGES

To produce needed change, these leaders . . . communicated their visions and strategies broadly in order to obtain understanding and commitment from a wide range of people. . . . They allowed people to challenge the messages—thereby establishing healthy dialogue to replace static, one-way monologue. . . . They kept their own actions consistent with the communication in order to bolster the message's credibility. . . . They became living embodiments of the new cultures they desired.[12]

John Kotter and James Heskett

Convincing a critical mass to accept the new vision is a more gradual process. Sometimes it is helpful at this point to use outside resources, such as a consultant, to help you walk through the process. Oftentimes it takes the voice of a key outside person affirming the direction of the church leadership to convince people of the validity of the vision. Also, consultants are usually trained to facilitate discussions and help develop implementation plans that will turn the vision into reality. Even if you choose not to use outside resources, develop strategies for the best times and places to share the vision, and share it often. The more people hear it, the more they will understand and begin to buy into it.

### SELECTING, PLACING, APPRAISING, AND REWARDING THE RIGHT PEOPLE

A vision cannot be established in an organization by edict, or by the exercise of power or coercion. It is more an act of persuasion, of creating an enthusiastic and dedicated commitment to a vision because it is right for the times, right for the organization, and right for the people who are working in it.[13]

Warren Bennis and Burt Nanus

One of the best ways to make the vision become reality is to affirm the new direction through the use of recognition and reward. Gradually begin to select, appraise, and reward those who buy into the vision. Let them be examples and leaders in their own right to promote the needed changes. As people see this process begin to take place, they will realize the necessity of making their own choice about where they stand. This should be particularly true of leadership positions. One of the major criteria for the selection of key positions should be the degree of commitment to the vision.

Having a balance of power, a loyal opposition, a devil's advocate, or a set of checks and balances may be fundamental to our democratic heritage, but it can destroy change movements. This is where the typical election process for board or council members can really cause problems. Rarely do people vote for someone on the basis of their ideas or the vision to which they are committed, and yet these may be the most important criteria for election in a church that is trying to implement change. If nothing else, the nominating committee, if there is one, should make an affirmation of the new vision one of the screening criteria.

### An Example of a Failure to Change

The Scriptures give us many examples of people who failed to change, but one that stands out is the people of Israel when Moses tried to lead them out of Egypt.

Moses had been given God's vision for his people. Even though he was a reluctant leader in many ways, Moses tried to convince the people of Israel to accept God's plan for their lives. They finally left Egypt, partly because of the vision Moses had shared but also because of the fear of the Egyptian army. Once they had seen the miracle of the Red Sea, you'd think they would have gotten the message. But we see time and again how they moved from faith to disbelief. They constantly grumbled against Moses and his leadership. Many began to dream about going back to Egypt. What they were forgetting was that in Egypt they had been slaves. Why would anyone want to go back to slavery? This just shows the difficulty of change, and how some people will want to return to the past, even if the past was hurtful.

The final sad chapter in the Exodus story is when Moses sends spies into the Promised Land. The spies see bountiful opportunities in this beautiful land, but ten of them focus on the obstacles involved in taking the new territory and convince the rest of the people the task is impossible. What an unfortunate choice God's people made. God became angry with his people and decided that none of those who were living at that time, with the exception of Joshua and Caleb who had kept their faith in the provision of God, would be allowed to enter the Promised Land. The people of Israel would have to wander in the desert until all of those who had been disobedient died. Then and only then would their children be allowed to fulfill the promises of God.

This passage reminds us of how difficult change is, in our own lives and in the lives of our churches. Change is not easy, but if it is change ordained by God, we need to focus on what he wants for us, not on our own fears and concerns. Otherwise, we will never see the fullness of what God intended for us.

### An Example of a Willingness to Change

The Council of Jerusalem marked a critical point in time for the church (see Acts 15). The church had to decide what rules and regulations it would impose on the new Gentile believers. Many believers with Jewish backgrounds wanted to see the rules and traditions that belonged to their past be part of the requirements for the Gentile believers.

However, under the wise leadership of the Holy Spirit, the apostles decided the Gentile believers did not need to follow Jewish rules and traditions to be fully Christian. This decision laid the foundation for an incredible expansion of the church into the Gentile world.

While this was a difficult transition for most people, including the apostle Peter if you read Paul's accounts, the church was able to adjust to the changing conditions, and great fruitfulness was the result. Had the church been unwilling to make this major change, it probably would have been ineffective among non-Jewish believers.

## Organizational Leadership

The third concept about organizations and institutions that needs to be understood has to do with leadership. Pastoral leadership, particularly in small rural areas, used to mean shepherding a small group of people, most of whom had direct contact with the pastor. Many churches carried this model into the urban environment. But nowadays in urban and suburban settings, the numbers of churchgoers are often too high for pastors to be in contact with everyone on a regular basis. Instead of shepherding everyone more or less individually, or at least family by family, pastors must shift their focus to a small core of leaders who do most of the individual ministering with church members. Many pastors and church leaders have been caught in the transition between the first and the second model.

### Rethinking Leadership Style

They [church leaders] are terrified that they might be perceived to
be too aggressive, too disruptive, or too dictatorial. They cling to
the myth that the less leadership they offer, the more empowered
Christians will be! In fact, the opposite is true.[14]

William Easum and Thomas Bandy

The vast majority of pastors and church leaders, as a result of
their training and the expectations of their congregations, are
using a leadership style that could best be described as *participative* or *supportive*. They see themselves primarily as facilitators
or consensus builders rather than leaders. They see their job as
doing a lot of listening and trying to make sure everyone gets a
hearing. To avoid dominating or being too authoritarian, they
often withhold their personal views or make sure they don't inter-
ject them until everyone else has had a chance to express his or
her own opinion. When they do try to lead, most act as managers
rather than leaders.

Another way of describing the typical leadership style and role
of most pastors is to call it a *chaplaincy* model of ministry. George
Hunter, in his book *How to Reach Secular People*, estimates at
least eight out of ten churches operate out of a chaplaincy model,
which he says is characterized by four basic assumptions:

- Primary ministry takes place inside the church, not outside
  in the world.
- The main object of ministry is believers, not non-believers.
- Ministry is the preserve of the clergy, not the laity.
- The validity of ministry is measured not by redeemed lives
  or changed communities but by vocational satisfactions of
  the clergy.

A study of most organizations would show they are very simply overmanaged and underled. While everyone involved in ministry or service will need to do both leadership and management,
it is the leadership practices that will make the most difference.

Why managing rather than leading is so dominant among pastors and church leaders is hard to say. It appears, however, that

many use this style in an attempt to fulfill what is termed the *servant-leader* model of leadership. While it is true that the biblical definition of a leader includes a willingness to wash disciples' feet and lay down one's life to protect the flock, this is only the servant side of the equation. A second side is equally important—the leadership part. Both are required to be a godly leader. Most pastors and church leaders confuse the concepts of power, control, and authority with leadership and therefore fail to lead. What they need to understand is that leading means assuming the responsibility to initiate.

While most pastors and church leaders would define their servant-leadership style as one modeling the life of Jesus, they fail to understand that while Jesus was willing to serve and give his life for his followers, he also had a plan and a strategy for what he wanted to do with his disciples. His leadership strategy was not to get up every morning, turn to his disciples and say, "I have no idea what we should do today, so what do you think? What would you like to do?" Jesus exemplified perfectly how to be both a servant and a leader. Most pastors and church leaders are trying to lead based on only the first half of the equation.

On the other side of the coin, very few churchgoers know how to be followers. In most churches we have too many captains and not enough crew members.

> You cannot manage men into battle. You manage things; you lead people.[15]
>
> Grace Murray Hopper

> Management is fine as far as it goes, but leadership is the way to win.[16]
>
> Noel Tichy and Stratford Sherman

> There's a big difference between leading and managing. You can manage inventories, but you lead people. You can manage from afar, with a fax machine and a cellular phone, but you better be up close and personal when it comes to leading.[17]
>
> Bill Parcells

## Visionary Leadership

Visionary leadership has three major characteristics—*intentionality, transformation* or *empowerment,* and *accountability.*

- *Intentionality* means we have a direction, a purpose, a reason for moving in a particular direction. We are not just going through the motions, but are seeking to accomplish specific ends. The degree of clarity for our destination may vary, but it is clear we are on a journey or a mission with specific outcomes in mind. Expanding on this point, Noel Tichy, in *Control Your Destiny or Someone Else Will,* writes, "This is leadership that transcends the mere management of what already exists, to create something fundamentally new. The field itself is new, a study not of heroes, but of the ways ordinary people can bring institutions through the convulsions of dramatic change."[18]
- *Transformation* or *empowerment* means a leader accomplishes his mission or vision by involving others. In a *Pastoral Psychology* article, Jack Balswick and Walter Wright explain, "Empowering leadership is the process of helping others to recognize strengths and potential within, as well as encouraging and guiding the development of these qualities. . . . Empowering leadership is the affirmation of another's ability to learn and grow and become all that they are meant by God to be."[19]
- *Accountability* means we not only know where we are going, we are willing to evaluate our progress. We hold ourselves and others accountable to ensure we are moving in the intended direction.

Visionary leadership, therefore, is not a mandate for autocratic leadership. It clearly affirms the legitimate role of leader in the laity and in the pastorate. In our society perhaps the best metaphor for visionary leadership is that of a coach.

### The Coaching Model for Leadership

The position that is now called the "pastor" of a church will be redefined. Those who fill that position will function more like the coach of a sports team rather than the owner.[20]

Bill Hamon

I think perhaps the best modern day idiom for pastor is "coach."[21]

Greg Ogden

In order for the church to be healthy and effective, it appears that pastors are going to have to learn a new leadership style. One term that seems to describe this role is *transformational leadership*, but I prefer to call it the *coaching* model.

Probably no area of American life has attracted more attention than the athletic field. To be sure, much of what is heard, seen, and done has entertainment value only, and sometimes not even that. But beneath the surface, particularly with many of the successful teams, lie some valuable principles that are transferable to any field, including ministry. Recently several famous coaches have started writing books aimed at corporate leaders, trying to demonstrate how the principles they use as coaches can apply to the operation of a business. Many of these principles of leadership are useful for pastors and church leaders today. Not surprisingly, we find these same principles used by great and godly leaders throughout Scripture.

The coaching model seems to balance the need for strong, visionary leadership with the need for team building. Coaches recognize that when the game starts, they will not be playing, only watching from the sidelines. Their job is to prepare the players, so they will do the right thing regardless of the obstacles they may face.

The coaching model of leadership does not require a certain personality. Personality is God-given, while leadership style is learned behavior. Regardless of personality, all leaders can adopt a coaching style of leadership. Too many falsely assume that the only kinds of leaders who get things done are those with more directive or charismatic personalities. The truth is that all personalities have certain qualities that help us and certain qualities that hinder us as we learn to lead. Certainly a study of men and women leaders in the Scriptures does not give us a picture of God using only directive or charismatic personalities.

Another issue related to the coaching model is that of accountability. The results of a coach's efforts are measured and reported on a scoreboard. There is no fuzziness or talk about the inability to measure progress. And while criteria and assessment often come from outside sources (e.g., owners, sports critics), wise coaches have their own evaluation techniques to measure the success or failure of their efforts.

We need to recognize that while the coaching model emphasizes certain common characteristics, there is also a lot of room for individuality.

The coaching model of leadership gets in touch with the deepest feelings and needs of an organization but at the same time sees the potential for growth. Coaches live in the tension between these two worlds. They must balance their time between meeting the needs of today and preparing for tomorrow. They recognize that for a vision to happen, they must initiate and lead. If their leadership style is genuinely transformational, people will follow. Bill Walsh, who led the San Francisco 49ers to three Super Bowls, has this to say about good coaches:

> There are different categories of coaches. One extreme is the administrative coach, who makes sure that everything is in place so his staff can coach the team. . . . Another type concentrates on a specific aspect of the team and then surrounds himself with staff who coach the other areas. . . . The coaches who have been the most successful are usually the ones actively involved in the on-the-field, day-to-day coaching. Players will sacrifice for a hands-on coach, because they identify with him as an integral part of the team. A head coach who sees his role only as motivating the team and organizing the staff is at the mercy of other people. Having spent so many years as an assistant coach, I became more and more aware that someone had to be the source of game strategy and tactics.[22]

### Basic Elements of the Coaching Style for Pastoral Leadership

Robert Coleman, in *The Master Plan of Evangelism,* described the training and mentoring process used by Jesus to equip his disciples for future ministry. The best coaches in any sport apply principles that are identical or at least very similar to the ones Coleman describes. What are these principles? Below are the essential aspects of the coaching model.

- *Commitment to leadership.* A coach initiates, leads, goes in front, and models what he believes.
- *Commitment to team development.* Few coaches are player coaches. Most spend their time coaching coaches and allowing players to play. The primary role of the coach is to ensure the overall development of the team.
- *Commitment to mentoring, training, and equipping.* Good coaches understand the necessity of having a process in place to improve the skills of both staff and players. Most training should be on-the-job training rather than in-a-classroom training. A major part of this commitment to training and equipping is the concept of multiplication. Just as most coaches see a significant turnover of athletes each year, most churches also experience a great deal of change. Only those church leaders committed to multiplying and reproducing other leaders are going to be able to keep pace and have the necessary numbers of leaders in place.

  In *Control Your Destiny or Someone Else Will,* Noel Tichy and Stratford Sherman wrote, "The world of the 1990's and beyond will not belong to 'managers' or those who can make the numbers dance. The world will belong to passionate, driven leaders—people who not only have enormous amounts of energy but who can energize those whom they lead."[23]

- *Commitment to accountability.* Whether coaches like it or not, whether it is always fair or not, coaches are measured, graded, and evaluated on a regular basis by the success or failure of their teams.
- *Commitment to excellence and results.* Coaches have clear definitions of success and develop specific plans and strategies to achieve that success. These plans are flexible enough to be adjusted as necessary during the course of the game.
- *Commitment to planning.* All coaches are committed to planning. They spend many hours putting together the plans they believe will best accomplish their goal of winning. This means not only studying themselves and figuring out what they do well but also studying their teams to determine how to place each individual.

- *Commitment to optimism.* Virtually all coaches start out with a view that they can be successful. They realize there are a number of variables in the process, but they believe that if they do the right things, in the right way, with the right people, the results will speak for themselves. Their optimism creates energy within their teams.

## Summary

The drive to significance is a simple extension of the creative impulse of God that gave us being. . . . It is outwardly directed to the good to be done. We were built to count, as water is made to run downhill. We are placed in a specific context to count in ways no one else does. That is our destiny.[24]

Dallas Willard

Churches in the United States are being forced to take a harder look at what they are doing and why. If the church had unlimited resources of people, dollars, and time, it might not be such a critical issue. But when we know we have limited resources and those resources are in fact declining, we begin to see the need in our churches for ministry that is much more focused, intentional, and proactive.

- *Focused* in the sense that there is a clear picture of where the church is going and why. If we don't know where we are going, we are bound to waste vital resources as well as create a general sense of apathy which further reduces those resources.
- *Intentional* in the sense that we know what we are attempting to accomplish and we allocate resources accordingly. We are willing to measure progress and hold ourselves accountable for results.
- *Proactive* in the sense that the church moves ahead aggressively before there are major problems rather than living from one crisis to another with a fire-fighting mentality. "Proactive" implies that we anticipate what problems or obstacles may keep us from fulfilling our vision and develop

strategies and action plans to circumvent or overcome these problems and obstacles.

The primary purpose for this book is to help pastors and church leaders assess where they are, where they want to go, and develop a game plan for getting there. While these issues are not the only causes for unhealthy or ineffective churches, they are ones that play a major role.

## Questions for Reflection

1. How would you rate the health and effectiveness of your church culture?
   - How is its strength? (How well is the culture understood and modeled by leaders?)
   - How is its appropriateness? (How well does the culture meet the needs and values of those it is trying to impact?)
   - How is its adaptability? (How well is the culture able to make needed changes as the environment changes?)
2. How would you rate the readiness of the church for change?
3. In change efforts attempted in the past, evaluate the degree to which the church leadership
   - helped people see the need for change
   - created a compelling picture of a new future
   - institutionalized the desired changes (i.e., made them a real part of the church culture)
4. How would you classify the leadership style of the pastor(s) and church leaders?
   - In what ways is it similar to or different from the chaplaincy model?
   - In what ways is it similar to or different from the coaching model?

# FOUR

# The Scouting Report

## *Discovery Phase*

The first step in any planning process is to understand thoroughly where you are starting from. For a church this includes both an understanding of the demographic context as well as an assessment of the overall health and effectiveness of the church's ministry. Many churches try to bypass this critical phase and move immediately to visioning or planning. However, until we thoroughly understand our ministry and context, we will not have the necessary data to do any effective visioning or planning.

Few coaches would want to take their teams into competition without having some type of scouting report on their opponents. Most also would want to know their own strengths and weaknesses in order to determine their best strategies for success. A successful game plan implies that you:

- Understand your opponent
- Know what you can and cannot do

101

- Have a game plan to maximize your opportunities and minimize your obstacles

The same is true in the business field. Few companies begin operation without thoroughly understanding the market conditions, their competition, and their own capacities and capabilities. These would be a key part of what they would call a "business plan." Any lending institution would require this kind of analysis before underwriting a business.

## Introduction to the Discovery Phase

> Be sure you know the condition of your flocks, give careful attention to your herds; for riches do not endure forever, and a crown is not secure for all generations.
>
> Proverbs 27:23 TLB

> Get the facts at any price, and hold on tightly to all the good sense you can get.
>
> Proverbs 23:23 TLB

It is important to do two kinds of discovery. In the business world the first is called *environmental analysis*. For a church, environmental analysis means looking at the community or ministry area in which the church is located and trying to understand this environment's implications for the church's ministry. Businesses spend a lot of money on such an analysis and feel it is essential to their business ventures.

The second kind of analysis most businesses use is what might be termed *internal analysis*. For a church, internal analysis is when church leaders evaluate every aspect of the ministry to determine strengths, needs, opportunities, and challenges (or SWOT—strengths, weaknesses, opportunities, and threats). The discovery phase provides the baselines and foundation upon which credible visioning, planning, and evaluation can take place.

The desire to move directly to visioning and planning is not unusual. We often see the same thing on the athletic field. It is a lot more fun to play the game than to do the planning, so some teams try to skip or minimize the importance of a good scouting report. Usually these teams end up losing. Similarly, businesses that don't have a good grasp of the market or their product line are usually the first to fail. It is obviously more exciting to set up shop and begin selling the product, but it can be disastrous if the necessary research has not been done before the business begins.

We need to know where we are starting from before we try to define where we are going. Many churches have developed game plans for their future but have badly miscalculated their starting point because they assumed too much. After attempting to implement their plans, they are often surprised to find few people following. The problem in many cases is simply a misunderstanding of the starting point.

### Developing a Planning Team

Refuse good advice and watch your plans fail; take good counsel and watch them succeed.

Proverbs 15:22 THE MESSAGE

Form your purpose by asking for counsel, then carry it out using all the help you can get.

Proverbs 20:18 THE MESSAGE

It is a good idea to organize a planning team to work through the development of a game plan. Normally this team consists of the senior pastor, the administrative pastor (if there is one), any other staff members that would like to be part of the process, and a few key church leaders from the church board. The remainder of the team should be as representative as possible of the people in your congregation.

In thinking about who should be included in this last group, try to include people who represent different age groups, different lengths of time in the church, new Christians as well as long-term Christians. This last group is usually ten to fifteen people in churches with smaller congregations. In larger congregations the size of the group may number as many as thirty. The role of this group during the discovery phase is to review the data collected and give *input* and *insight* concerning that data. Someone, usually this is someone from the staff, should put together reports based on an analysis of the data collected and then distribute these reports to the planning team. Otherwise you will spend too much time trying to understand the data and even longer developing conclusions. Usually a couple of people on the team like to think analytically, and they could be used to assist the senior pastor (and his administrator, if there is one) in preparing the reports for the group.

For the planning team to function at peak efficiency, the following guidelines have proven helpful.

- Limit the entire strategic-planning process to no longer than six months. It is hard to keep a team together longer than this, and the results do not improve significantly with a longer process.
- Limit meeting times to an hour and a half to two hours. This seems to be the maximum period of time people can stay focused and maximally productive. Additionally, team members greatly appreciate starting and ending meetings on time.
- Regarding how regularly to meet, the best approach seems to be to meet once every two weeks. This gives adequate time between meetings for people to complete their assignments. It's possible to meet every week, but most people feel the meetings plus the outside work require more of a time commitment than they can afford.

The discovery phase of the planning process involves taking an objective look at any and all relevant data. From this data, the planning team tries to spot significant trends, either positive or negative, and draw conclusions that will help in later phases of the planning process. Much of the data you collect will simply tell you that you are normal or average. But pay particular attention to where feedback is very positive, very negative, or surprising. If you knew these areas ahead of time, you wouldn't have to gather as much information or use as many assessment tools. But you don't, so it's better to gather more information and allow the results to speak for themselves.

What you are looking for primarily is information in one of four categories:

- *Strengths.* What are the things we are doing that are better than would be expected and show promise for the future?
- *Needs.* What are the things we are doing that are worse than would be expected and that must be addressed if we are to achieve maximum health and effectiveness?
- *Opportunities.* What are the opportunities that God seems to be providing which show considerable promise for the future?
- *Challenges.* What are the challenges that if left unchecked could prevent us from achieving maximum health and effectiveness?

Whether you are an athletic team, business, or church, you need to know yourself well enough to evaluate your strengths, needs, opportunities, and challenges.

### Key Questions to Keep in Mind during the Discovery Phase

As you gather information for your church, keep in mind the following questions:

- Does the information seem accurate based on your perceptions?
- If not, why not?
- What are the implications of this information relative to the future of the church?
- Are you missing any information that would be essential to your planning for the future?

In many cases you will want to compare your results with that of other churches. However, some cautions are in order as you do this comparison.

- *In what ways is the average church not a good standard against which to compare your church?* Are there good reasons why you would not expect to match or exceed the data of an average church? In what areas would you expect to

exceed the norms, in what areas would you expect to match
the norms, and in what areas would you expect to be below
the norms?

- *Why is your church above the norm, about average, or below
  the norm?* What does the data and summary tell us about ourselves? Are we satisfied with where we are, or do we sense a
  real need to change? What is the commitment level of the congregation for such change?
- *How well is this information already known and understood
  by the congregation?* If the information is not known or understood, how important is it to get this information communicated, and what are the best channels for communication?
  Why is it not understood?

The information derived from your analysis will help you to
generate some very important observations about your church.
As in most research, you're likely to have more questions when
you finish than when you started. However, the value of this type
of analysis should not be underestimated.

## Tools for the Discovery Phase

Churches have found several analytical tools helpful to carrying out the discovery phase. You can use as many or as few of
these tools as you like. You may not decide to do as extensive an
analysis as is suggested here, but the more you do, the more you
can be sure you have all the information you need. You may think
of other tools that would work better in your setting. The key is
to get the information you need.

While the following list of tools is long, this does not mean the
discovery phase should be a long drawn-out process. Normally,
ten to twelve weeks (five to six meetings) are enough to gather
and evaluate the necessary data. A description of each tool is followed by an explanation of how it can be used to help the church
in its discovery process.

## Demographic Analysis

In the past, a lot of Methodist pastors were trying to be like the Sears Roebuck catalog, all things to all people. But in the greatest mail-order period in history, that catalog went out of business. In targeting a church's efforts, you have to get very clear on who you want to try to reach. I always start with a demographic analysis, and try to help churches target the largest market segment that other churches are not reaching.[1]

                                                        Jack Heacock

Virtually every conscientious pastor is committed to the church he serves. Few and far between are those pastors who are equally committed to the community in which their church is located.[2]

                                                        Peter Wagner

Perhaps the most important research tool you will use is a demographic study of the church's ministry area. Several companies specialize in doing such demographic research. Perhaps the best known is Percept Ministries (formerly CIDS—Church Information and Development Services), 151 Kalmus Drive, Suite A-104, Costa Mesa, CA, 92626, (800) 442-6277. According to Percept, their information is accurate and up-to-date, revised at least annually. You can set the designated area for your study by a radius of so many miles, by zip codes, or by simply drawing a specified area on a map.

The primary purpose in securing demographic information is to determine the ministry potential of the area the church is trying to impact. Several factors need to be analyzed in order to determine this potential.

1. What are the major demographic characteristics of the ministry area?
   - Do these characteristics match the demographic characteristics of the church, or are there any important differences? The degree to which the church's demographic characteristics match those of the community increases the likelihood that the church can reach large numbers of unchurched people in the ministry area.

- Are there significant demographic groups in the community that are not represented in our church, and do we have the desire and resolve to try to reach these groups? Trying to reach different demographic groups usually requires a significant change in ministry style and significant costs as well.

2. Are there common demographic characteristics in the ministry area, or is the area characterized by lots of different kinds of people with different kinds of demographic characteristics?

   - The more common the demographic characteristics of an area, the easier it is for the church to reach and impact that community. Typically, urban areas have substantially more demographic diversity than do suburban or rural areas.

     The larger the church, the more capable it will be of reaching and assimilating a diverse body of churchgoers. Reaching different groups requires diverse ministries and styles. Some churches are much more flexible in this regard than others. Depending on the size, resources, and flexibility of the church, it may be necessary to reach some of the demographic groups in the community through church planting or working with other church and parachurch ministries in the area, rather than trying to reach and assimilate these groups into the existing congregation.

3. Are the demographic characteristics of the immediate ministry area similar to that of the church, or are they different?

   - If the demographic characteristics of the immediate ministry area are substantially different than those of the church, it may mean the church should consider relocation or changing its ministry style.

A major problem most churches have with demographic data is this issue: "To what degree should the demographics of our ministry area affect or influence the ministry of our church?" There is no simple answer to that question, but let's approach the subject from two different perspectives.

The first is the approach most missionaries would use when beginning their work in a different culture. To them, demographics are critical. Most missionaries take one to two years trying to understand the culture before formulating a clear ministry plan. They see their primary role as contextualizing a faith that is based on eternal truths but adaptable enough to reach and be lived out in any culture. Missionaries who try to skip this basic step often encounter serious resistance or obstacles. So understanding the demographics (Who lives there and what type of people are they?) and psychographics (What do they think and believe?) is critical to virtually all missionary efforts. Many pastors in the United States feel they can bypass this step because they mistakenly assume they already understand the demographics and psychographics of the people in their ministry areas.

The second approach wrestles with the question, "Are we called to reach all the people in our ministry area, the largest demographic groups, or only a subgroup of the population?" Demographics and psychographics give you a snapshot of the community. They don't dictate the vision, but they certainly will impact the vision. While it is unusual, some churches have a vision to focus on a very small demographic group within their ministry areas. Most churches find themselves ministering to the predominate demographic groups. Either way, the church needs to know the demographics and psychographics that are at work in its community as well as the implications of those factors on its ministry.

For example, let's look at a church that happens to be located in a community that is drastically changing in its ethnic makeup. What are the church's options?

- They could choose to minister to a declining niche group and make plans accordingly.
- They could choose to plant other churches among the different cultural groups in the community.
- They could develop different ethnic churches using the facilities on their own campus.
- They could develop a ministry aimed at meeting a more diverse cultural makeup, a ministry that purposely crosses cultural barriers.

The church could choose any of these strategies based on the unique vision of the church. But to ignore the data and stick to the old tried-and-true ministry of the past without any consideration of the changing demographic context is indefensible.

### Congregational Survey

An important part of any analysis you do is some type of congregational survey. It is important to understand the attitudes, opinions, and beliefs of the members of your church. Several such surveys are on the market. An excellent one is published by the Church Consultants Group (CCG), 3416 Huron View Court Suite A, Dexter, MI, 48130, (734) 424-2720. It has eighty-four questions and allows you to add fourteen additional questions. There is also provision for written comments. The survey includes two kinds of questions—*evaluative* (How do you feel we are doing?) and *planning* (What do you feel we should be doing?).

The congregational survey is a particularly important document because the information comes from people in your church. It is their perception of the way things are or the way they would like them to be. While the statistical significance of their answers depends on the number of people who respond and who those people are (i.e., Is there a representative sample, and is it large enough to be statistically significant?), most churches find the data from the congregational survey to be very informative.

Perhaps the most important feature of the survey is its ability to compare the answers from your congregation with those of other congregations CCG has surveyed. The other churches represent both large and small churches, as well as urban, suburban, and rural churches. They also represent a wide variety of denominations. This comparison provides much better information than just numerical scores. It allows you to see how your congregation feels about a particular item compared to data from a large number of churches.

CCG also can supply a demographic breakdown of how different groups in your church answered specific questions. This is particularly helpful when you are trying to understand why the congregation scored particularly high or low on a specific question. This information can be difficult for people to understand but can yield a wealth of information. Because of the analyzing capability of computers, it is possible to compare how different groups in the church answered different questions. These groups are determined by the demographic data supplied by each respondent (age, marital status, length in the church, giving, and so on). The computer takes a look at all the different groups and tells you whether or not significant differences exist between different groups in their responses to particular questions. It is not unusual to find certain groups do in fact have considerably different views about the church than other groups. For example, different age groups often have considerably different perspectives on what is going on in the church or what they would like to see go on. Likewise, those with children may see things much differently than those who do not have children.

Other surveys you may also consider using for this analysis include the following:

- CIDS, previously mentioned in the section on demographic analysis, has their own congregational survey that is available for purchase.
- George Barna and the Barna Research Group have developed a congregational survey that can be purchased from them by writing to or calling Barna Research, 2487 Ivory Way, Oxnard, CA, 93030-6290, (800) 55-BARNA.
- Church Smart Resources, the company that markets the materials associated with *Natural Church Development* resources, have their own congregational survey that is based on the eight characteristics from the book, *Church Smart Resources*. Write to or call them at Church Smart Resources, 390 E. St. Charles, Carol Stream, IL, 60188, (800) 253-4276.

### Composition Analysis

The composition of a congregation can tell us a great deal about the health and vitality of the church. To assess the implications of a church's composition, a helpful tool is one originally available from the Charles E. Fuller Institute in Pasadena, California—*Affiliation History* by Chester Ainsworth. This tool gives you a picture of the composition of the church at a given moment in time. This allows you to analyze the church from several different perspectives.

Gathering the necessary data for the composition analysis is a relatively simple process. It involves handing out a small survey during the worship services, which can be filled out in about one minute. A sample is shown below.

---

### SAMPLE SURVEY CARD

Year of Birth _____ or Age _____

Year you began attending this church regularly _____

Which of the following best describes you when you began attending the church (mark only one):

_____ Had not been attending any church regularly for at least two years

_____ Had been attending another church in the area

_____ Had been attending another church in another area (moved here)

_____ Was brought here by my parents

Which of the following are reasons why you came to this church (mark as many as apply to you):

_____ Location

_____ Denominational affiliation of church

_____ Was invited by a friend, relative, or work associate

_____ Came on my own without an invitation

_____ Came for a special event held at the church

_____ Came for financial help from the church

_____ Came for counseling help from the church

_____ Came because of first attending a home group in the church

Which direction is your home from the church?

_____ North

_____ South

_____ Southwest

_____ West

_____ Northwest

_____ Northeast

_____ East

_____ Southeast

Approximately how long does it take you to drive to church?

_____ minutes

---

From the information that is gathered you will be able to do several different analyses.

### Decadal Group Analysis

The initial purpose of decadal group analysis is to identify the age distribution characteristics of the church. Another purpose of this analysis is to measure the age group trends in the congregation. This tells us what groups are growing and what groups are declining in size. You do this by comparing the percentage of people in each decadal generation (ten-year segments) who have come to the church during the last three years (these are "new constituents") with the percentage of people in each age group in the church. A positive number indicates that the decadal group is increasing in relative size to the congregation. A negative result indicates the decadal group is decreasing in relative size. The significance of the difference varies with the percentage of new members. The higher the percentage of new members, the more significant the shifts become.

### Institutionalization Analysis

Institutionalization is the process by which a group becomes rigid and opposed to change. The purpose of this analysis is to identify the degree to which this process is affecting the life and vitality of your church. To do this analysis, you divide the congregation into three groups according to how long they have been in the church. The relative sizes of groups combined with the data from the decadal group analysis gives important clues about the basic openness of the church to change.

Institutionalization is a normal and natural process that every organization must face. The question is not whether a church will have to face this issue, because every church does. However, it is important for the church to recognize when this is happening and to know how to counter it.

The three groups that can be identified in this analysis are:

#### Family Group

This group is really two separate groups, the *pioneers* and those who came to the church just after the pioneers. For practical purposes you can lump the two groups together with the label *family group*. The key to deciding who should be in this group depends on the age of the church. If the church is less than thirty years old, those who came to the church during the first five years are part of the family group. If the church is more than thirty years old, those who have been coming to the church for more than twenty years are in the family group.

This family group represents the long-termers in the church. They planned and sacrificed to build the original buildings. They usually have a high sense of ownership. Family group members are highly committed and very loyal to the church. However, they are often excessively possessive of the church and try to hold on to their power positions. They unintentionally keep new members from feeling included in the church. In many churches they pass this status and position on to their children.

In a church that is over thirty years of age, the family group should not consist of more than 20 percent of the congregation. If it exceeds 20 percent, it's probably a sign of serious problems. Even if the church is less than thirty years old, this group should have the smallest percentage of the three groups.

### Intermediate Group

These are the people who have been in the church more than three years but less than the family group. The size of this group and their distribution gives important clues about the attitudes and openness of the church to new people. It tells whether these new people become a significant part of the church's life. It usually takes about three years before a person is fully assimilated and feels a genuine part of what is going on. The number of people in the intermediate group tells a lot about how the church is keeping and assimilating those it attracts.

A typical church loses 10 to 15 percent of its members every year. Many of these simply move out of the area. But many others just quit attending. The most common reason given for why these people drop out is a failure to feel included. The intermediate group should be the second largest group in the church if the church is at least ten years old.

### New Constituents

These are the people who have been in the church three years or less. The size of this group is a good indicator of the attractiveness of the church. It is also a good indicator of the church's ability to reach new people.

In order for the church to grow, this group needs to be at least 30 percent of the congregation and probably closer to 40 percent depending on the percentage of people leaving each year.

By looking at the various sizes of these three groups, you can estimate the degree of institutionalization that is taking place in your church.

### CONGREGATIONAL PROFILE

Looking at the size of the various age groups in the church and comparing them with those in the church's ministry area can provide some interesting results. For example:

- What age groups are overrepresented in the congregation? What are the implications for the future ministry of the church?
- What age groups are underrepresented in the congregation? What are the implications for the future ministry of the church?

Churches most easily reach people who are like the current members. This gives the church advantages in certain age groups and disadvantages in others. Most churches assume they can reach all groups with equal success. This is seldom the case. Simply recognizing the realities of the age profile can be helpful to a church.

### PASTORAL LEADERSHIP POTENTIAL

The purpose of this analysis is to identify the degree to which the church is willing and ready to accept visionary, pastoral leadership.

Research shows that for virtually every church a major leadership crisis occurs sometime during the third to sixth year of a pastor's ministry. This explains why the average tenure of pastors is in that range. Until recently, it was not clear what was causing this crisis. The issues varied from church to church, but the time of the crisis was amazingly consistent. We now know that the basic reasons are sociological, not theological. We can predict the timing as well as the severity of the crisis by analyzing two factors.

### Degree of Institutionalization

Using information from the previous section, it is possible to estimate the degree to which the church has an institutionalization problem. Larger than usual percentages in the family group, along with smaller than usual percentages in the intermediate and new constituent groups, usually indicate an advanced stage of institutionalization.

What this means for pastoral leadership potential is significant. The people of a church that is institutionalized are usually looking for more of a chaplain model of pastoral leadership. They see the primary job of the pastor as maintaining the functions of the church and taking care of the members. This situation usually means that the real decision-making power is in the hands of a few church leaders, with the pastor having little or no say. Any attempt to change the existing system will meet active or passive resistance.

### Tenure and Age of the Pastor vs. Tenure and Age of Church Members

By comparing the tenure and age of people in the church with the tenure and age of the pastor, we can learn much about any leadership crisis that may take place. Certain characteristics are common in most churches:

- People who have been together a long time have much stronger ties and loyalty to each other than they do to a new pastor. This is especially true if the new pastor is significantly younger than those who have been in the church before him.
- New people are more accepting of pastoral leadership than those who have been in the church a long time. New people usually become part of the church because they like the style and leadership of the pastor. Thus, they easily identify with him and expect him to be the leader of the church.
- People are more likely to attribute authority to those who are older rather than those who are younger.
- Those who have joined since the pastor came and are older than the pastor are an interesting group. They usually will accept pastoral leadership if the pastor shows respect for their age.

- Those who have joined since the pastor came and are younger than the pastor are normally open to pastoral leadership. An exception would be the well-churched person who has seen many pastors and churches. They know by experience that the pastor is often not the actual leader in the church.
- Those who came before the pastor and are older see the pastor as their chaplain only.
- Those who came before the pastor and are younger have the most complex relationship with the pastor. If the younger-priors are children of the older-priors, they will usually side with the views of their parents. If they don't have these ties, they accept stronger pastoral leadership.
- The real crisis occurs when the numbers of those who see the pastor as leader begin to approximate the numbers of those who see the pastor as chaplain. A power shift takes place. There is a sociological battle over who is going to rule.

In most churches those in power are overrepresentative of those who have been around the longest. Thus, the battle can get mean and ugly. The chance for a smooth and orderly change of power is difficult to judge and depends on several issues.

One issue is the pastor's leadership style and ability. Another is the willingness of everyone involved to listen to the Holy Spirit rather than their own emotions and feelings.

Fast-growing churches usually have the easiest time of change. This is because the change of power takes place so fast there is no time to organize any real resistance to it. In cases where growth is slow, the situation is more difficult. Any change will take longer or may never take place at all.

### How and Why People Come to the Church

The composition analysis offers information about two aspects of how and why people come to the church. The first has to do with people's previous church attendance; the analysis will tell you how many people fit into each of the following categories:

- *Unchurched.* People in this category had not been attending any church for at least two years prior to coming to the church. The norm for this category is about 15 percent.

- *Transfer from another church in the area.* This is the least desirable form of growth since it means people are simply moving from one church to another. In some cases this percentage may represent people who are coming from a church where the gospel message was not clearly preached and who now are able to hear and respond to that message. However, studies indicate that for most churches this is a very small number. The norm for area transfers is about 44 percent.
- *Transfer from another church in another area.* These are people who have moved to your area and have chosen to attend your church. The norm for out-of-area transfers is about 31 percent.
- *Biological growth.* This category is comprised by those who were brought to the church by their parents. The norm for this type of growth is about 9 percent.

The second category of information the composition analysis offers has to do with what prompted people to begin attending the church. The various reasons listed on the sample card, and the normal percentage for each, is shown below:

- Came because of the location of the building—about 19 percent
- Came because of the denominational affiliation of the church—about 28 percent
- Came because of the invitation of a friend, relative, or work associate—about 49 percent
- Came on own without an invitation—about 39 percent
- Came for special event—about 5 percent
- Came because of ad in newspaper or phone book—about 3 percent
- Came for financial help from the church—benevolence ministry—about 1 percent
- Came for counseling help from the church—about 1 percent
- Came because of first attending the small group ministry in the church—about 2 percent

The reason the total of percentages is greater than 100 is because people are allowed to mark more than one of the choices if it applies to them.

### GEOGRAPHICAL DISTRIBUTION OF CONSTITUENTS

From the composition analysis we can get a rough idea of where people live and how far they drive to get to church. This is helpful in determining whether or not the present location of the church is a positive or negative factor. It is also helpful for getting an idea of the scope of the church's ministry area and for showing what areas are the most over- or underrepresented. The typical drive time for churches across the country is about eleven minutes.

## Space Analysis

Facilities and space usage are two major factors related to the health and effectiveness of any church. Many times we underestimate the importance of these. The church needs to make sure it has the necessary facilities to carry out its mission and vision. It's important that the church regularly assess its facility needs and then compare those needs with existing space. Several factors should be considered in assessing your space needs. Four are essential.

### WORSHIP SPACE

Because worship space is so central to the mission of the church, we need to start here. A beginning guideline for how much worship space to have is twelve square feet per person. This includes room for some platform space but not much more space than is required for actual seating. If the church is planning extensive ministry on the platform for singers, musicians, drama, and so on, you will need to allow more square feet. You need to analyze several subtopics when calculating the necessary worship space.

1. What type of seating are you using? The type of seating does make a difference for seating potential. Chairs usually provide the most seats for the smallest area. Theater seats provide the second most seats per square foot even though on

paper they provide less than pews. You should therefore adjust the twelve-square-feet rule somewhat upward if you are planning on using pews (perhaps to thirteen to fourteen square feet).

2. How many services are you running and what are the time frames? Most churches are now finding that the economics of church construction require them to go to multiple services before they expand or build new facilities. Many find they can expand comfortably to three services. Beyond three services, the wear on the staff and volunteer workers may be counterproductive. Several churches, however, have been able to run more than three identical services successfully. Remember, the more services you run, the more time the church staff must spend on these services, and there is a longer recovery time. The organizational culture in some churches allows for more flexibility in this regard than others. You need to answer several questions.

   • Is it possible to hold back-to-back services? If so, you can obviously have more services than if you need to have Sunday school one hour and church another.

   • Is Sunday morning the only acceptable service time? Can you use Friday evening, Saturday evening, or even Sunday evening to hold duplicates of the Sunday morning service?

3. What are the time frames of the services? Any service is perceptually full when it gets to 80 to 90 percent of capacity. When you reach these attendance levels, people (particularly newcomers) begin to feel like the service is full. People will start to avoid services they perceive to be overcrowded. Ordinarily, only services that start somewhere between 9:00 A.M. and 11:15 A.M. have the potential to fill to the maximum capacity of the facility. Services that start before the 9:00 time frame will usually not reach capacity.

   There are exceptions, but a good rule of thumb is to expect the potential of the third morning service to be 55 percent of capacity. Figure every service after that at 40 percent, including evening services. Using this method, if you ran three services, you could expect to fill one to the 90-percent level, one to about 80 percent, and one to 55 percent. The total of these services would then be 225 percent, indicating that realistically you could grow until the population of churchgoers is 2.25 times the seating capacity of your facility.

### CHILDREN/YOUTH EDUCATION SPACE

Here again we need to use some standards in figuring the necessary space. For children two years and less, thirty-five square feet per child is a common figure. This includes room for storage, cribs, diaper-changing areas, and so on. For children of preschool age, the figure is usually thirty square feet. For grade-school age children, you need to figure twenty-five square feet per person. This figure assumes self-contained classrooms. You could use a smaller figure if the teaching concept was a large group setting (i.e., children's church). For junior and senior high groups, the figure is more like twenty square feet per person.

These figures represent the necessary space for seating and minimal storage. They do not include additional rooms for breaking into smaller groups or bringing groups together in larger settings. They also do not include storage rooms for teaching materials or hallways. Normally you can figure you will need to add an additional 30 percent beyond your regular space to cover these items. Remember that the same 80 to 90 percent rule that applied for worship applies here as well. That is, when the rooms are 80 to 90 percent full, you should consider them maximally full. This allows space for newcomers as well as providing some flexibility for those Sundays when attendance is abnormally high.

In your planning, try to accommodate the number of children at the largest service, not an average service. If you check your historical records, you will find that one service traditionally runs a higher percentage of children than the others do. You need to factor this in when assessing the necessary children's space. At the largest service the number of children and youth is usually 30 to 40 percent of the adult attendance in the worship space, although this varies a lot from one congregation to another. That is, if you are running 150 adults in the worship space, you will need to provide for about 50–60 children and youth.

### ADULT EDUCATION SPACE

Here you need to take into account the number of adults you will have in classes at the same time as the largest service. The reason you figure it this way is because you are trying to determine the maximum number of people that will be on the site at one time. This determines the maximum building and parking space needed. Many churches hold adult education classes at a different time than the services. If you do, you may find you still need additional space. For adults, you can figure fifteen square feet per person.

### ON-SITE PARKING SPACE

There may be some exceptions when people can park in large numbers on surrounding streets, but most churches need to plan on having adequate off-street parking or direct-access off-site parking. You will need to plan on approximately one parking space for every 2.4 people in attendance (including children). If you have many single people in your congregation, you will need additional parking, as many of them will be coming in their own cars. If you have many families in your congregation, you may be able to provide slightly less parking space, as the ratio of people per car will be higher. The same 80 to 90 percent rule holds true for on-site parking. Also, ideally open parking spaces will be visible from the street. What you're dealing with is perception. Long-standing church members don't pay nearly as much attention to these factors as visitors do. But we must provide for the needs of all people, not just the regulars.

## Staffing Analysis

Another critical issue relative to church health and effectiveness is staffing. There are two basic levels.

### MINISTRY STAFF

Ministry staff includes all those who are involved in ministry in one of two capacities:

- Responsible for an age group or specific group of people in the congregation (e.g., children's pastor, youth pastor, singles pastor, senior pastor, associate pastor, and so on).

- Responsible for a specific area of ministry in the church (e.g., music pastor, evangelism pastor, pastoral care pastor).

### SUPPORT STAFF

This includes those who work with or facilitate the work of the ministry staff (e.g., administrative assistants, secretaries, receptionists, maintenance workers, and so on). As you evaluate your staffing ratios, keep the following in mind:

- In many churches the lines between ministry staff, support personnel, and church leadership are not clear. For example, many secretaries may have some pastoral responsibilities, and many pastors find themselves doing considerable amounts of support activities.

- The philosophy of ministry and style of ministry seriously affect staffing ratios. For example, if the church works hard at empowering, recruiting, deploying, and monitoring volunteer workers, it may be able to get by with fewer support staff.

  If the church is *pastor* focused, like the *chaplain* model discussed earlier, you can also get by with less staffing as the congregational expectations allow for a more traditional model of ministry.

  On the other hand, if the ministry style of the church dictates many events and activities at the church building, you will need to have increased staffing. Also, if the church is in a rapid-growth mode (15+ percent per year), it would need a higher level of staffing to keep up with the growth. Conversely, a church that is plateaued or declining requires less staffing.

- Third, the level of pay affects the staffing ratio. If a church pays its staff at wages comparable to a corresponding job in the secular market, the level of staffing will probably be less. On the other hand, if the church pays its staff at wages considerably below market value, the level of staffing could be more.

- Fourth, the amount of contracted services affects the staffing ratio. If the church contracts out significant portions of its work (e.g., custodial work, landscaping, printing, secretarial), the level of staffing would be less, but the expenses for overhead would be higher. Many churches are using more contracted labor for three reasons: (1) they need to contract only for the hours needed to complete the job, (2) they don't have to bring on a full-time person with benefits, and (3) in the case of economic slowdowns, it is much easier to eliminate contracted personnel than to terminate a staff member.

As you can see, many factors need to be considered in regard to staffing. However, for purposes of analysis, you can use some general figures that apply in an average situation.

- One ministry staff member for every 150 people (including children) in attendance on Sunday morning
- One support staff member for every 170 people

### Organizational Effectiveness

If the church is going to operate with maximum effectiveness, you'll need certain organizational aspects in place. While some of these seem mundane and obvious, it's amazing how many churches ignore these and assume they can operate without them. Consider these four key principles.

- First, every organizational unit (every ministry, department, team, or committee) should have its own mission, vision, or purpose statement. Without a statement of purpose showing how this organizational unit is going to fulfill the mission and vision of the church as a whole, it tends to operate to meet its own ends rather than as a coordinated and integrated function of the church's overall ministry. Without clear direction, any one unit may stray away from the original vision and purpose over time.
- Every organizational unit should have specific objectives and measurable standards. Objectives are generalized statements of what the organizational unit hopes to accomplish. The standards show how success will be defined for these objec-

tives. They are objective criteria that set measurable benchmarks.

- Third, there needs to be a system in place to evaluate every organizational unit at least annually. Assuming the objectives and standards are in place, they would become the major criteria for this evaluation. Every organizational unit should be expected to justify its existence each year and demonstrate the degree to which it is accomplishing its function in the church.

- Finally, each organizational unit should have a well-organized training and equipping strategy. This training allows new people to be involved in the ministry and receive the training they need to function effectively. Such a strategy ensures that new people are in fact recruited and that the organizational unit has the necessary people in place. If the church is not reproducing leaders, it will become stagnant. The qualified few can only do so much, and they will become burned out very quickly if they are expected to take on the whole load without any help. Having a mentoring process in place in each unit will produce additional leaders in the church.

### Small Group Analysis

By analyzing the small group ministry of the church, you will be able to see how well your church is set up to meet the relational needs of its members. You'll find out whether there is a good balance between the types of groups that are available and whether or not some new groups should be established to meet the needs of those in the congregation who are not involved. You also will see if your vision is being realized in the groups that are presently functioning.

Collect the necessary information by having each small group leader fill out a brief survey that asks what type of group it is, how many are in the group, their ages, and how long they have been in the church and in the group. There are two aspects of the small group analysis:

- The first is the variety of types and sizes of the existing small groups in the church.

- The second area of concern is the health and effectiveness of the small (or cell) groups in the church. The average church in the United States has only about 15 percent of the congregation involved in small groups, and for most that percentage is declining. Many of the churches that stress small group ministry have not been able to get more than 25 percent involved although a few have managed to get a 50-percent involvement. It is an unusual church that gets more than 50 percent involved. It takes considerable effort and planning to move beyond these levels.

As you collect the information on your small groups, you should be able to ascertain the health and effectiveness of these groups by asking the following questions:

- How many people are involved in small groups on a regular basis?
- How many groups of each of the following types do we have: Decide, Task, Learn, Love, Support, and Mission? How many should we have of each? The following are brief descriptions of each of these types of groups:
  *Decide.* Makes decisions that affect the whole church. This would include finances, programs, staff, property, worship, and so on.
  *Task.* Performs some task. This would include caring for children, being on the worship team, greeting, ushering, caring for the grounds, and other tasks.
  *Learn.* Studies the Bible, a biblical topic, a book, and other relevant topics.
  *Love.* Builds and sustains friendships. Fellowship and sharing are key aspects of each meeting.
  *Support.* Deals with problems of addiction, compulsion, or dysfunctional backgrounds.
  *Mission.* Ministers to people outside the church.
- Are the groups growing and adding new people or are they staying with the same people?
- Are the different demographic groups in the church participating in the small group ministry? Are the differing needs

of the congregation being addressed? If they aren't, what types of new groups need to be started?

- Are the groups reproducing leaders and new groups?
- Are the groups adding people who are new to the church as well as those who are long-term?

### *Financial Analysis*

Many areas relative to finances can be analyzed. You may need to use several resources to recover this information.

#### GIVING

To give you a starting figure against which you can compare your tithes, offerings, and missions income figures, the national average for giving to churches of all kinds in 1994 was 2.72 percent of total income. The figure for evangelical churches was closer to 4 percent. The figure for churches with fast growth rates (10+ percent per year) was about 3.5 percent. You can get the figures for average household income from your demographic research or from census data. A better figure, if you can get it, is the median household income (the figure above which half of all households make more and below which half of all households make less). You should be able to determine the number of family or household units from your giving records. But if you want to use a rough estimate, you can use one half of your total attendance. For example, if your total attendance including children and youth is 300, you can estimate an attendance of 150 household units.

Another way to look at the tithe or offering numbers is to determine the average giving per person (including children). Comparative figures would be:

- Average of all churches—$12 per person per week
- Average of growing evangelical churches—$15 per person per week
- Average of evangelical churches—$18 per person per week

A third way to evaluate giving is to determine how many people are giving at certain levels. You can set whatever categories you want, but some of the questions you might want to ask of the data include:

- How many people or families gave something to the church last year? What percent of your total church body is this? Is the percentage growing?
- How many people or families are giving at a tithe level? What percent of your total church body is this? Is the percentage growing?
- Are long-term church members giving at higher levels than those who are new? Are people growing in their giving if they stay in the church for several years?
- What do the top 10 percent give? What percentage of the total giving is this? What about the second 10 percent? Third? And so on.

You may be surprised to know the national averages are as follows:

- The top 10 percent of donors give 50 percent of all donated funds.
- The top 20 percent of donors give 65 percent of all donated funds.
- The bottom 50 percent of donors give only 12 percent of all donated funds.

### EXPENDITURES

To give you some basic guidelines for determining budget allocations, note the following average expense figures for churches across the country:

- Personnel—40 to 55 percent
- Debt Servicing/Leasing—15 to 25 percent
- Facilities/Maintenance—5 to 10 percent
- Overhead—7 to 10 percent
- Ministry Expenses/Departmental Expenses—10 to 15 percent

- Missions/Benevolence—5 to 10 percent
- Denominational Giving—5 to 10 percent

As you compare your expenses with the norms above, use the following questions for analysis:

- In what areas are you particularly high? What are the implications? What does it say about your real priorities?
- In what areas are you particularly low? What are the implications? What does it say about your real priorities?

### Church Growth and Loss Analysis

Analyzing the church's growth and loss patterns can be informative. It helps us to understand the past as well as make projections for the future. It can identify key trends or patterns.

As you look at the data, ask yourself the following questions:

- What have been our growth trends in worship attendance over the last several years? What are the implications of that pattern for our future growth potential?
- What have been our growth trends in Sunday school attendance over the last several years? What are the implications of that pattern for our future growth potential?
- Do the worship-attendance trends and the Sunday school attendance trends coincide, or are they different? What are the implications of this data?

### Volunteer Analysis

The two basic types of volunteer workers include those whose work primarily meets the needs of people who regularly come and give to the church (called in-house or maintenance positions) and those whose work primarily meets the needs of people who do not regularly come or give to the church (called outreach positions). It is important to evaluate both when talking about volunteers.

Normally these measurements cover only those programs and ministries sponsored by the church and not activities outside the church such as social or political action groups, Christian schools, and others. As you look at the results of your survey, ask yourself the following questions:

- How many total volunteers do we have? What percent is that of our total adult attendance? What are the implications? A good percentage would be 50+ percent involved. An average church has approximately 35 percent involved. If a church has 50+ percent volunteers, but workers appear to be over-worked, or there does not seem to be enough workers to meet the needs of vital ministries, you may have to think about reallocating your volunteers from other ministries or reducing the number of volunteers in some ministries.

- How many total hours are the volunteers putting in? What is the average per person? What are the implications? It is not unusual to find too small a number of people doing too many jobs. This is bound to end up in burnout or at least in severe frustration. An average volunteer spends approximately two hours per week in their ministry assignment.

- What percentage of the workers is maintenance versus outreach? What are the implications? It is not unusual for the maintenance volunteers to be 90+ percent of the total volunteer force. Many churches feel this is far too heavily weighted toward the needs of the existing members and try to get the outreach volunteer percentage up to 20+ percent.

### Executive Summary

It is a good idea to take the results of all your analyses and compile them into the form of an executive summary. The purpose of this document is to summarize in one place the findings from the entire discovery phase. For some people, the analysis is information overload, and it is difficult for them to see the big picture when they are bombarded with a lot of data. Hopefully an executive summary would provide that big picture.

Divide your executive summary into four basic categories:

## STRENGTHS

This section details what aspects of church life are much stronger than you would expect or much stronger than would be true in the typical church. These strengths are important for the church to consider. Many times we dwell so much on the negative that we forget to affirm the positive. These strengths are foundational to the church's future. They represent the building blocks on which effective ministry can be based. These are the things that you are already doing well, and therefore, without much additional effort, can continue to do well. These strengths often represent the most effective bridges to your community.

It is important that the average person in your congregation understand these strengths. During the visioning phase, you will want to identify some of these as ways your church is distinct from other churches in the area. This information may help you more clearly define what it is God is already doing in your congregation, or what it is he is calling you to do in the future.

## NEEDS

This section identifies what aspects of your present church life are weaker than you would expect or weaker than would be true in the typical church. One of the key determinations during the remaining phases is to identify which of these needs should be addressed or corrected. The needs identified represent potential areas of concern or areas that may be limiting the effectiveness of the present ministry. Some obviously will be identified as more important than others. But if a church finds it has some definite needs, and these needs are negatively impacting the effectiveness of the church, these should be addressed as soon as possible.

## OPPORTUNITIES

This section details the particular aspects of your church ministry that seem to provide the greatest opportunities for your church to expand its current ministry. These are the doors that it seems God has opened for the church, if it desires to increase its ministry and impact. They represent things your church should consider in your planning process. Normally these opportunities are the most cost-effective areas to address as they are the easiest and most potentially fruitful.

### CHALLENGES

This section identifies the particular aspects of your church life that seem to provide the greatest challenges for your church to expand its ministry. These are the challenges that could keep you from fulfilling the mission and unique vision God has determined for your church. You will need to decide how much you think each of these challenges is in fact impacting the present ministry of the church. You'll also need to decide how much they will impact the ministry of the church in the future. In the planning phase you will need to identify particular strategies to address the most critical challenges. In most cases these challenges will not remove themselves; it is up to the church to figure out how to remove them.

It is very important that as you summarize your work during the discovery phase you do not miss any major information. Because you will be using this information as a baseline in all of your future planning, you cannot be too careful in making sure you have not missed anything during this first step.

## Summary

After reading through these tools for the discovery phase, you may be a little overwhelmed. Remember, you don't have to use all of these tools. However, it is good at this point to remind ourselves why we are doing all this research.

- We are trying to get as accurate and complete a picture as possible of what is going on in the church. We are trying to be as objective as possible in our research to make sure we don't allow our opinions to color the data.
- We are gathering information that later can be used to help move the church toward change. One of the best ways to create a climate for change is to give solid information that shows the need for change.

## *The Example of Nehemiah*

We have already listed Nehemiah as a biblical example of a leader who believed in planning. He probably is the best example of someone who did his homework before beginning his actual ministry.

In Nehemiah 1 we see the steps that Nehemiah took. After hearing of the conditions in Jerusalem he did the following:

- He grieved
- He fasted
- He prayed
- He repented
- He planned

In chapter 2, when he is asked by the king, "What do you want?" we see that Nehemiah had obviously been planning for some time.

> "If it pleases the king and if your servant has found favor in his sight, let him send me to the city in Judah where my fathers are buried so that I can rebuild it."
>
> Then the king, with the queen sitting beside him, asked me, "How long will your journey take, and when will you get back?" It pleased the king to send me; so I set a time.
>
> I also said to him, "If it pleases the king, may I have letters to the governors of Trans-Euphrates, so that they will provide me safe-conduct until I arrive in Judah? And may I have a letter to Asaph, keeper of the king's forest, so he will give me timber to make beams for the gates of the citadel by the temple and for the city wall and for the residence I will occupy?" And because the gracious hand of my God was upon me, the king granted my requests.
>
> Nehemiah 2:5–8

But Nehemiah was not through with his planning. When he arrived in Jerusalem, he did more research and planning.

> I went to Jerusalem, and after staying there three days I set out during the night with a few men. I had not told anyone what my God had put in my heart to do for Jerusalem. There were no mounts with me except the one I was riding on.
>
> Nehemiah 2:11–12

Nehemiah realized the need to examine for himself the conditions that he was facing before he came up with an appropriate plan to remedy the situation. After personally inspecting the walls, he was able to devise a strategy that was both unique and appropriate. When he presented his plan to the leaders and the people, their response was, "Let us start rebuilding" (Neh. 2:18).

The analysis done by Nehemiah while he was in the Persian capital as well as the research he did when arriving in Jerusalem provided him with the information he needed to begin planning, and to convince the people to join in his efforts. These are the purposes of the discovery phase.

## Questions for Reflection

1. If you were to do a major planning effort, would you use a planning team? If so, who should be on it?
2. What demographic research do you have on your ministry area? What additional information do you need?
3. When was the last time you had your congregation respond to a major survey? What do you want to know about what the congregation thinks or believes?
4. What research tools described in this chapter would be helpful for evaluating the health and effectiveness of your church's ministry?
5. How will you do the necessary research but at the same time keep the discovery phase down to no more than two to three months?

# FIVE

# Team Philosophy (Part 1)

## *The Pre-Visioning Phase*

"For I know the plans I have for you," declares the LORD, "plans to prosper you and not to harm you, plans to give you hope and a future."

Jeremiah 29:11

Write down the vision and make it plain, so those who read it and run may stay on course, for the vision pertains to the future.

Habakkuk 2:2–3

Once you have completed the discovery phase, you have an accurate picture of where you are as a church. While you could always do more research, there comes a point where you need to move on to determine your future. Introspection is a worthwhile process, but it needs to have an end point. The main reason for the discovery phase is to establish clear baselines.

In the pre-visioning phase you begin to look at the future. You begin to think about and meditate on what kind of future God intends for the church. It is particularly important that everyone involved in the process understands two fundamental assumptions:

- The future is not a composition of what people want individually for the future but what the church believes God wants for its future. It therefore means putting aside personal agendas as much as possible. It's okay to recognize what those agendas might be, but the idea is to keep them from interfering with the visioning process.
- The future is not just an improved version of past history. While God has obviously been laying a foundation for the future in the present ministry, people at church should not automatically assume the future will look like either the past or the present. People need to keep their minds and hearts open to what God wants to do, which could mean a significant amount of change for the future. If the history of the early church is any indication of what the future might look like, everyone is in for more than a few surprises.

Before beginning a discussion of some of the steps you might want to take in the pre-visioning phase, we need to explore the concept of *vision* in some detail. While it has been fashionable for churches as well as secular institutions to decide that a vision is necessary for their future, many people have misconceptions about what vision is and how it should be formulated.

## Understanding the Why

The most important problem in the church today is a fundamental lack of clear, heart-grabbing vision. The church in America has no vision. It has programs and institutions and property and ministers and politically correct hymnals, but no vision.[1]

Mike Regele

Action without vision is stumbling in the dark, and vision without action is poverty stricken poetry.[2]

Burt Nanus

If you stacked these teams up against one of the perennial contenders, the talent gap might not be as great as you'd expect. It's the philosophy gap that separates them. The losers lack something vital: a sense of purpose.[3]

Bill Parcells

God's vision for the future of your church is not a fad. It is not something brand new, neither is it something that is going to pass away. Many have pondered why it is so important to capture a specific vision for the church. Perhaps the simplest answer is that if we don't have a picture of where we are going, we are bound to be overcome by our circumstances.

If a farmer wants to plow a straight furrow, he cannot look at the ground immediately in front of him; he needs to focus farther on, on some point at the end of the field or on the horizon. That point provides direction and guidance and keeps him going in a straight line rather than wandering all over.

Businesses have discovered it's not enough to have a great product or even a great location. The number of new businesses that fail each year is a testimony to the difficulty of surviving in a very competitive marketplace. And the opposite is also true. Many of the truly great companies in the United States today were started by men and women who overcame unbelievably difficult circumstances and yet not only survived but thrived in the same market setting. Many who have researched these successes and failures point to the essential role vision, or lack of vision, played in the outcomes of these companies.

In the athletic arena we see the same thing. The differences in athletic ability between professional teams are truly minimal. And yet we see certain teams that continue to dominate, while others continue to fail. Studies have shown that it is not the team that spends the most money or even has the most talented athletes that stays at the top. Instead, books written by coaches and players alike point to the intangibles and in particular the vision of the coach or organization that made the difference.

In my own research on church health and effectiveness, I have found no factor more important than vision. And yet, we see virtually nothing written about this concept in contemporary Christian books. Seminaries and Bible colleges teach little if anything about it. In fact, if a pastor wants to learn about this concept, he will have to turn primarily to books from the business and athletic fields. This concept reminds me of Luke 16:8: "For the people of this world are more shrewd in dealing with their own kind than are the people of the light."

The number of activities in which a church is involved or the level of its activity is a poor measure of its health or effectiveness. Activity without purpose drains all the resources of the church. Without definite direction and purpose, the ministry of the church is little more than a fire-fighting job for its leaders. The pastor and church leaders are forced to spend the majority of their time trying to solve problems within the body, with little or no time to dream, plan, or minister in any significant way. The result is stagnation, lack of growth, and poor health. What's needed is a compelling picture of a future for your church or what is best described as vision.

The most familiar Bible passage regarding vision is Proverbs 29:18, "Where there is no vision, the people perish" (KJV). A more accurate translation states, "Where there is no revelation, the people cast off restraint" (NIV). This verse reminds us of the biblical analogy of Christians as sheep and the church as a flock. Flocks of sheep need shepherds to guide, protect, and give direction to them. Without shepherds, the sheep will become unrestrained, either running off and getting hurt or turning on one another and fighting. What a sad but accurate picture of the church that lacks a clear vision. Where there is no direction, no dream beyond self-preservation and maintaining the status quo, we run off and get hurt or turn on one another.

Satan knows it is useless to try to destroy a church from the outside. Persecution only causes the church to get stronger. The only way the enemy can destroy a church is from the inside. And one of his favorite ploys is to cause the removal of the shepherd, so the flock will be divided.

The apostle Paul is perhaps our best example of a man captivated and compelled by a vision. It's interesting as you study his life and ministry to see the focus, direction, and sense of destiny that characterizes his life and ministry. It is truly inspiring. We ought to be careful not to write this off to the fact that he was gifted as an apostle. Gifted he was, but he was driven to use those gifts to fulfill a special and unique call of God upon his life—a *vision.*

> This all fits into Paul's affirmation that God has a plan for every life, that we each have been created unto good works which God has before ordained that we should walk in them (Ephesians 2:10). Through daily prayer and communion, the leader must discover the details of the plan and arrange his work accordingly.[4]
>
> J. Oswald Sanders

> Growing, healthy churches have a clear cut identity. They understand their reason for being; they are precise in their purpose. They know exactly what God has called them to do. They know what their business is, and they know what is none of their business.[5]
>
> Rick Warren

> The mission has to be clear and simple. It has to lift up people's vision. It has to be something that makes each person feel that he or she can make a difference—that each one can say, I have not lived in vain.[6]
>
> Peter Drucker

## Why Churches Lack Vision

If vision is so important to effectiveness in ministry, why is it that so few pastors and church leaders have a vision that is empowering and compelling? There are at least four possible reasons.

### *Churches Misunderstand the Source of Vision*

> Just as no great painting has ever been created by a committee, no great vision has ever emerged from the herd.[7]
>
> Warren Bennis

Vision is not the result of consensus; it should result in consensus. In a church, it is important that people own the vision for ministry, not that they create it. . . . Grasping God's vision for the church's ministry is not a committee process.[8]

George Barna

So the point is not to become a leader. The point is to become yourself, to use yourself completely—all your skills, your gifts and energies—in order to make your vision manifest. You must withhold nothing, you must, in sum, become the person you started out to be and to enjoy the process of becoming.[9]

Warren Bennis

Vision doesn't come from committees, it comes from God. It is not given to groups. It is initiated by a leader and confirmed or affirmed by those around him or her.

A review of both the Old and New Testaments does not show a single example of vision by consensus. Yet most churches try to define their vision by forming a committee of those they think are the most mature or the most spiritual. The only possible vision that can come from that kind of process is a watered down series of ideas that are acceptable to all but compelling to none.

God's plan is to impart the basic outline of a vision through a leader. Then those around that leader have the right to affirm or deny the vision. In some cases people may reject the vision and the visionary, even though the vision is valid, and the vision may be delayed or fulfilled in a totally different way. The visions of many Old Testament prophets were rejected. In other cases, such as those of Joshua and Paul, we see godly leaders who affirmed and confirmed the vision, and great things were accomplished.

Pastors themselves often misunderstand the source of vision and choose to copy someone else's vision rather than determine their own. This approach is virtually doomed to failure because:

- Someone else's vision cannot exactly match your own circumstances.
- Even if the circumstances were similar, pastors will not be able to carry out someone else's vision simply because of their own unique personalities and God-given gifts.

- When you accept someone else's vision, usually you're only getting the surface material. Behind that vision are many assumptions that you may or may not understand. To adopt the vision without fully understanding the underlying assumptions is likely to cause failure.

## Most Pastors Are Afraid to Lead

We need people who influence their peers and who cannot be detoured from their convictions by peers who do not have the courage to have any convictions.[10]

Joe Paterno

He who floats with the current, who does not guide himself according to higher principles, who has no ideal, no real standards—such a man is a mere article of the world's furniture—a thing moved, instead of a living and moving being—an echo, not a voice.[11]

Henri Frederic Amiel

To get profit without risk, experience without danger, and reward without work is as impossible as it is to live without being born.[12]

President Harry Truman

There's a fine line between delegating authority and turning the asylum over to the inmates. You want to be a fair, attentive, confident leader. You want to encourage people to take initiative, put forward original ideas, take the calculated risk. But if you go too far, you can wind up accommodating people. You can find yourself stepping back to keep the surface appearance of unity—and to avoid confrontation with people who are staging a house rebellion.[13]

Bill Parcells

In an effort to meet all the various needs and demands of the ministry, pastors have abdicated their God-given responsibility to lead. In an effort to live the life of a servant-leader, as they understand it, pastors have forgotten or neglected their leadership responsibility. We should not be surprised by these pastors' reluctance to lead when we remember the reluctance of God's chosen leaders such as Moses, Gideon, Jeremiah, and Esther when they were called.

When the angel of the Lord appeared to Moses, he was told, "So now, go, I am sending you to Pharaoh to bring my people the Israelites out of Egypt" (Exod. 3:10). Even though the Lord had spoken directly to him, Moses' response was a series of fearful questions.

- "Who am I, that I should go to Pharaoh and bring the Israelites out of Egypt?" (Exod. 3:11).
- "Suppose I go to the Israelites and say to them, 'The God of your fathers has sent me to you.' And they ask me, 'What is His name?' Then what shall I tell them?" (Exod. 3:13).
- "What if they do not believe me or listen to me and say, 'The LORD did not appear to you'?" (Exod. 4:1).
- "O Lord, I have never been eloquent, neither in the past nor since you have spoken to your servant. I am slow of speech and tongue" (Exod. 4:10).
- "O Lord, please send someone else to do it" (Exod. 4:13).

After the last question above Scripture records, "The LORD's anger burned against Moses" (Exod. 4:14). Moses certainly was not overly eager to lead the nation of Israel out of Egypt even though he was God's chosen instrument. Moses' reluctance may have been the result of his previous experiences, when he had come to the aid of a fellow Hebrew but was rejected by his own people.

Gideon wasn't much better. The Lord told him, "Go in the strength you have and save Israel out of Midian's hand. Am I not sending you?" (Judg. 6:14). Gideon's response? "But Lord . . . how can I save Israel? My clan is the weakest in Manasseh, and I am the least in my family" (Judg. 6:15).

The Lord promised to be with him, and still Gideon demanded a sign and later tested the Lord with a fleece.

When the Lord spoke to Jeremiah, he declared, "Before I formed you in the womb I knew you. Before you were born I set you apart; I appointed you as a prophet to the nation" (Jer. 1:5). Jeremiah responded, "Ah, Sovereign LORD . . . I do not know how to speak; I am only a child" (Jer. 1:6).

Mordecai asked his cousin Esther "to go into the king's presence to beg for mercy and plead with him for her people" (Esther 4:8). Her response was to say it was too dangerous and risky for her to do it. Mordecai's response included the famous phrase, "And who knows but that you have come to royal position for such a time as this?" (Esther 4:14). Esther's reply was that she would go. "I will go to the king, even though it is against the law. And if I perish, I perish" (Esther 4:16).

This pattern existed among God's chosen leaders in the past, so it should not surprise us to see it today. But shouldn't we profit from the wisdom of Scripture and avoid having to relearn these lessons the hard way?

A fear of leading or feeling inadequate to lead is not unnatural or uncommon. However, failing to deal because of such is contrary to God's will. You will remember God's displeasure with Moses' continual questioning and his reluctance to fulfill the vision God had given him. Also, remember Paul's warning to Timothy: "Don't let anyone look down upon you because you are young. . . . Do not neglect your gift, which was given you through a prophetic message when the body of elders laid their hands on you" (1 Tim. 4:12–14).

It is essential that pastors deal with their fears and move beyond them. The fear will limit the degree to which the pastor is able to hear the vision of God and communicate it to others.

Many pastors fear they do not have time to develop their own vision. Already consumed by the tyranny of the urgent, they don't see how they can take the time to determine their own vision or carry it out. J. Oswald Sanders points out that Jesus did not have this treadmill mentality about ministry. "The secret of his serenity lay in his assurance that he was working according to his father's plan, a plan that embraced every hour, made provisions for every contingency. His calendar had been arranged and through communion with his father he received both each day the words he was supposed to say, and the works he was supposed to do."[14]

### Most Churches Are Organized So Pastors Cannot Lead or Provide Vision

Authority and authoritarianism should not be confused. Authoritarianism says, 'This is right because I say so.' Authority says, 'I say this because it is right.' A good leader has authority on his side, but he is not an authoritarian.[15]

Joe Ellis

The polity of the United Methodist Church, which is organized around distrust of individuals, makes it impossible for anyone to serve as the wagon master.[16]

Lyle Schaller

Why is it that so many churches are organized so that the pastor cannot lead? There are probably many reasons, but two seem to be most prominent.

### PAST ABUSES OF POWER

Many churches are trying to protect themselves from leadership abuse by making sure leaders cannot lead. They have regulated leadership into obscurity and rendered it powerless. The whole issue of authority has become confused with authoritarianism, and the baby has been thrown out with the bath water. Let's face it, no set of regulations can totally eliminate the possibility of abuse of power.

What I've seen is that the Holy Spirit is capable of making good things happen in spite of all the obstacles the church sets up. One church I worked with had a membership of 150 and a church board of 74, and most of the positions on the board were legislated by the denomination. Not surprisingly, the pastor said he found it difficult to get anything accomplished.

However, the enemy also can use people to circumvent the church's best governmental systems and cause chaos and destruction in the church. So, removing authority from pastors is not the answer to abuse.

### BECAUSE OF OUR ENAMORMENT WITH THE DEMOCRATIC PROCESS

The divisive effect of the vote is one which cannot be tolerated in the church, for the church is uniquely one. It cannot be forced to take sides and remain true to its nature. The vote approach to decision making must always do just this; it must force individuals to

argue and attempt to convince, rather than help them work together to reach mutually agreeable solutions.[17]

F. F. Bruce

Most of America has become an extension of some committee. Well,
you can't run a company as a democracy. It's more of a benevolent
dictatorship. You set the direction and let people run.[18]

Ralph Burnett

What do the words committees, elections, majority rule, boards,
board members, parliamentary procedures, voting, and vote have
in common? None of these words is found in the New Testament.
We have imposed an American form of government on the church
and, as a result, most churches are as bogged down in bureaucracy
as our government is.[19]

Rick Warren

To observe most United States churches, you would think concepts ingrained in the democratic process must be foundational
biblical truths. But they're not. Biblically, a better case can be made
for casting lots than for voting.

Concepts such as checks and balances, parliamentary procedure, rule by the majority, and so on are simply not biblical principles for church organization. For example, a study of the Old
and New Testaments would show the majority was wrong far
more times than they were right.

This is not to say there aren't certain principles in the democratic process that are biblical. It's also not to say a church cannot or should not vote on various issues. However, the idea that
all decision making done in the church should be democratic is
wearing out leaders and congregations alike. The only way pastors can survive in these systems is to become astute politicians,
carefully lobbying their views and making sure they get what
they want passed. This is not the role God intended for these
shepherds.

We need to recognize that the democratic system may very well
be given by God, but it is a system that is designed primarily to
work in a world that is largely ungodly. It is not designed for the
church.

Because of overreliance on the democratic process, many churches have regulated away their vision. They have made it impossible for vision to be the driving force of the church. Instead, rules and policies drive the church. The result is ultimately a bureaucracy with endless meetings and committees. People that get along best in a church like this end up being miniature politicians who *talk* about the work of the ministry but never have enough time to *do* the work of the ministry.

### Pastoral Turnover

Pastors of growing churches are generally characterized by longevity in the ministry.[20]

Peter Wagner

On average, today's pastors last only four years at a church and the average length of a pastoral career is just fourteen years—less than half of what it was not long ago.[21]

George Barna

A long pastorate does not guarantee a church will grow, but changing pastors every few years guarantees a church won't grow.[22]

Rick Warren

If pastors are to lead and guide the church as well as be the primary initiators of vision for the church, obviously they will need to remain in their positions for some time to gain the confidence of the people and to convince themselves of their true calling as shepherds. Several studies have indicated that the most fruitful years for pastors do not begin until the fourth or fifth year, yet few pastors remain that long.

Carl George pointed out an interesting phenomenon about pastoral turnover. In what he calls the "Berry-Bucket Theory," most churches go through a significant crisis somewhere between the fourth and sixth year of a new pastorate. This crisis may have to do with several issues, but the underlying cause is the same in most cases.

When the "new guard" approaches the "old guard" in voting power, the "old guard" perceives a threat. Sometime after four years a congregation begins to realize the new pastor's agenda for the future may contradict some of the long-time members' agendas.[23] Lyle Schaller has described this tension as the classic conflict between the "pioneers" and the "homesteaders."

Most pastors, when facing this crisis, cannot understand the underlying pressure that causes the crisis, and they leave the church. The result is great insecurity and fear on the part of people in the church. Subconsciously, many lay leaders say to themselves, "We must be the only true shepherds of this flock. These other guys come and go. We are the only ones who remain with the flock, regardless of the circumstances." Pastors who come and go on a regular basis are viewed as wolves in sheep's clothing who are not to be trusted, and who certainly are not to be allowed to lead.

Unfortunately, many pastors are viewed more as hirelings than they are as shepherds. Recognize that much of this is subconscious among lay leaders. There is no conscious plan to keep the shepherd from leading. In fact, in most pastoral interviews, the leaders will express a real desire to grow and be led by vision. However, when the pastor begins to lead, he encounters all kinds of resistance, the source of which both sides are often unaware.

Thus, we see a vicious cycle of pastoral turnover that creates insecurity and fear, a lack of trust, and an unwillingness to allow pastoral leadership and vision, which leads to more pastoral turnover.

This cycle must be broken if the church is to function as God intends. All sides need to face the issue openly and not give the enemy a foothold where he can cause apathy and dissension in the local church.

> We must rediscover our role as clergy, and it will probably be more similar to the role of coach than that of chaplain or strong, authoritarian leader. As clergy, this means change. It means wrestling with a new self-image of the pastoral role. It also means challenging our congregations in their image of the pastoral role.[24]
>
> Mike Regele

## The Power of Vision

> There is no more powerful engine driving an organization toward excellence and long-range success than an attractive, worthwhile, and achievable vision of the future, widely shared.[25]
>
> Burt Nanus

Some people see things the way they are and ask why. I see the way things could be and ask why not.

President John F. Kennedy

How can we create the sense of purpose, possibility, and mutual commitment that will inspire ordinary individuals to feats of collective heroism?[26]

Gary Hamel and C. K. Prahalid

For most entrepreneurs, certainly for me, the primary pull is the vision. You are simply passionately compelled to make it come about. . . . It's as if you already handled the risk ahead of time in your mind, so you can go where angels fear to tread, because you've already skipped ahead to the gain.[27]

Larry Wilson

To understand the importance of vision in the life of the church, we must understand the power of a dream. Two movies that powerfully demonstrated the importance of a dream are *Field of Dreams* and *Rudy*.

*Field of Dreams* was the story of a farmer who heard a voice telling him to build a baseball field in his cornfields. "If you build it, he will come," a voice says. Many elements in this film demonstrate the importance of a dream.

- The dream allowed the farmer to do far more than he ever thought possible.
- The dream kept him going when everybody said it was impossible and crazy.
- The dream allowed him to get in touch with the deepest parts of himself, which in turn made him a healthier and more complete person. In a way the accomplishment of the dream became almost secondary to the personal fulfillment and sense of meaning brought about by the dream.
- The dream allowed him to involve thousands of others who were in search of a dream for their lives.

*Rudy* was the true story of a young man from a town where almost everybody worked for a large industrial factory. Virtually no one went on to college. In fact, no one in Rudy's family had gone to college. Rudy, however, has a dream and not just a dream to go to college, but to go to Notre Dame. Not only that, Rudy wants to play football for Notre Dame. At the end of the film a footnote scrolls up to say every one of Rudy's younger brothers and sisters graduated from college. Rudy's dream not only changed him, it changed his whole family, forever.

While there are obviously hundreds of examples of visionaries and the power of vision, these films give us a good picture of why vision is so important.

> If you can dream it, you can do it. Always remember that this whole thing was started by a mouse.[28]
>
> Walt Disney

> Do not underestimate the power and importance of a dream. It will be impossible for your church to get out of its holding pattern without a dream. Someone must have vision of the good, the wonderful, and the possible that is in the future of your church. . . . Dream big dreams. You can never achieve more than someone dares to dream.[29]
>
> Charles Chaney and Ron Lewis

### The Example of Joshua

> It's easy to get diverted by all the variables outside of your control, to let them eat away at your vision and self-confidence. But detours will doom you. Lose faith in yourself, and you'll fulfill your own worst prophecy.[30]
>
> Bill Parcells

Perhaps the best biblical example of the power of vision, and the pain that comes when vision is lost, is found in the Book of Joshua. In Deuteronomy 31:23 we see Joshua receiving his commissioning by God: "Be strong and courageous, for you will bring the Israelites into the land I promised them on oath, and I myself will be with you." Joshua had proved his faithfulness to God as well as to Moses, thus he was chosen to lead the people of Israel into the Promised Land.

In Joshua 1, we see Joshua receiving his specific instructions (his vision) from God:

> "Moses my servant is dead. Now then you and all these people, get ready to cross the Jordan River into the land I am about to give to them—to the Israelites. I will give you every place where you set your foot, as I promised Moses. . . . No one will be able to stand up against you all the days of your life. As I was with Moses, so I will be with you; I will never leave you nor forsake you.
>
> "Be strong and courageous, because you will lead these people to inherit the land I swore to their forefathers to give them. Be strong and very courageous. Be careful to obey all the law my servant Moses gave you; do not turn from it to the right or to the left, that you may be successful wherever you go. Do not let this Book of the Law depart from your mouth; meditate on it day and night, so that you may be careful to do everything written in it. Then you will be prosperous and successful. Have I not commanded you? Be strong and courageous. Do not be terrified; do not be discouraged, for the LORD your God will be with you wherever you go."
>
> verses 2–9

For awhile it struck me as odd that God had to warn Joshua so many times to be strong and courageous and not to be discouraged at the same time he promised he would be with Joshua and bring him great victory. The crossing of the Jordan (chapter 4) and the taking of Jericho (chapters 5–6) were spectacular in many ways, and obviously reinforced Joshua's role as leader and proved the validity of his vision. However, in chapter 7 we see the reason for the warnings in chapter 1. Because of Achan's sin, the military units sent to take the small city of Ai were defeated and forced to retreat.

Joshua's immediate reaction, along with that of the elders of Israel, was to put on sackcloth and ashes and to get on his face before God. Joshua's prayer as recorded in chapter 7 is particularly interesting.

> "Ah, Sovereign LORD, why did you ever bring this people across the Jordan to deliver us into the hands of the Amorites to destroy us? If only we had been content to stay on the other side of the Jordan! O Lord, what can I say, now that Israel has been routed

by its enemies? The Canaanites and the other people of the country will hear about this and they will surround us and wipe out our name from the earth. What then will you do for your own great name?"

verses 7–9

Notice first that Joshua blames God for bringing them into the land to die! And then he tells God he will look bad because the people of Israel have been defeated! What a contrast to the inspiring visionary of chapter 1 and the military hero of chapter 6. And what is God's reply?

"Stand up! What are you doing down on your face? Israel has sinned; they have violated my covenant, which I commanded them to keep. . . . That is why the Israelites cannot stand against their enemies; they turn their backs and run because they have been made liable to destruction. I will not be with you anymore unless you destroy whatever among you is devoted to destruction."

verses 10–15

Paraphrased, God's response is, "Joshua, I'm not impressed with your prayers or your mourning. I have not changed my mind about what I have called you to do or what inheritance I intend for the people of Israel. Get back on your feet, take care of the sin in the camp, and carry out the vision I gave you." Evidently Joshua got the message, as the rest of the book tells us the story of the great victories that took place.

An interesting conclusion to the story is found in chapter 23. This is where Joshua is about to die, and he gives his final address to the elders of Israel. If you compare his message (what could be called his vision) with that of chapter 1, you will see they are virtually identical. Joshua learned to hold on to the vision. It had guided him in good times and in bad. He could say at the end of his life, as did Paul, "I have fought the good fight, I have finished the race, I have kept the faith" (2 Tim. 4:7).

What a powerful thing a vision is and what a difference it makes whether we have it or not. Can you see how this kind of passion, dream, or vision could literally transform the life and culture of a local church?

## Steps in the Pre-Visioning Phase

> In most companies employees don't share a sense of purpose above
> and beyond that of short-term unit performance. Lacking a com-
> pelling sense of direction, few employees feel a compelling sense
> of responsibility for competitiveness. Most people won't go that
> extra mile unless they know where they are heading.[31]
>
> Gary Hamel and C. K. Prahalid

As we have already said, it is clearly the job of the leader to initiate the vision. But in almost every case where vision has made
a difference there have been key people around that leader who
helped to shape that vision. Visioning is not just a one-man
process. Usually God puts together a team to pull off the vision.

In the church there are several key pieces of groundwork that
need to be laid before the pastor leads the church in producing a
strategic planning document. Some particular questions can help
elicit key information that should not be ignored. While the number of those questions may vary from church to church, you will
find several suggestions on the following pages. The key is to ask
the right questions.

Bob Buford of the Leadership Network has rightly pointed out
that one of the positive roles of mega-church pastors around the
Unites States has been to break other churches out of their status quo. He points out that mega-church pastors are like a cue
ball in billiards. A cue ball breaks up the rest of the balls and scat-
ters them around the table. A mega-church pastor breaks up the
status quo.

Buford also points out that most churches miss out on what
they could learn from these mega churches because they look for
the wrong things. Most pastors who visit these churches or listen
to the pastors of these churches are looking for methods and
strategies they can walk away with and install immediately in
their own churches. Unfortunately, the track record is not great
on the success rate for this kind of wholesale adoption of someone else's ministry ideas. What Buford so accurately points out is
that the key to the success of mega-church pastors is that they
ask the right questions! If pastors who want to learn from mega-
church pastors would simply focus on asking the right questions

and spend time answering them for themselves, they would be much richer for the experience.

In the pre-visioning phase, we want to ask the right questions, and in particular we want to capture the insights of those who are intimately involved in the ministry of the church. You might want to use three groups to get this input:

- The first would be the governing board or *leadership team* in the church. Normally this would include ministry staff, board members, and key lay leaders. Because this group has the assigned responsibility of helping to oversee the ministry of the church, it makes sense that their input would be very helpful in the visioning process.
- The second would be a selected *planning team* who represents a cross section of the congregation. While it might be helpful to involve every single member of the congregation, it makes more logistical sense to select a planning team who can meet together on a regular basis and give the necessary feedback.
- The third group would come from selected groups within the *congregation*. It is helpful to involve as many people as possible from the congregation in some form of data-gathering or focus-group settings. Many churches use existing groups such as Sunday morning adult classes or small groups. Others choose to set aside a special Sunday night or Wednesday night to obtain congregational input.

For the congregation and leadership team of the church, you can use a four-question format that can be done in approximately one hour (15 minutes per question). The group is divided into smaller groups of five to seven people, and one person acts as a recorder. The sequence of the questions is:

- As we think about our future for the next three to five years, what do we want to maintain or keep? What are the key aspects of the ministry today that you believe God would like to see us keep or maintain in the future?

- What do we want to avoid, or make sure we don't do? What are the main things you believe God would like to make sure the church does not do? What should we make sure we avoid?
- What do we want to achieve or accomplish? What are the main things you believe God would like to make sure we achieve or accomplish?
- What should be the distinctives or unique features of our church that will make it different from other churches in our community? What are the distinctives God wants our church to have?

Notice the emphasis here. We are not just asking people, "What do you want?" We are asking them, "What do you believe God wants?" That is a much different question and will elicit significantly different answers.

I learned this lesson the hard way in a church where I was consulting. The church was losing all of its younger people (those forty and under), and the leaders were concerned enough to call in a consultant. Many of the issues centered on the ministry style of the church including worship style. When we had a congregational meeting, I posed the question, "What do you want for the future?" After we summarized the results that showed the orientation of the older people in the congregation, I was challenged by one of the oldest women in the congregation. She said, "Young man, you are asking us the wrong question. If you ask us what we want, we will describe the kind of church we want which is exactly what we just described. But you didn't ask us what do we think God wants for this church or what we would be willing to give up if we could keep our families together in the church. If you ask those questions you will find different answers." She was absolutely right and taught me a great lesson.

Plan how to present the results of this data gathering to those who participated. You could do this by simply handing out a compilation of the results, or you may want to schedule a special time to start a discussion. The important thing is to demonstrate to those who participated that you value their input and are willing to communicate the results.

For the planning team, you can use a series of exercises, which I'll be describing. These exercises are designed to obtain some very detailed input. Some churches use all of the exercises I'll describe, others only a few. For the group to process the information, I've found each exercise requires a minimum of thirty minutes. It is often a good idea to have the group review the assignment and come prepared with their ideas rather than start from scratch, but don't expect everyone to have done their homework assignment. A subgroup collates the results of each of these exercises and the results are given to each member of the planning team and leadership team. They are also given to the senior pastor for review and to contribute to the pastor's own visioning work.

If there is time, you may want to collect the key information from each group and put it on overheads or on flip charts that can be pasted around the room, so each group can see how similar or different their ideas were from other people in the room. Most church leaders are surprised to see how similar the work of each group really is.

After the headings of the following sections are step-by-step instructions for exercises that are designed for your planning team.

### *Who Are We? (Your Church History)*

To understand who you are as a church, it is often helpful to look back over your past history. One of the ways you can do this is to imagine the history of the church as a book with many chapters.

- First, identify the chapters (or key time frames) in the life of the church. Every church has significant events, happenings, or occurrences that symbolize the start or end of a particular phase of its life. Try to think of five to seven of the most memorable or important dividing points in the life of your church.
- Second, give a title to each of these phases or chapters.
- Third, write some key phrases, ideas, or thoughts that symbolize the most important aspects of that particular chapter in the life of the church.

- Finally, assign a small group of people to take this information and turn it into a one to two page narrative of the church's history.

### What Should Be Our Primary Values?

A good value is biblical, passionate, shared, constant, clear and implementable, and congruent with all others.[32]

Aubrey Malphurs

The key point is that an enduring great company decides for itself what values it holds to be core, largely independent of the current environment, competitive requirements, or management fads. Clearly, there is no universally "right" set of core values.[33]

James Collins and Jerry Porras

Values are the things we believe are nonnegotiable. They are the foundational principles upon which you intend to develop your ministry. Values reflect how you want things to be, not necessarily how they are now.

Values are another one of the foundation stones upon which our vision for the church should be developed. One major source of tension and division in churches is a failure to agree on these underlying values. Members assume they are in agreement on these values when in fact there may be significant differences.

The benefits of identifying these values are:

- They allow us to challenge an idea and not a person.
- It is easier and more efficient to handle differences of opinion at the value-building stage than when they occur later in the planning process.
- When it is determined that no one knows for sure if a value is valid or true, this is a sign that more research is required. Doing this research up front will save time and energy later.
- By researching unanswered questions linked to values, the planning team can be better prepared to answer the probable questions and concerns of the congregation.

- Congregation members are more likely to understand the church's vision if they understand the fundamental values upon which the vision rests.

To help the planning team come up with ideas, I give them a sample list from other churches. This usually helps them generate ideas easier than just starting with a blank sheet of paper. Following is a sample list:

1. We value an environment characterized by love, acceptance, and forgiveness.
2. We value creativity characterized by the willingness to create and express our God-given talents and skills.
3. We value risk-taking—the adventurous expression of faith (i.e., a pat on the back for a good try is more important than safe, methodical steps).
4. We value the right of people to choose for themselves and to make up their own minds on issues related to their personal lives. This is a nondirective approach to Christian leadership.
5. We value the management of our resources to the highest good of God's kingdom.
6. We value a strong personal home life. We contend that local congregational life should be enhancing rather than destructive to the strength of the home.
7. We value accountability. The systems of accountability within and outside the church are valued very highly and considered essential to the maintenance of all we stand for as the church.
8. We value holiness. We believe in our right standing before God, through Christ, as being righteous, without sin; and we contend for a life free of willful sin and disobedience.
9. We value each individual's personal relationship with Christ.
10. We value the spontaneity of the Holy Spirit—the free expression of his gifts. We are committed to a serendipitous approach to the walk of the Holy Spirit, always being aware of the possibility of his intervention.

## *What Should Be Our Distinctives?*

The process of figuring out which characteristics will most effectively provide your business with a competitive advantage is the
central decision in . . . our strategic decision-making process.[34]

Caryn Spain and Ron Wishnoff

Distinctives can be defined as:

- Unusual or unique attributes of the church as it sees itself in
  the future.
- Unusual or unique attributes of the church that make it different from the church down the street.
- Special things God seems to be doing or wants to do in the
  church. You'll see this in the gifts, talents, and abilities of
  those God has placed in the congregation. You'll also see it
  in the special burdens or concerns of the people in the
  church. In order to be classified as a distinctive, it must be
  something that is believed or demonstrated by a significant
  number of leaders and constituents.

God places every church in a specific community for a specific
purpose. In other words, the church fulfills a special purpose and
therefore needs to understand its uniqueness.

Examples of answers to the question, "What are your church's
distinctives?" from planning teams who have done this exercise
include the following:

1. Discipleship and mentoring takes place both officially and
   unofficially in our body. Many Christians are taking on the
   responsibility of training, discipling, and mentoring others.
2. Our church services are encouraging and uplifting to all who
   come.
3. The preaching in our church allows for practical implementation of Christianity throughout the week.
4. Our congregation has an unusual number of gifted intercessors that have demonstrated that gift repeatedly over the years.
5. Our church is one of the leaders in developing prayer relationships with other churches in the city.

6. Our people develop significant relationships with unchurched people.
7. The worship services in our church are encouraging and understandable to unchurched people.
8. Our people understand the concept of sacrificial over-and-above giving.
9. People in our church feel that the communication channels between the leaders and the congregation are open and helpful.
10. People in our church feel that caring is everyone's responsibility, not just that of the pastoral staff.
11. God has placed in our body an unusual number of caregivers who use their gifts both inside and outside the church.
12. We have small groups that are open and inclusive to new people.

### What Should Be Our Assumptions?

Unfounded assumptions are, I believe, one of the most widespread causes of disaster in organizations. Accepting and acting upon bad assumptions undermines many leaders.[35]

George Barna

Assumptions can be defined as:

- A belief or a conviction that is taken for granted about the way things ought to be
- Claims and presumptions supported by either individuals or groups, but may not be objectively verifiable
- Perceptions of facts that are held as truth until they are effectively challenged
- Things people believe to be true or should be true that help define priorities and values
- Beliefs that help define a church's identity

Examples of answers to the question, "What are the church's assumptions?" from planning teams who have done this exercise include the following:

1. We assume that disciples have a responsibility to be involved in helping others grow.
2. We assume that effective discipleship will produce growth in believers at any level of spiritual maturity.
3. We assume that music, drama, and other art forms are a means of adoring God, teaching, edifying the body of Christ, and proclaiming the Word of God.
4. We assume that pursuing quality in all that we do means skillfully using our God-given gifts with all our hearts.
5. We assume that not everyone understands all the different types and methods of prayer.
6. We assume that prayer is a discipline that must be learned and developed over time.
7. We assume that people who reject church may not necessarily reject God.
8. We assume that outreach must be an intentional strategy of the church using a variety of methods and strategies.

## Consult the Prophets

One potential source of input for this pre-visioning phase that I did not mention is people who are proven intercessors or those who have prophetic gifts. In several cases church leaders have identified such people, brought them together in a meeting format, and given them the assignment to pray and discern God's will regarding the future of the church. They are asked to avoid sharing vision-related information with one another until the appropriate time. Then you can use one of two strategies:

- Have each person write up any conclusions or insights they have received from God and present their insights to the planning team or pastor or both.
- Gather the group together and have someone facilitate the meeting and compile the insights from the group. This method has the advantage of allowing each person to test his or her gifts and learn to use them in actual ministry. It also allows the group to sort through the information to come up

with key statements that they believe God is speaking to the church.

## Summary

By understanding the need for vision in our churches and by asking ourselves some hard questions, we prepare ourselves for the next step, which is to clarify the actual vision for the church.

## Questions for Reflection

1. What are the key assumptions, values, and distinctives that underlie and define the present ministry of our church?
2. What do you believe are the key assumptions, values, and distinctives God wants for the church in the future?
3. What are the implications of our present ministry style for our overall health and effectiveness?
4. What are the key priorities of our present ministry? What's first, second, third, and so on?
5. What do we believe are the priorities God wants for our church in the future?
6. What is the unique call of our church in its community? What are we called to do and be that is different from other churches in the same area?
7. What specific contextual features of our community and our church are central to the church's vision?
8. What are the key tasks our church is trying to accomplish? How do we define success?
9. What does our church budget say about the real mission and vision of our church?

# SIX

# Team Philosophy (Part 2)

## The Visioning Phase

The noble man makes noble plans, and by noble deeds he stands.

Isaiah 32:8

I cry out to God Most High, to God, who fulfills his purpose for me.

Psalm 57:2

For it is God who is at work within you, giving you the will and the power to achieve his purpose.

Philippians 2:13 PHILLIPS

Now we are ready to produce the strategic plan. A study of the biblical process of visioning demonstrates that God conveys vision

163

primarily through a single individual and then the vision is
affirmed by those around the leader. Thus, the assumption of this
book is that the senior pastor will initiate the visioning process
by writing a draft of the strategic plan. Several factors need to be
taken into account in the preparation of this document.

## Defining Vision

Dynamic individuals and vital groups of people have at least one
characteristic in common. They know where they are going, they
have a plan for getting there, and they work wholeheartedly at the
job. . . . The effective congregation has a high sense of mission. It
is in the world as an alien community and as a task force with a
God-given objective. This objective dominates, directs, and drives
such a church to the extent that it is likely to be considered radical by the world (and by innocuous churches). It refuses to accept
the role accorded to it by its culture, to accommodate a less virile
image.[1]

Joe Ellis

Vision is having an acute sense of the possible. It is seeing what
others don't see. And when those with similar vision are drawn
together, something extraordinary occurs.[2]

Shearson Lehman/American Express

Defining vision seems like it should be a relatively easy chore.
But it's not as easy as one might think. You won't always be sure
how much vision your church has, but you'll know if you don't
have it. Duke Ellington said it best when he defined rhythm: "If
you got it, you don't need no definition. And if you don't got it,
ain't no definition gonna help."
Here are some definitions for vision.

- Jim Dethmer (formerly a pastor at Willow Creek Community Church): "A memorable picture of a preferred future
  rooted in the person and plan of God."[3]
- Warren Bennis and Burt Nanus: "To choose a direction, a
  leader must first have developed a mental image of a possible and desirable future state of the organization. This image,

which we call a vision, may be as vague as a dream or as precise as a goal or mission statement. The critical point is that a vision articulates a view of a realistic, credible, attractive future for the organization, a condition that is better in some important ways than what now exists."[4]

- George Barna: "A clear mental image of a preferable future, imparted by God to His chosen servants, based upon an accurate understanding of God, self, and circumstances."[5]
- James M. Kouzes and Barry Z. Posner: "Visions, then, are conceptualizations. They are images in the mind. They are impressions and abstractions."[6]
- John Kotter: "Vision is not mystical or intangible, but means simply a description of something in the future, often the distant future, in terms of the essence of what it should become."[7]
- Aubrey Malphurs: "It's a mental picture of what the ministry's tomorrow will look like. It's a snapshot of the church's future and all its exciting possibilities."[8]
- Markus Pfieffer: "Seeing an idea or image of a God-designed future or outcome imparted to His open and chosen vessel."[9]
- Webster's Dictionary: "the ability to perceive something not actually visible, as through keen insight."
- My Personal Definition of Vision: A compelling picture of God's preferred future for us—what God wants us to look like and be like as we fulfill his mission in our unique context.

Vision and mission are different. Mission consists of mandates derived from the principles of the New Testament that apply to all Christian churches. While the labels may differ from church to church, most would agree that the mission of the church, as described in the Scriptures, includes the following:

1. Assimilation
   - Small group ministry
   - Visitor follow-up
   - New member classes/orientation
2. Discipleship/Spiritual Growth
   - Preaching/Teaching

- Christian education classes
- Spiritual disciplines
- Mentoring

3. Evangelism/Outreach
   - Evangelism training
   - Evangelistic events/activities

4. Missions
   - Local, national, and international missions
   - Benevolence for those in need outside the church
   - Church planting

5. Pastoral Care
   - Short-term counseling
   - Crisis care/counseling
   - Benevolence for those in need inside the church
   - Recovery groups

6. Training and Equipping
   - Spiritual gifts discovery
   - Volunteer involvement
   - Ministry training

7. Worship
   - Drama
   - Music
   - Celebrative Arts

Vision, however, is different. It is the unique plan of God for a particular church in a particular location. It is the specific game plan of God which guides and directs the local church to maximum fruitfulness and effectiveness. It is nothing less than God's dream for a specific congregation.

While there is a great deal of literature about how to implement vision, surprisingly little information is available on how vision is formed or developed.

A false assumption on the part of many pastors is that only a few are gifted with vision. According to their way of thinking, some have it, others don't. However, this would mean God has a dream and plan for those churches fortunate enough to have a visionary pastor, but not for others. That makes no sense at all.

The problem escalates when pastors listen to one another or read how a pastor "received a vision" for his church. Not surprisingly, when a pastor shares how he determined what his church's vision was, in most cases the vision follows his own theological assumptions about how God speaks to people. This confuses pastors who have a different set of theological assumptions. It shouldn't though, because obviously God can communicate with us through whatever vehicles he wants to use. Therefore, the systems and strategies by which one pastor determines his vision are not necessarily transferable to all pastors.

There is no one right way to write a vision statement. The key is to write one that is *meaningful* and *compelling* to you. Remember that what you are trying to define is a clear and compelling picture of God's preferred future for your church.

## Writing a Draft of the Strategic Plan

> Opportunities that at first blush seem evolutionary will prove to be revolutionary. Today's new niche markets will turn out to be tomorrow's household appliance. There is no way to create the future, no way to profit from the future, if one cannot imagine it.[10]
>
> Gary Hamel and C. K. Prahalid

> After the completion of Disney World, someone remarked, "Isn't it too bad that Walt Disney didn't live to see this!" Mike Vance, creative director of Disney Studios replied, "He did see it—that's why it's here."[11]

At this point the senior pastor has a couple of choices. His assignment is to produce a preliminary strategic plan for the church along with some supporting documentation. This material will be presented to the planning team for review, or to the leadership team of the church if you don't use a planning team. Few pastors feel confident enough to produce a strategic plan solely by themselves. However, it is up to the pastor whether he chooses to work alone or with a small group of people he personally selects.

The key is that the senior pastor must lead and initiate the process. That is the responsibility of leaders. We are not talking about issues of power and control but the right and responsibility of leaders to lead and initiate.

If you choose the small group method, the group is usually no more than three to four people. It should include someone who has excellent writing skills. This group should be composed primarily of people who thoroughly know you and understand your philosophy of ministry.

## *Vision Statement*

Creating a vision for your organization is similar in many ways to these initial stages of planning an expedition. It begins with a vague desire to do something that would challenge yourself and others. As the desire grows in intensity, you realize that it isn't a passing fancy but something that you are determined to do. The strength of this internal energy forces you to clarify what it is that you really want to do. The end result becomes clearer and clearer. You begin to get a sense of what you want the organization to look like, feel like, and be like when you and others have completed the journey. An image of the future begins to take shape in your mind.[12]

James Kouzes and Barry Posner

I believe that vision development is the primary domain and responsibility of the point person on the ministry team because of leadership. The ability to craft and communicate a clear challenging vision is a key aspect of what it means to be a leader.[13]

Aubrey Malphurs

There are three kinds of companies. Companies that try to lead customers where they don't want to go (these are companies that find the idea of being customer-led an insight); companies that listen to customers and then respond to their articulated needs (needs that are probably already being satisfied by more foresightful competitors); and companies that lead customers where they want to go, but don't know it yet. Companies that create the future do more than satisfy customers, they constantly amaze them.[14]

Gary Hamel and C. K. Prahalid

First and foremost, find out what it is you're about, and be that. Be what you are.[15]

Norman Lear

The thing is to understand myself, to see what God really wants me to do; the thing is to find a truth which is true for me, to find the idea for which I can live and die.[16]

Søren Kierkegaard

Instead of, "You are what you do," calling says: "Do what you are."[17]

Os Guinness

Vision is shaped and defined by four primary variables.

- *Senior Pastor Personal Profile.* This refers to the unique characteristics of the senior pastor of the church. It includes the personal history, training, experience, abilities, gifts, personality, attitudes, and opinions of the senior pastor.
- *Community Demographics/Psychographics.* This refers to the types of people in the church ministry area as well as their attitudes, opinions, and interests.
- *Congregational Profile.* This refers to the demographics/psychographics, abilities, and gifts of the people already in the congregation.
- *Ministry Style.* This refers to the way in which the church carries out its mission. It defines the unique culture and personality of the church, how it approaches ministry, and how it defines itself.

These four elements interact in various ways to enhance or discourage the ministry of a local church. The health and effectiveness of the ministry of the church is basically determined by the degree to which these four variables are in alignment. Unfortunately the opposite is also true. Many churches are not familiar enough with these variables to understand how they interact, and the result is ministry that is ineffective at best. Developing a vision for your church begins by examining each of these four areas and then determining how the church can align itself with them.

### Senior Pastor Personal Profile

Every pastor is different and unique. It only makes sense that God would use the unique combination of personal history, training, experience, abilities, gifts, personality, attitudes, and opinions of the senior pastor to help shape the ministry of the church.

A review of your past can be extremely helpful in understanding where you have been as well as where you are going. Books by Ralph Matson and Arthur Miller *(Finding a Job You Can Love)*, Bobby Clinton *(The Making of a Leader)*, and John Trent *(Life Mapping)* would be excellent resources to help you in this assessment.

A good first step of the visioning process is for the senior pastor to do a fairly detailed self-analysis along with an extended time of prayer. Some of the key questions that need to be answered include the following:

- Who are the people who most influenced your life? What did they have in common?
- What have been the highlights of your life? What types of activities have you enjoyed the most? What have you disliked?
- What types of people do you relate to the best? What types of people do you have trouble relating to?
- What is your personality style?
- What are your spiritual gifts?
- What skills or abilities are your strengths? What are your weaknesses?
- What motivates, captivates, and challenges you?
- If you knew you couldn't fail, what would you try for God?
- What are your likes and dislikes in terms of church ministry?

### *Community Demographics/Psychographics*

In the discovery phase I pointed out the importance of gathering data on your community's demographics and psychographics. Now you will want to reflect on the results of that work and ask yourselves several questions:

- If we chose to minister primarily to the largest demographic groups in our community (the norm for most churches), who would they be? What are their demographic characteristics? What are their psychographic characteristics?

- Would we consider ministering primarily to a demographic group that is not predominant in our community? If so, why? What are their demographic characteristics? What are their psychographic characteristics?

## Congregational Profile

In the discovery phase you evaluated the congregation from several perspectives. Now you need to reflect on the results of that work and ask yourself a few questions:

- What demographic groups are most represented in our congregation? What are their psychographic characteristics? (What do they think? What do they believe?)
- Are these groups the ones we want to focus our ministry on? Why or why not?

### MINISTRY STYLE

In the Body of Christ, diversity is a positive quality. In a family of churches, each local church is different and is known by its individual characteristics.[18]

Peter Wagner

The number one rule of business strategy is: you cannot be all things to all people.[19]

Caryn Spain and Ron Wishnoff

In Appendix A you will find an exercise that will help you clarify the desired ministry style of the church. Take as much time as necessary to complete each of the steps. The steps can be done by the senior pastor alone, by the senior pastor and a small group of leaders, or by the planning team.

### VISION EXPANSION

Some pastors and churches choose to take key words from their vision statement, define them in more detail, and make them part of their strategic plan. You may also want to include scriptural references that support this aspect of the vision statement.

### CHURCH CULTURE

Church culture has to do with the ideas, values, assumptions, distinctives, and so on that are essential to your vision. Remember that what we are trying to define is what culture God wants to prevail in your church, not just a consensus of what people want. Sometimes church culture is simply defined by describing key elements of your church's ministry style. I suggest the following three steps for determining the culture for your church. First, answer two very difficult questions.

- What are the things that your church will do that most churches would never or seldom do?
- What are the things that your church will seldom or never do that most churches would normally do?

Second, answer the following questions and determine what the answers mean relative to your desired culture.

1. If a visitor to your church asked the following questions of one of your members, what answers would he or she receive?
   - What are the most important things in the history of this church that have an impact on what it is today?
   - Why is the church successful or unsuccessful?
   - What kinds of people come here?
   - What kinds of people don't make it here?
   - Why do the people who leave do so?
2. What does a person have to do to get recognized or to be moved into a leadership position? What does the church reward (e.g., certain attitudes, performance, loyalty)?
3. Think about the best stories you have heard lately that had something to do with your church. What patterns do you see in these stories? How often are the same stories told by different people in the organization? How pervasive are they?
4. Identify two or three heroes of the church. What characteristics do they have in common?

5. If you wanted to provide a new member with a really accurate picture of the church and how it works, to whom in the organization would you send them? Why?
6. If someone asked you to describe in just a few words the most important things about your church, how would you respond?
7. If someone asked you to state the most important values held by your church, how would you respond?

Third, define the absolutely critical organizational assumptions, values, and distinctives that will make your church the unique place that God intends it to be.

As part of the pre-visioning phase you had the members of your planning team identify what they felt were the key assumptions, values, and distinctives that God wants for the future. Review these and add your own ideas. Finally, review all the work you have done in these exercises and make a list of the top ten to fifteen items that best define your church's unique culture.

### *Vision Implications or Strategic Initiatives*

Despite the comprehensiveness of the material you have written to this point, as you begin sharing it with people you will find many people still aren't quite sure what it means for the future. It's a good idea, therefore, to add a section that gives a list of implications or strategic initiatives that define the meaning and intent of the vision statement. The following is an example of what one pastor identified as the implications or strategic initiatives of his vision:

- *The value of relationships*. We will take new practical steps to develop an atmosphere where personal, deepening, supportive, faith-building relationships of love are highly valued as expressions of our passion for the supremacy of God's love.
- *Urban-suburban partnership*. We will strive to forge a mutually enriching urban-suburban partnership, in which a significant range of racially, educationally, and economically diverse people feel at home, as they grow in their passion for following God.

- *Interracial reconciliation.* Against the rising spirit of indifference, alienation, and hostility in our land, we will embrace God's love to take new steps personally and corporately toward racial reconciliation, expressed visibly in our community and in our church.

- *Diversity in God-centered worship.* Sunday morning worship is a corporate expression of our passion for God. We sense God's leading to develop this expression in such a way as *(a)* to allow for a more focused and free lingering of love in the presence of the Lord; *(b)* to reflect musically the diversity of our congregation and our metropolitan culture; and *(c)* to interweave the values of intense God-centeredness and more personal ministry to each other in the power of the Holy Spirit.

- *Good news to the poor.* We will develop new strategies for proclaiming God's all-satisfying love and justice to the poor through: *(a)* personal involvement, *(b)* a more welcoming atmosphere, *(c)* local missionary strategies of urban disciple making; and *(d)* equipping missionaries for unreached urban peoples.

- *Challenging church and culture with the truth.* We will challenge our culture and the wider Christian movement in fresh ways with biblical truth by means of courageous Christian action and speech in the secular world.[20]

## Communicating the Strategic Plan

In an unstable environment, it is especially vital for leaders to articulate their vision for the organization—clearly, explicitly, and often.[21]

Bill Parcells

It is especially frustrating to visit a church where the leader has God's vision for the church's ministry, but has simply overlooked a crucial step in the process: disseminating the vision so it can be owned and implemented by the congregation.[22]

George Barna

The visioning phase is not complete when the strategic plan is written. In some ways, that's the easy part. The hard part is communicating it to others in a way that they can hear it, understand it, and internalize it.

As you consider how you are going to communicate your strategic plan, one of the things you should take into account is personality style. A number of tests assess personality styles. An excellent resource is the "Personal Profile System," put out by the Carlson Learning Company. Many pastors and church leaders try to sell the strategic plan with a style and demeanor that is totally contrary to their basic personality style. It may be fear, or a desire to compensate for the weaknesses of their particular style, but whatever the reason, they choose to communicate in a manner that is out of character with who they really are. This is an ineffective approach.

One thing you don't have to worry about is whether you are charismatic enough to communicate the strategic plan. In *Leaders: The Strategies for Taking Charge,* Warren Bennis and Burt Nanus write, "Charisma is the result of effective leadership, not the other way around. Those who are good at effective leadership are granted a certain amount of respect and even awe by their followers, which increases the bond of attraction."[23] And James Collins and Jerry Porras, authors of *Built to Last,* have this to say: " 'What if high-profile, charismatic leadership is just not my style?' Trying to develop such a style might be wasted energy. . . . Our research indicates that you don't need such a style anyway."[24]

### Sharing the Strategic Plan with the Planning Team

When God imparts the vision to the leader, He works through a variety of people and circumstances to enlarge the scope and perspective of the leader. People play a critical role in the development of vision, although it is not a committee-based activity. Other godly individuals are needed as a sounding board (i.e., counselors) to evaluate the vision. . . . The pastor is the point person and central figure in the process, but capturing God's vision for ministry is certainly not a solitary process.[25]

George Barna

You want to be careful how and when you share your strategic plan. Remember that you have spent countless hours thinking and dreaming about it. You own the strategic plan, heart and soul. Oftentimes, if you begin to share it too early, you are disappointed to find out others are not as excited about it as you are.

Remember this is a two-way process. You should be truly interested in getting an accurate assessment of how on target you are and getting input on how you can better communicate your ideas.

One way of doing this is to present a draft of the strategic plan first to the planning team. Depending on the kind of input you want from the planning team, you can use either one of the following feedback options.

### FEEDBACK OPTION A

Have the members of the planning team read completely through the strategic plan and do the following:

- Make a list of any items *included* that they feel *should not* have been included.
- Make a list of any items *not included* that they feel *should* have been included.
- Underline key words or phrases that are confusing or unclear.
- Bracket or box words or phrases that they feel are unnecessary.
- Add words or phrases that they feel are necessary.
- Make a list of the five items in the church-culture section that they feel are the most critical.

Have them turn in their feedback prior to your meeting with them. Then at the meeting discuss some of the major issues that came up. It is important for the planning team to understand that their role is to give *input* regarding the strategic plan. You will take the results of their input and rewrite a second draft of the strategic plan. Obviously it will be impossible to incorporate every person's ideas into the final draft of the strategic plan.

### FEEDBACK OPTION B

Have the members of the planning team read completely through the strategic plan and come to a meeting having prepared answers to the following questions.

- Is there anything in the strategic plan that you did not expect to see? What are the implications?
- Is there anything missing from the strategic plan that you expected to see? What are the implications?
- What stands out in the strategic plan? What do you think are the implications?
- Does this sound like what Jesus would be saying to our congregation? Does this sound like what he is saying to you?
- What words or phrases are confusing or difficult to understand?
- What stands out as particularly compelling, challenging, or motivating?
- What words are particularly powerful in conveying what it is God wants to do with our congregation?
- If we fulfill the strategic plan, will it make a significant difference in our lives, the lives of the congregation, and the outside community?
- Does the strategic plan clarify who we are and explain the unique features of our congregation and our community?
- Is the strategic plan worth the sacrifices and intentionality of focus that it will take to pull it off?
- Would the strategic plan motivate the congregation to get involved? Does it challenge and motivate you?

Have the planning team discuss their observations in groups of no more than five and make specific suggestions for revision. Also, give this group the opportunity to respond individually to the strategic plan in written form. Many people are overwhelmed with the initial presentation and feel intimidated to respond immediately. Many need time to pray and reflect before they can respond. It's best to give them a short time frame for this assignment (one week or less).

After reviewing the recommendations the senior pastor will usually want to incorporate some of the ideas into a revised strategic plan. The revisions are normally presented to the planning team at the next meeting.

### Sharing the Strategic Plan with the Dominant Coalition

Earlier in this book I mentioned a group of people found in every church called the *dominant coalition.* These people are the key opinion makers in the congregation. For this group, it is essential that you present your strategic plan in the idea stage and in a one-on-one setting. Usually these people prefer to meet in a *neutral* setting such as a restaurant.

Explain to them that you are going to present your ideas to the leadership team and would value their input. It's important that once you present your ideas, you do not go into a defensive posture. Remember, you genuinely want to hear what they have to say and you absolutely must not try to justify, rationalize, or argue why you are right and they are wrong. If they don't seem to respond, ask probing questions. If possible, affirm the values and assumptions they have that are in line with your own.

### Sharing the Strategic Plan with the Leadership Team

The first task in enlisting others is to find out what you and your constituents have in common. No matter how grand the dream of the individual visionary, if others do not see in it the possibility of realizing their own hopes and desires, they will not follow. It is incumbent upon the leader to show others how they too will be served by the long-term vision of the future.[26]

James Kouzes and Barry Posner

Paint a compelling picture of this vision in the minds and hearts of the people so as to catalyze them to work together to bring about God's plans for your ministry.[27]

Jim Dethmer

Another group that definitely needs to give input is the leadership team. This usually consists of the governing board, staff, and key lay leaders. You can do this in one special meeting, a series of meetings, or in a retreat format.

You might want to use specific questions like you did when you shared the vision with the planning team. Depending on the policies and bylaws of the church, you may need to have your final draft voted on and adopted by the board.

By the end of your session or sessions with the leadership team, you will have a good idea of the level of acceptance of these key leaders.

### Sharing the Strategic Plan with the Congregation

You can present the strategic plan to the congregation in a number of ways. The first and most important decision is whether you want to present it as a draft document, about which you want congregational input and reflection, or as a finished document, endorsed by the church leaders and staff. Either way can work, depending on how decisions are usually made in the church.

Timing is key at this point. If you share the strategic plan too early in the process, you may spend an inordinate amount of time trying to answer questions and concerns from the congregation. If you wait too long, you may not create the momentum you want to carry out the strategic plan. Remember, according to the Pareto principle, if you can get 20 percent of the people committed to the plan, you can accomplish 80 percent of your results with this group.

When you take the results of your work to the congregation, use two separate vehicles.

#### VISIONING SUNDAY

Because this is such a critical juncture in the life of the church, I recommend that you plan a special Sunday or series of Sundays, when the senior pastor can share the key aspects of the strategic plan with the church. Some churches have had a response form of some kind and asked people to commit themselves to the strategic plan and sign their name. One church I know of had a large copy of the vision portion of the strategic plan printed and then had it mounted in the foyer. People were asked to sign their names on the poster-board background so everyone who came to the church saw this as they entered the sanctuary.

It is a good idea to have the strategic plan in written form, so it can be handed out on Visioning Sunday or sent to homes a week before. It may be a good idea to have the word "draft" written on the cover to indicate these materials are still in process.

### CONGREGATIONAL MEETING

You should provide a separate session where people in the congregation can ask questions and give their input (usually a Sunday evening or a Wednesday night). Make sure you announce this meeting ahead of time and during the services.

It is a good idea to have every member of your leadership team in attendance at this meeting and be available to answer any questions. A definite time frame should be set for this meeting (approximately one and a half hours), so it does not drag on. The senior pastor or chairman of the board should preside at this meeting and make sure that one or two individuals do not dominate the discussion.

It's important that the leaders not be defensive as they respond to questions and comments. The purpose of the meeting is to answer questions and get input, not defend the work. By this point you will have spent a great deal of time on each of the issues and have a lot invested in the results. Thus, it is easy to be overly sensitive when people criticize or challenge your work. However, you also must remember that most people adapt slowly to change. For most people in the congregation, this is their first opportunity to see the strategic plan and the natural reaction of some will be to look for something they do not like. The key is to allow them to have their say.

You could pose questions to the group as a whole or break the group into subgroups of five to seven and have them discuss key questions and write out their observations and suggestions. This method allows everyone to voice their opinion instead of a few people dominating the meeting.

By the end of such a session, you will have a good idea where you stand with the congregation. You may have some good ideas suggested by the group that you would want to incorporate into your final draft. Going through this process will show the congregation that you really do value their input. However, make sure that the additions or modifications do not alter the heart of the vision unless you are convinced that this is God's leading.

## Special Circumstances

At least four special circumstances need to be discussed regarding visioning. These circumstances require some special treatment as they can change the visioning process significantly.

### *When the Pastor Is New to the Position*

Hopefully, in the interviewing process pastors have shared some of their philosophy of ministry, and the church has indicated a desire to move in that direction. However, this should not be interpreted as a blank check for moving ahead. Remember that in most cases the subconscious thought process, particularly among church leaders, is to avoid allowing pastors to lead. This is generated out of their fear of losing control and a desire to protect the flock. Therefore, new pastors should expect significant resistance, if not openly, subconsciously, because new pastors have not had an opportunity to earn their spurs, so to speak. They obviously have to move slower and more cautiously. They may want to begin sharing their vision more gradually and in many different settings.

A new pastor will need to spend time developing a core of leaders who share a similar burden for the ministry. This may include the present leadership team or new people who are not currently in leadership positions. Developing such a core can be done in one-on-one settings or in small group meetings. The key is for new pastors to invest in the lives of faithful people so that a core of lay leaders will learn to love and trust their leader, as well as share the pastor's passion for ministry. A year or two of developing this kind of team will save a new pastor much grief. There is no way pastors can pull off the vision by themselves. They will need to have a group of people who can not only help fulfill the vision but share it with others.

## When the Pastor Has Encountered Serious Resistance to the Strategic Plan

Leaders learn by leading, and they learn best by leading in the face of obstacles. As weather shapes mountains, so problems make leaders.[28]

Warren Bennis

To be an effective leader, you not only have to get the group of followers on the right path, but you must be able to convince them that whatever obstacle stands in the way ahead, whether it's a tree or a building that blocks the view, you're going to get around it. . . . All journeys are filled with potholes and mines, but the only way we can move beyond them is to approach them, and recognize them for what they are.[29]

Norman Lear

Resistance should not surprise pastors. Recognize that most people have great difficulty with change. Especially when faced with new and challenging ideas, many people express resistance simply as a way of buying time to deal with the implications of those changes. Remember also that unless there is significant resistance among the leadership team itself, the church can usually move ahead even if there are several people who don't agree with the new direction.

However, if the resistance is firm, and particularly if those resisting are in the leadership team itself, pastors have at least two options:

- *Assume that those who are resisting won't change and the pastor is not willing to change either.* In this case the best resolution for all concerned may be for the pastor to move on to another church or another location. One option would be to start another church (assuming the pastor possesses the necessary skills). However, I recommend that the pastor start a church in a different ministry area because starting one in the same area could be divisive and is bound to cause confusion in the community. Many pastors have left with a splinter group of supporters who later turned on them and wanted someone else. As John Wimber, the founder of the

Vineyard movement once said, "You may be dealing with a bunch of unhappy people looking for a new place to be unhappy." By starting a new church, a pastor has the luxury of starting with people who hopefully buy into the vision from the start. The main disadvantage is the financial struggle to start a new work. Moving to another church has its own risks.

- *Assume those who are resisting will change over time.* In this case pastors should invest themselves in such a way that people will gradually accept the vision. The risk here is that those who are opposed to the vision may not change their view regardless of the pastor's investment, and then he would be back to square one. However, in most congregations there is a 10 to 15 percent turnover every year, which means that even if you just maintain the size of the church, 50 percent of your congregation is likely to be new in a few years. These new people are more likely to accept the new vision.

### When the Pastor's Leadership Style Isn't Intentional Enough

If the leadership style of the pastor is more participative than initiating, or if the church has an established system of consensus decision making that will not allow pastors to take an initiating role, the pastor is faced with a serious challenge. If the issue is the leadership style, pastors have at least two choices:

- *Gradually modify the leadership style to more of a coaching role.* This role allows for plenty of input from others but requires pastors to take the initiative to present their ideas early on in the process. They must move from a role where they primarily facilitate and build consensus to where they initiate change, review, and action. In other words, to a great degree these pastors set the agenda.
- *Keep the leadership style,* recognizing its limitations, and gradually expose those on the leadership team to new ideas, hoping they will agree and begin to push for implementation. This could be done through books the pastor has people read or by

visiting other churches together that have a similar vision. The chances for success with this strategy are marginal at best.

If the issue is the organizational style within the church, pastors have a couple of choices:

- *Begin implementing their style of leadership, hoping the church will gradually go along with it.* Actually this works in a lot of situations, because often the church is looking for someone with vision and direction and a coaching style appeals to them. Recognize they probably do not understand the implications of this change and that there will be some major bumps in the road before the process is completed. But it's possible the pastor can create enough momentum in the new direction that the process becomes irreversible.
- *The other option is for the pastor to accede to the present organizational style* and attempt to work though it in a gradual fashion. Again, this strategy appears to have limited potential for success unless the pastor is willing to wait four to six years to see the vision happen.

### *Where a Radical Shift of Ministry Must Take Place*

Here lieth one whose soul sometimes burned with great longings. To whom sometimes the curtain of the Infinite was opened just a little, but who lacked the guts to make any use of it.[30]

Malcom Muggeridge

It is nothing to die. It is an awful thing never to have lived.[31]

Jean Valjean, *Les Misérables*

A fourth and very difficult challenge is when the pastor has an intentional leadership style and the church has an organizational style that allows the pastor to lead, but the pastor and church leaders have come to the conclusion that a radical shift of vision must take place.

This is a very difficult situation for a pastor, but it is not uncommon. Several pastors of significant churches have had to walk through the same kind of crisis.

- The reality is if such pastors follow their convictions, they're likely to lose several people in the church, many who love and appreciate the pastor's ministry. The phrase they are likely to hear is, "You've changed." And that's true, they have. The vision and philosophy of ministry with which some in the church are comfortable is now being changed, and people adapt slowly to change. Some people can barely handle any change. So if pastors choose this strategy, they need to be prepared for the consequences.
- The other option is really not an option at all. It's for pastors to give up their convictions and live out their ministries under a vision they no longer agree with and do not find fulfilling. Sadly, more pastors than you might expect have succumbed to this mentality.

## Summary

The purpose of this chapter is to give pastors and other church leaders some help with leading a church through a visioning process. The methodology is not as important as the destination. The final product of this phase should be a vision that is compelling and paints a clear picture of what God wants the church to look like and be like in the future. Pastors must initiate the process but can use others to help them craft the actual vision. This vision becomes the focus of all future planning efforts of the church.

## Questions for Reflection

1. To what degree does the church believe in being vision-led or vision-driven?
2. To what degree is the church ready and willing to have the senior pastor initiate and lead a visioning process?
3. Do any of the special circumstances discussed in this chapter come into play?
4. How clear a vision does the senior pastor have regarding the future ministry of the church?

5. What additional work needs to be done to clarify the vision?
6. What process will work best for your church during this visioning phase?
7. What steps need to be made in communicating the vision to the church?

SEVEN

# Developing a Game Plan (Part 1)

## Ministry Planning

■ Gap Analysis
■ The Need for a Serious Planning Effort
■ Steps for Ministry Planning
■ Summary

Once the strategic plan is in place we have completed the two ends of the planning process. We know exactly where we are starting from as a result of the discovery phase, and we know exactly where we are going from the visioning phase. Now we need to develop courses of action that will move us from where we are to where we want to go.

## Gap Analysis

Some planners call the initial stage of the planning phase a gap analysis. What you are doing is comparing the two pictures you

187

developed from the discovery and visioning phases and determining how large a gap exists between the two. Once you have determined the size and nature of the gap, then you develop plans that will gradually move you away from where you started and closer to where you want to go.

As you evaluate this gap, one of the questions you should be thinking about is, "How difficult is it going to be for us to get from where we are to where we want to be?" While there are no easy answers to that question, there are ways to evaluate the difficulty level for your future. Below are some tests that have been used to help measure the level of difficulty.

1. *How much does the church we saw in the executive summary differ from the church as defined in our strategic plan?* This helps you determine how difficult it will be to get agreement and consensus on the new vision. Ask yourself the following questions:

   • Based on the results of the discovery phase, if we continued our present course, where would the church be in ten years and what would it look like?

   • If the new strategic plan was accepted and the church operated with it for the next ten years, where would the church be and what would it look like?

2. *What degree of change do you anticipate you will be making as you implement the new strategic plan?* There are four possible degrees of change:

   • *Minimal.* The new strategic plan will require the same programs and reach the same people but with some minor adjustments and improvements.

   • *Moderate.* The new strategic plan will require new programs. However, they will be targeted at the same people.

   • *Significant.* The new strategic plan will require the same programs but require us to reach new people.

   • *Severe.* The new strategic plan will require new programs and reaching new people.

3. *What is the degree of unity that now exists within the leadership team?* While this is at best a guess, use the following scale to rate the degree of harmony and unity between the paid staff, board, and influential lay leaders.

- *Significant unity.* There is a good consensus and significant trust has been demonstrated.
- *Moderate unity.* There is some consensus and some trust depending on the issues involved. Significant discussion, however, is required to make changes.
- *Moderate disunity.* There is little consensus and little trust has been demonstrated. Significant time is required to get agreement on major issues.
- *Significant disunity.* There is virtually no consensus and trust. The relationship is basically adversarial.

4. *What is the degree of pastoral leadership potential?* In the discovery phase we measured this through the composition analysis. Looking back at these results, rate the degree of pastoral leadership potential.

5. *What is the readiness for change on the part of the leadership team and the congregation?* Use the following criteria:
    - *High opportunity.* The leaders and congregation are demonstrating a strong readiness for change and show little resistance. The prognosis is very positive.
    - *Moderate opportunity.* The leaders and congregation are demonstrating a moderate readiness with some resistance. The prognosis is positive if the implementation strategy can compensate for the leaders' concerns.
    - *Caution.* The leaders and congregation exhibit a general anxiety about change. Successful implementation of change can only occur when the forces open to change outweigh the forces resistant to change. When the forces are equal, as they are in this category, there exists the risk of investing a great deal of effort to accomplish very little. Each positive move is countered by an equally negative reaction. This may result in the appearance of movement when in fact no real change is occurring.
    - *Moderate danger.* The leaders and congregation are demonstrating a low level of readiness with considerable overt resistance. The prognosis for success is low unless the implementation strategy can modify the negative climate concerning change.

- *High danger.* The leaders and congregation are demonstrating virtually no readiness for change and extremely high levels of resistance. The implementation strategy must totally reverse the resistance atmosphere or the prognosis for success is extremely negative.

Using these five criteria you should have a good idea about what level of difficulty to expect as you begin implementing the new strategic plan. This is helpful to leaders, because with this information they won't be surprised by the difficulty of persuading various groups to take ownership of the new direction. As I pointed out earlier, it is not necessary to have 100 percent of the people in agreement with the new direction. However, it is essential that a substantial number agree that this is a valid direction. It's particularly important for the leaders to see this as a positive direction for the church.

It is not unusual for a few significant lay leaders to have reservations about the new direction. Their ownership may take some time to develop. If a severe problem exists, it may be necessary for the church to secure the services of an outside resource such as a consultant for additional help in resolving the conflict.

## The Need for a Serious Planning Effort

Now it is required that those who have been given a trust must prove faithful.

1 Corinthians 4:2

"His master replied, 'Well done, good and faithful servant! You have been faithful with a few things: I will put you in charge of many things. Come and share your master's happiness!' "

Matthew 25:21

Each one should use whatever gift he has received to serve others, faithfully administering God's grace in its various forms.

1 Peter 4:10

Successful coaches learn early in their careers that it is not enough just to know your capabilities, know the capabilities of your opponent, or even have a clear and compelling strategic plan for the future. Somehow you have to develop the necessary game plans that will allow you to accomplish the vision. If professional coaches don't do this, they are just operating by hope and chance, which probably won't keep them employed very long. Coaching plans usually focus on several key aspects:

- The personnel changes that will be necessary (and remember that not every team can simply get rid of all their players and buy players who are much better)
- The skill development that will be necessary to improve performance and take the team to the next level
- The specific plays and strategies that will work best given the talent and abilities of the personnel

Normally teams will develop plans in all these areas. In fact, most coaches set aside specific times each year when they will go through a complete planning process.

In business we see a somewhat similar but usually more complex planning process. Depending on the type and size of the business, plans are developed that move the company toward the vision.

In the church we cannot ignore the need for planning. Three major areas must be addressed during the planning phase:

- ministry planning
- facility and financial planning
- organizational planning

We will cover the first one in this chapter and the last two in following chapters.

## Steps for Ministry Planning

Every church ministry or program committee needs to develop a clear picture of what part it plays in fulfilling the mission and vision of the church. In other words, each of these groups needs to define clearly what success means. How will they know if they are fulfilling their part of the church's vision? It's amazing to me how few are the churches that have any definition of success or any way of keeping score of how they are doing.

Clearly defining what you are trying to accomplish and how you will measure progress helps ensure that the church is focused and intentional about what it is doing. Doing this accomplishes several critical functions that are foundational for effective ministry:

- The energy and activity in the church is on target and purposeful. The church knows exactly what it is trying to accomplish and why.
- The church knows what effectiveness means. It has clearly defined and measurable criteria for success.
- All resources (time, people, and dollars) are used effectively and efficiently.
- There is accountability through regular, systematic evaluation of every ministry in the church.
- The focus of every ministry area is clearly upon fulfilling the church's unique vision. There are no competing agendas.

As we look at the ministry carried out in most churches, there seem to be two distinct types of ministry going on. The first is the *people* side of ministry. This deals with the *"who"* or *pastoral* side of ministry. Ministry staff on this side are generalists who are responsible for specific age or life-stage groups (i.e., children's ministry, singles, and so on).

The second is the *task* side of the ministry. This deals with the *"what"* or *mission* aspects of ministry. Ministry staff on this side are specialists who are responsible for a specific area of ministry that crosses all age groups in the church (i.e., worship, evangelism, and so on).

Most churches have found it best to establish ministry-planning teams based on the organizational design of the church. Thus, churches usually have ministry teams that represent both sides of ministry referred to above.

In many cases you will recognize after the completion of the visioning phase that changes need to be made to the organizational structure of the church. However, it is best to complete the planning process and then tackle the problem of organizational redesign later. While the ideal would be to do these two steps in the reverse order, most churches have found that if they attack the organizational structure first, they end up in a long and arduous process that dredges up a lot of fear and conflict. Because this could derail the entire planning process, my feeling is that you should go ahead and use the present structure the first time through and then work on changing the structure after the planning process has been completed for the first time.

In most cases ministry planning teams should be led by ministry staff members (pastors) for two reasons:

- The primary responsibility of ministry staff members should be to lead and initiate, not just do the work of the ministry.
- Most lay leaders do not have the perspective or time to provide the necessary leadership.

If there is no staff leadership available, you will need to use lay leaders to head the ministry planning teams. Also, you can recruit additional people that should be involved in the process including board members, elders, deacons, and people in charge of strategic ministries.

The church should use a four-step process during the planning phase. These steps include:

- Determining Objectives
- Developing Standards
- Establishing Benchmarks
- Determining Action Plans and Strategies

### Determining Objectives

Teams break when they don't have a goal or the goals aren't clearly defined by the leaders. Goals have to be firmly entrenched, otherwise people begin to operate as independent entrepreneurs in a system that really needs cooperative work.[1]

Lew Richfield

The second tenet of strategic decision-making is, just because you can, does not mean you should. . . . A strategic plan is a tool to clarify if you should—and if the answer is yes, then what is the best way to go about it.[2]

Caryn Spain and Ron Wishnoff

The first step is to develop objectives for each area of ministry. Objectives can be defined a number of ways:

- They are generalized statements indicating a desired target or goal at some future date.
- They are statements indicating a desired or preferred future.
- They are challenging statements that summarize the most appropriate targets for ministry.
- They are statements indicating what you intend to accomplish over the next one to two years.

Perhaps the easiest concept for people to grasp is that of a *target*. It automatically conjures up the picture of something toward which we are aiming. Objectives *may* or *may not* be measurable in and of themselves. I will show how to measure objectives later. To begin with, it is easier if you do not make your ministry teams develop objectives that are immediately measurable. Let them simply state what it is they want to see happen in the future. By putting these objectives into simple sentences, you are able to identify which ones are the most crucial.

Defining objectives is vital for several reasons:

- Objectives help us clarify what it is we want to see happen.
- Objectives provide direction and intentionality for our ministry.
- By narrowing down what it is we want to see happen to only a few objectives, we force ourselves to prioritize what it is we want to do.

### CLARIFYING THE FOCUS

As each ministry seeks to fulfill the church's vision, the focus of the objectives should be to define the desired outcomes for the next one to two years. Generally speaking, objectives should be stated in terms of the results we want, not just a generalized statement that may or may not get the desired results.

An example of an objective that clearly defines a desired future might be, "Increase the number of volunteers in the church." An example of an objective that is too general would be, "Provide increased opportunities for volunteer involvement in the church." Regarding the second example, it is possible to increase the number of opportunities and not actually increase the number of volunteers, which is the real objective. When possible, try to state your objectives with clear results in mind.

Another example that may help clarify this point is in the area of Christian education. For a long time churches assumed that if you provided classes for people where they could *learn,* they would *put this learning into practice.* Many church leaders and pastors have learned the hard way that this is seldom true. Objectives, therefore, need to focus on what specifically we want to see accomplished.

Common action words used to start objectives are: increase, grow, expand, enlarge, extend, improve, develop, create, make, cause, produce, ensure, enhance, facilitate, build, maintain, ensure, train, or equip.

Examples of objectives for a number of categories include:

1. Assimilation
   - Develop an increased attitude of warmth and acceptance in our fellowship by increasing contact and interaction between members and newcomers.
   - Increase the number of individuals who are exercising their spiritual gifts in service and ministry.
2. Care
   - Improve staff and lay caregiver training that emphasizes application and practice for ministry.
   - Expand our programs and systems for care giving by focusing on specific groups in need.
3. Communications
   - Enhance the communication activities in the church.

- Ensure consistent and reliable feedback from the congregation.

4. Operations
  - Increase the average giving of individuals who are regular constituents.
  - Ensure financial accountability.

5. Outreach
  - Increase the number of constituents who are equipped for outreach.
  - Individually and corporately reach out to the surrounding community with the gospel of Jesus Christ.

6. Prayer
  - Increase participation in personal and corporate prayer.
  - Increase satisfaction in the personal prayer life of the constituents of the church.

7. Public Services/Worship
  - Create an atmosphere that encourages people to worship personally and corporately.
  - Plan high-quality, uplifting, creative services, offered in a spirit of celebration and adoration, and integrated to support the thrust of the sermon.

8. Spiritual Growth
  - Develop a disciple-making strategy through a coordinated effort of children, youth, and adult ministries.
  - Provide continuous training and mentoring of leaders for the various ministries of the church.

9. Children's Ministry
  - Develop an increased atmosphere of warmth through love, acceptance, and fun.
  - Increase personal contact with students and parents outside of the normal Sunday school time frame.

10. Youth Ministry
  - Improve our contacting of absentees.
  - Develop outreach and communication skills of regular constituents to welcome visitors during the Bible fellowship hour.

11. Adult Ministry
   • Develop and implement a plan for tracing the ongoing integration of each constituent, for the purpose of personal development and retention.
   • Enhance the "newcomer friendliness" of all our adult groups.

### WRITING OBJECTIVES

Big Hairy Audacious Goals (BHAGs): Commitment to challenging, audacious—and often risky—goals and projects toward which a visionary company channels its efforts (stimulates progress).[3]

James Collins and Jerry Porras

The best way to write objectives is to get a small group together who is responsible for a specific area of ministry. Then have that group brainstorm ideas about the things *that will help them fulfill the overall vision for the church* during the next one to two years. You would be surprised how many ministry-planning teams start listing what they would like to see happen without taking into consideration the church's overall vision. You must make sure this does not happen, otherwise your church will be like the wagon whose horses are pulling it in many different directions.

Also, first you should get everyone in a ministry-planning team to share his or her ideas on paper, so everyone in the group can see what has been said. *Do not* allow discussion until all ideas have been exhausted. It only takes one person to tear apart or criticize someone else's idea to stop the brainstorming process. People in the group end up deciding it is better not to suggest anything than to look stupid.

Once the ideas are written for everyone to see, facilitate a discussion that focuses on how the group might change or improve the ideas to make them more closely align with the vision. This is where it is okay to rephrase the ideas.

Another caution is to make sure objectives are objectives and not action plans or strategies. An example of a strategy is, "Integrate Evangelism Explosion into our church." This is a strategy because it tells *how* to do something and limits the solutions to one answer. When in doubt, ask yourselves the question, "What are we really trying to accomplish with this objective?" This will usually lead you to a true objective.

While there is no magic number for the amount of objectives, two to three is more than adequate. If you have many more than that, people will forget what the objectives are and you will have ideas on paper that never get implemented. In my own opinion, two is better than three, but each group has to decide the number that best fits for them. Each group should ask themselves, "If we were able to accomplish only one thing relative to the church's vision during the next one to two years, what would we want it to be?"

Then ask the question, "If we could accomplish only one more thing, what would it be?"

The result should be a short list of objectives that gets at the heart of what that ministry is trying to accomplish.

### Defining Standards

For each person to take responsibility for his or her own contribution and for being understood requires standards. . . . Standards have to be set high; you cannot ease into a standard.[4]

Peter Drucker

It is certainly to our detriment that we focus solely on quantitative growth. You can have numerical growth in spite of sub-par quality. But I have yet to see a church that fails to realize quantitative increases in spite of top-notch quality. Maybe we cannot determine if the chicken or the egg came first, but I think we can ascertain that quality ought to precede quantity when it comes to building a true community of believers.[5]

George Barna

Visionary companies, we learned, attain their extraordinary position not so much because of superior insight or special "secrets" of success, but largely because of the simple fact that they are so terribly demanding of themselves.[6]

James Collins and Jerry Porras

Standards are the evaluation tools we use to know whether we are meeting our objectives. The easiest way to make sure accountability takes place is to define standards of effectiveness that relate directly to our objectives.

Standards allow us to keep score, and don't underestimate the importance of score keeping. Imagine bowling where a curtain blocked your view halfway down the alley. You'd roll the ball and hear pins fall, but you would never know how many pins you knocked down, so you couldn't keep score. It wouldn't take long before you would quit bowling.

What is it about ministry that makes us think it isn't important to measure or assess effectiveness? Most churches have some assessment tools, particularly for the senior pastor and staff members, but how often is this evaluation truly objective? Most of what takes place is exclusively subjective.

Standards should define the measuring criteria you are going to use during the *next year*. Your objectives identified targets that you wanted to accomplish over the next one to two years. But your standards need to be set for a shorter period of time so you can measure progress almost immediately.

Word your standards in such a way that they do not limit the creativity of action plans or strategies. Standards should not be prescriptive but evaluative.

Standards are important for several reasons:

- They are clear, simple statements of the criteria used to measure the degree to which an objective is being accomplished.
- Their purpose is to provide a measuring rod for objectives.
- They tell us how the measurement is to take place.
- They answer the basic questions: how many, how much, and/or when.

Standards are beneficial because they:

- Help members clearly picture what it is they are trying to accomplish
- Remove the mystery and vagueness of general desires, aims, or purposes
- Motivate people into action
- Provide an objective way of measuring progress

There are two different types of standards:

1. *Declarative/Objective.* These standards include dates, numbers, or some other quantitative criteria that allows a given group to know whether it is accomplishing its objectives. More specifically, these standards may include numerical growth within a ministry; the number of people a group intends to recruit, train, or deploy; or dates by which a group will accomplish a stated objective.

2. *Affective/Subjective.* These standards are used for objectives that reflect feelings, opinions, or attitudes. Normally they are measured by asking people to tell how they feel about something or how they view something. More specifically, they may elicit statements about the clarity of church bulletin's presentation, effectiveness of a certain plan, or the degree of satisfaction with a Sunday school class.

Below are examples of standards in several categories, as defined by ministry planning teams in other churches. These examples should help you formulate your own standards.

1. Assimilation
   • Date for development of strategy and methodology in each ministry area
   • Percent of congregation leaving the church
2. Care
   • Frequency and number of training opportunities in the area of care
   • Frequency and number of training opportunities for small group leaders to assist them in their care giving
3. Communication
   • Number of church informational publications per month
   • Effectiveness of communication
4. Operations
   • Degree to which giving information is brought to the attention of the congregation
   • Increase in overall giving
5. Outreach
   • Number of visitors who attend as the result of an invite by a constituent
   • Degree of outreach training required for ministry leaders

6. Prayer
- Number of ministries with a prayer support team
- Degree of satisfaction with personal prayer life

7. Public Services/Worship
- Degree to which parts of our service support the sermon and promote meaningful worship
- Degree to which there is support for the development of worship, drama, and other fine art ministries

8. Spiritual Growth
- Date of implementation of a centralized plan for disciple making
- Number of leaders trained and deployed

9. Children
- Number of children who attend two or more times per month
- Degree of satisfaction of parents

10. Youth
- Degree of contact with students after they have been absent
- Number of new youth who visit more than once

11. Adults
- Date by which computer data base program is implemented to track attendance in worship or Sunday school
- Elapsed time between a first-time visit and personal follow-up contact

### WRITING STANDARDS

Each objective should have at least one standard. Some may have two. The idea is to have a way of measuring the progress of each objective, but not to have so many measuring devices that you create a paper factory. Because you are going to write only one or two standards, make sure you use standards that will tell you the degree to which you are accomplishing the objective.

Again, this usually is done in a group setting. Questions you can use to help define the standards include:

What would we consider observable evidence that we are moving ahead?

How would we know if we are making progress on our objective?

What would be the best way to measure whether or not we
really are accomplishing this objective?

### *Establishing Benchmarks*

Every employee must have a personal scorecard that directly relates
his or her job to the challenge being pursued in a particular time
frame. This might be a quality benchmark, an indicator of timeli-
ness, or a productivity number.[7]

Gary Hamel and C. K. Prahalid

Benchmarks measure the degree of success. They set the height
of the bar at which you're aiming. They are objective measurements that tell how successful you have been in accomplishing
your objective and fulfilling your vision.

Each standard should have three levels of benchmarks rather
than just one. The reason for this is that the accomplishment of
objectives often depends on outside resources (i.e., amount of
publicity, size of the budget, and necessary space). The extent to
which a ministry receives these resources usually makes a big difference in terms of what can be accomplished. By setting only
one benchmark, you don't take into account some very important
variables that can affect your performance. The following are
three suggestions for benchmarks:

- *Minimum* is the lowest level of performance the church will
  accept without requiring major changes. Any evaluation that
  scores below this minimum means major revisions must be
  made in the action plans and strategies, or there must be a
  significant revision in the objective, standard, or benchmark.
  It assumes no increase in the amount of resources currently
  dedicated to accomplishing the objective (e.g., no new
  money and no additional communication).
- *Acceptable* is the level of performance you would consider
  successful within the next year. It assumes some increase in

resources such as funding, publicity, additional facility usage, and so on, but not large amounts.

- *Exceptional* is the level of performance that you consider the absolute best you could do if you had all the necessary resources and the Lord significantly blessed your ministry. Most groups usually set this level where they want to be two years from now.

Below are two examples of how you would move from objectives to standards to benchmarks.

1. *Objective:* To increase the number of small groups in the church
   *Standard:* Number of new small groups
   *Benchmarks:*
   - Minimum—two new groups
   - Acceptable—four new groups
   - Exceptional—eight new groups
2. *Objective:* To increase the satisfaction of the members of our congregation in their personal prayer life
   *Standard:* Degree of satisfaction
   *Benchmarks:*
   - Minimum—On a five-question survey filled out by members of the congregation the average rating of satisfaction is 40 percent or above
   - Acceptable—The average rating of satisfaction is 60 percent or above
   - Exceptional—The average rating of satisfaction is 70 percent or above

### Developing Action Plans and Strategies

Setting a goal is not the main thing. It is deciding how you will go about achieving it and staying with that plan. The key is discipline. Without it, there is no morale.[8]

Tom Landry

Once we have the objectives, standards, and benchmarks in place, we are ready to develop specific action plans and strategies that will accomplish the objectives, meet the standards, and fulfill the vision. Unfortunately, this is where most churches *start* when they do planning. Hopefully you can now see why this is a huge mistake. Without any knowledge of where you are starting from, without any knowledge of where it is you are trying to go, without any definition of what that future should look like, how can you develop action plans and strategies? All you can do is try to come up with some kind of program that supposedly moves the church in a positive direction.

Now you are ready to decide what activities, events, programs, ideas, and so on will best fulfill the vision of the church, accomplish objectives, and meet standards. These are called *action plans* and *strategies*.

### DEFINITION

- Action plans and strategies describe methods the church intends to use.
- Action plans and strategies describe how limited resources such as money, people, materials, and facilities will be used.
- Action plans and strategies are our best estimate of what it will take to accomplish the objectives and meet the standards.
- Action plans and strategies are ideas we hope will work, but if they don't, we will develop new plans and strategies as necessary.

### BENEFITS

- Action plans and strategies describe the major activities, events, and ideas on which we have agreed.
- Action plans and strategies describe who will be responsible and the specific methods we will use.
- Because action plans and strategies are normally fairly detailed and straight forward, they allow us to involve others in the congregation. (By definition they should not require experts to implement them.)
- Action plans and strategies are excellent tools for training and equipping the congregation for ministry.

- Action plans and strategies allow us to take the focus off personalities and put it where it belongs—on accomplishing the objectives and meeting the standards.
- Action plans and strategies allow us to provide accountability at every level.

Obviously there are an unlimited number of possibilities for how a church can accomplish its objectives and meet its standards. Your job is to decide which ones are best for your church. Take into account the resources available in your church, but do not limit your ideas solely on these criteria. It may be that you'll need to increase your resources to make a vital action plan happen.

If you decide to use a program that has been developed by another church or a parachurch ministry, you still should go through the process of developing an action plan or strategy. You should then purchase the necessary materials, attend a training seminar if one is available, and interview churches that have used the program successfully.

Any program you use that comes from outside the church needs to be filtered through your specific needs and adapted to fit your unique situation. The primary reason for failure of these types of programs is failure to spend the time necessary to adapt the program to the unique needs of an individual church.

You should start your thinking by brainstorming with your group, asking everyone to contribute their ideas on what would be some possible action plans or strategies that would best accomplish the objectives. Don't forget to include the programs, events, and so on you are already using. Don't assume you have to throw out everything you've already been doing. While it is likely that your group will come up with a lot of new ideas, you also will be using existing ideas. If costs are involved, you should estimate the costs for the next year and write it down next to your recommended plans.

After you have generated a list of items (for some ministries, this list may be four to five items, for others forty to fifty items), you should prioritize the list, asking yourself the question, "If we could only do one of these action plans or strategies, which one would it be?"

As you prioritize your action plans and strategies, look for the ones that will have the greatest leverage.

- Plans or strategies that will most powerfully fulfill the vision
- Plans or strategies that will accomplish multiple objectives and standards
- Plans or strategies that will have the greatest impact in the shortest period of time
- Plans or strategies that do not require extensive new resources

These are the ones that should get first priority and the ones you should promote first. And these are the ones for which you should recruit your best people for implementation purposes. The old saying is true: "If you want the best person for the job, look for someone who is already busy."

For churches who have not had significant experience in the planning process, you may choose to stop the planning phase once the prioritization of action plans and strategies is complete. With your prioritized list, you should be able to produce the necessary data for the ministry portion of the church budget.

Where money is necessary, interaction should take place between your ministry-planning team and the appropriate budget group in the church. If a plan requires reallocation of funds, the two groups should discuss this. If a plan requires allocation of new funds, obviously this is more difficult. If it is impossible to get the necessary funds during the present budgeting period, the necessary funds should be provided during the next period, if possible. It is the responsibility of your ministry-planning team to make sure the necessary input is given in any future budgeting process, so the team can carry out its assignments.

Future budget preparation should take into consideration the objectives, standards, action plans, and strategies that have been prepared. After the fixed expenses of the church are accounted for, the action plans or strategies that best fulfill the mission and vision of the church should be funded first. This is one of the ultimate goals of the planning process—that the church would be clearly focused on what it is trying to accomplish, and that everything the church does, including the budgeting process, would be in alignment with the vision. In some cases this takes a while to develop.

### *Defining Steps for Accomplishing Action Plans/Strategies*

Some churches choose to take an additional step once they have identified specific action plans and strategies. They develop detailed plans for their major action plans and strategies. If you decide to take this step, each ministry-planning team needs to start with their highest priority plan or strategy and list every action or activity that is necessary for implementation.

Ask everyone to contribute ideas or activities and write each on a post-it note. Don't worry whether they are in order sequentially. Just have people name anything they think needs to be done and pile the notes on a table. When ideas stop, ask the question, "Is there anything else we need to do to implement this action plan or strategy?"

The next step is to organize the ideas or activities in chronological order. You can use a large piece of butcher paper and simply sequence the notes in the order you want them—from what needs to be done first to what needs to be done last. You may begin to see some natural divisions that could be used to create different simultaneously occurring "tracks." For example, you might see several items that relate to communications and other items that relate to facilities.

Once all the ideas or activities are posted, it might be a good idea to look at your chart and ask yourself again whether or not you have included *every* necessary action or activity. While it is understood that you cannot predict everything, the more complete your planning at this point, the easier it will be to implement your strategy.

After you are sure the chart is complete, transfer the results to paper, showing each action or activity, the date by which each is to be completed, who is responsible, and any costs associated with that action or activity.

## Summary

The primary purpose of ministry planning is to ensure that all aspects of church ministry are in alignment with the vision. Another purpose is to provide clear direction for each ministry, so it can accomplish the church's vision. And finally, ministry planning should provide the framework for realistic accountability.

## Questions for Reflection

1. How many ministries within your church have objectives showing how they will fulfill the church's vision? Assuming you want to have these kinds of objectives, what's the best process to develop objectives within the next year?
2. How many ministries within your church have standards and benchmarks indicating how they will measure progress on their objectives? Assuming you want to have these kinds of standards and benchmarks, what's the best process for developing them within the next year?
3. How many ministries within your church have a prioritized list of action plans and strategies? Assuming you want to have such a list, what's the best process for developing one within the next year?
4. To what degree would you say your present budgeting process is vision driven? Assuming you want to have a budget that is vision driven, what's the best process to get this accomplished within the next year?

# EIGHT

# Developing a Game Plan (Part 2)

## *Facility and Financial Planning*

- Site Development Analysis
- Developing a Facilities Plan
- Space Options
- Developing a Financial and Facility Game Plan
- Summary

Facilities and finances are two of the most critical areas involved in the strategic planning process for any church. Many churches find themselves stifled by one or the other at critical junctures. Only if the church has a detailed plan for each of these areas can it achieve maximum health and effectiveness. In this chapter I will briefly discuss both facilities and finances, giving not only theories but also practical steps to take.

## Site Development Analysis

One vital piece of knowledge is the development potential for a church's existing site. This helps to determine whether or not relocation is going to be necessary at some point.

One of the questions church leaders need to ask themselves is, If we developed this site to its maximum capacity and then relocated, who would be willing to buy the existing site and what would they be willing to pay? Many churches have miscalculated these numbers and as a result have ended up overestimating the value as well as the ease of sale for their existing site. Obviously the best buyer is another church. However, remember that there aren't that many churches shopping for buildings. If they are presently leasing space, they may want to build a facility that is designed to meet their unique needs. Your building and property may not match those needs. Smaller churches are possible buyers, but oftentimes they don't have the money, and it is doubtful you would want to finance the loan for them.

Appraisers assume that a church building is worth virtually nothing. They look at the land and its development potential, given local zoning regulations, and then determine its value. You definitely do not want to overbuild a site because you will never be able to sell it for the value of the existing buildings and land.

Having said that, how do you determine the maximum development potential of a given site? Assuming you do not have any unusual problems with your site (unusual setback requirements, areas where you cannot build because of water or terrain, etc.), you can count on accommodating 125 people on campus per acre for a single service. This figure assumes the necessary worship, parking, education, and office space.

For example, if your church had ten acres of property, and the full ten acres could be developed, you could make the following assumptions:

- You can accommodate an auditorium that will seat about 750 people.
- Assuming you were willing to run three worship services, you can project the number of people in attendance as follows:
    1. largest service—675 (90 percent of capacity)
    2. second largest service—600 (80 percent of capacity)
    3. third largest service—413 (55 percent of capacity)

- Your space for children and youth education would need to accommodate the following numbers of people (based on 40 percent of total attendance):
  1. largest service—450
  2. second largest service—400
  3. third largest service—275
- This means with three services you can accommodate a total attendance of 2,813 or approximately 2,800.

As you do your projections for growth in the future, you will need to predict when you will hit the 2,800 figure and begin to plan for relocation well before that time. Obviously, two other alternatives exist. One would be to get additional property adjacent to your present property, and the other would be to add more services. Remember, however, that this last option provides only minimal help because any service after your third service will fill only to about 35 percent of capacity because of the time frames available for such services.

## Developing a Facilities Plan

Peter Wagner, author of *Your Church Can Be Healthy,* has used the term "sociological strangulation" to describe facilities that are inadequate to meet the needs of the church. He writes, "What is sociological strangulation? It is the slow-down in the rate of church growth caused when the flow of people into a church begins to exceed the capacity of the facilities to handle it. In other words a church, like a plant, can become pot bound. If the root system gets too big for the pot, the plant will grow less and, as Japanese gardeners know, what growth there is may turn out to be grotesque. This is an interesting diversion for gardeners, but not for churches. Healthy, vigorous church growth requires space."[1] Four interesting phenomena take place when churches run out of needed space.

- While many people can handle overcrowding, many others cannot. It's not just a matter of the overcrowding being disruptive. It is actually stressful to many people. People can't explain why they feel like they do, but they feel totally over-whelmed. It doesn't make a difference whether the person is elderly or young; the dynamics are the same. When faced with this kind of pressure, the only alternative is to avoid coming. Adults simply choose not to come to the church, although they might not be able to explain why they don't come, and they might use reasons other than space to jus-tify their decision.

- Young children don't have the choice whether or not to go, so they have a variety of techniques to help convince their parents not to take them; everything from temper tantrums to simple crying is effective in letting their parents know they are unhappy. And there is more than ample research to show that if parents see their children having a negative experi-ence in Sunday school, they aren't likely to go to that church.

- In a crowded environment, only certain types of people thrive. They tend to be the more aggressive types that are jokingly referred to as church *piranhas*. They view the over-crowding as a challenge. They have a mentality that says, "I don't care how crowded it is; this is my church and I'm going to survive here no matter what it takes." Actually, to survive overcrowding people must subconsciously drive away oth-ers to make room for themselves. Thus, overcrowded churches are overly representative of aggressive personality types.

- Another negative effect of a crowded environment is a feel-ing of helplessness. People develop a survival strategy that says, "I can't fight the situation, so I guess I'll have to cope with it." The result is often apathy, lack of involvement, and so on—all things the church cannot afford to have happen. If the church remains in this condition too long, this apathy reaches a point where people see no reason and have no moti-vation to change the situation. When church leaders finally decide to expand, they often are surprised by how little church members are interested in the expansion.

For all of the above reasons and others, it is essential that the pastor and church leaders stay on top of the facility and space needs. A constant evaluation of the facilities must take place and adjustments need to be made quickly when there is a problem.

## Forecasting

One of the most difficult areas of facility planning is trying to forecast the future. Yet, if we can't obtain an accurate picture of the future, we will never have the necessary staffing, facilities, or resources for maximum effectiveness. Most churches respond to needs on a reactive rather than proactive basis. The result is crisis planning that is always too late and limits the health and effectiveness of the church. It is imperative that churches desiring to be maximally effective plan for the future. A key part of this planning is projecting or forecasting future needs of the church, so that leaders can make sure the church has the resources necessary to meet those needs.

Forecasting is the task of anticipating future conditions based on past and present realities. While a certain element of guessing or estimating is involved, much of what is termed forecasting is based on mathematical calculations. Because of the nature of forecasting, it's important to update these forecasts on a regular basis, at least semiannually and perhaps quarterly.

A number of advantages come with preparing forecasts using a computer spreadsheet program:

- It's easy to make changes and adjust data based on new information. Good forecasting involves constant fine-tuning and revision, so it is important to work in a format that allows for easy alteration as new information becomes available.
- Spreadsheet programs such as Excel or Quattro allow you to view hypothetical futures or alternate scenarios with relative ease. Simply changing certain basic variables in your model will give you new forecasts in a matter of seconds. This is particularly helpful when you are dealing with multiple variables that may affect your forecasts.

### COLLECTING DATA ON PAST HISTORY

The first step is to gather data on the past and present history of the church that will provide baselines for the future. Several pieces of information will help you forecast the future; an example of these is in Appendix B. I recommend gathering averages for each category for the last three to five years. If some of this data is unavailable, use at least the last several months' numbers.

### Projecting Future Growth

The next step is to project your growth rates for the next ten years. This is highly subjective but should be based on a combination of your past history plus your present potential.

Some guidelines are in order:

- If you have seen phenomenal growth during the last five years, is it realistic for you to continue at these growth rates? Are your facilities at the point where they can sustain the rapid growth? Do you have the necessary staff and lay leaders to continue to care for those coming in? These and other similar questions should be answered before you decide you will be able to sustain the same kind of growth for the next ten years.

- If you have seen steady but slow growth during the last five years, what do you see as the potential for the next ten years? If you do the same things you have been doing, you can expect to see the same kind of average growth each year. The only potential limitations are facilities, staffing, and number of lay leaders. If you feel your church has untapped potential for the future and should be able to increase its growth rate from the past, plan on a gradual increase rather than a dramatic jump during a single year.

- If growth has plateaued during the last five years (i.e., you have seen little growth but also little decline), do you see this pattern changing? If so, how much? Remember, if you are projecting a significant increase in your growth rate based on new potential, make sure you project a *gradual* increase. It takes time to turn things around, and momentum tends to generate itself. Stagnation tends to generate further stagnation; growth tends to generate growth.

- If you have experienced decline during the last five years, what is the prospect for the next ten years? Obviously, if nothing different is done, you can continue to expect a decline.

This will have as many consequences for your planning as a growth cycle. If you see the church turning its negative pattern around and beginning a growth cycle, be sure to project this as a gradual transition. The first step is to see the decline stop; in future years you can begin to project increases.

The goal is to project your future realistically. Some churches like to have three projections: a best-case scenario, worst-case scenario, and projected-case scenario. This is not absolutely necessary, but there is a range of possibilities for your future. Churches that do the best planning take in all the information they can about the past and present, and they put together their best estimates for future years.

Remember that you will be doing this process annually. The first year is the hardest. In subsequent years your projections will be more and more accurate.

The hard work is determining the growth rates for each year (see Appendix C). You can normally assume that the ratios for the various age levels will hold pretty constant over the next several years unless the demographics of the community change severely or you make specific efforts to increase certain age groups through staffing, programming, and other methods.

## Space Options

Based on your conclusions and projected growth rates for each of the next ten years, you can determine the present and future space needs for your church.

### *Worship Space*

If you find your worship space is inadequate, you have several options.

1. *The most obvious option is to add services.* The economics of church construction dictate multiple services in the average church today. You simply will not find the resources necessary to build a facility that will house only a single service

unless you have a very unusual congregation. Having said this, you can ask only so much of your staff. Two to three services seems reasonable, but many churches have successfully held more.

Planning the timing of your services is of particular importance. As pointed out earlier, services that begin between 9:00 and 11:15 usually have the potential to fill to capacity. There are exceptions to this time frame based on certain areas of the country, but this would be the norm. Therefore, when you are considering the best time for a third service, generally speaking your guidelines should be as follows:

- If you could hold another service at a second site that started during the prime time on Sunday morning, this would give you access to the most people. This would require overlapping the services so the pastor could preach at all services, or you could use different pastors at different sites.
- Most churches have found they can get more people to a Saturday night service than they can to an early Sunday service.
- Sunday evening seems to be a poor time for a service, unless it is fairly early, like 5:00 or 6:00 P.M.
- Any new service that you start should attempt to be at least 40 percent full, otherwise it will have a difficult time growing. People will sense that it does not have the dynamics of other services and will drift back to them. Also, an unusual dynamic takes place in a very small service. Preachers tend to increase their intensity and volume in an attempt to make something happen. Worship teams, however, do the opposite. They usually become more reserved because not much seems to be happening. The combination is a service that does not have the feel of a normal service. While a few people will like the new format and remain, the service will be more of a drain than a help.

2. *The best alternative may be adding new space.* This is obviously a major decision that requires a significant amount of analysis. But with the amount of time now required for

permits, design, dealing with environmental issues, and so on, it is imperative that the church provide the lead time necessary for any proposed building projects. In many areas of the country, even the simplest building project may require three years from the start of the design process to the actual occupation of the building. As you consider expansion, make sure you take into account the space needs for worship, education, and parking. To expand one without taking into account the others may undermine the reason for the expansion.

3. *The most radical solution is to relocate the church to a new site.* This should not be undertaken unless you are convinced that the space limitations at your present site are insurmountable. This means that you have evaluated every possible alternative for your present site (including buying surrounding property, moving offices off-site, etc.), and have come to the conclusion that the site is simply not workable for future expansion. If you reach this conclusion, you must be very careful in the selection of your new site. First of all, you cannot move very far without substantially restructuring your congregation. Second, you need to make sure that the new site will meet all your projected needs, so you do not end up in the same situation again.

4. *Get creative.* Some churches have used creative alternatives as temporary measures to solve their worship space needs while they build or relocate.

- Have certain portions of the congregation rotate and meet in home groups on certain Sundays to free up space at the church site.
- Teleconference the worship service to an alternate site or theater complex.
- Divide the church into multiple congregations that meet at multiple sites. Periodically hold services at a rented facility that accommodates the entire congregation.
- Rent facilities and meet as a large group only once a month. On other Sundays meet in small groups.

### Parking Area

If you find that your parking area is inadequate to meet the demands of parking during both worship and Christian education classes, you have several options.

1. *Limit the number of adult classes during worship services.* This is probably the number one solution for this problem. Adult Sunday school attendance has decreased over the last ten years, but part of the problem has been facility related. By not having adult education classes on Sunday mornings, the church is able to provide more classroom space for kids and decrease the need for parking at the same time.

   One potential problem with this strategy has to do with the busy schedules of many church members. It's getting more and more difficult for people to come to church more than once a week. Many people prefer to come once and get everything done at the same time. Because of the parking issue it may be necessary to have a second site nearby for education and training purposes. The only other alternative would be to have enough parking spaces to take care of both the worship and educational needs at the same time. This can be an expensive option.

2. *Another alternative, used successfully in some areas, is off-site parking with shuttle buses running people to and from church.* While this tends to work better in warmer climates than it does in colder areas, it can work in both. However:

   - You must have at least three buses for each route (one waiting at the church, one on the way to the church, and one waiting at the off-site parking area). People simply will not wait for a long period of time at a secondary site for transportation to the church, particularly if the weather is bad.
   - Convince your staff, key leaders, and workers to use the shuttle system. Because they are your most committed people, they should understand the need and be most willing to make the sacrifice. If they won't, you are unlikely to convince others to do so.

3. *Have the staff, key leaders, and workers carpool from an off-site parking area.* This is a less radical solution than the one above. Carpooling is sometimes difficult to coordinate because of people's differing time schedules. However, remember for every car you park off-site, you have provided room for two or more new people at the church site each service.
4. *Have the staff, key leaders, and workers park off-site and walk to the church from surrounding areas.* The only problems here are weather and neighbor sensitivity. If you can get around these two problems, it is a good alternative.
5. *Build a multilevel parking garage.* While this is an expensive option, if you have limited potential for acquiring additional land, or if land is so expensive that it does not make sense to purchase it, building a parking garage is worth considering.

### *Education Space*

If you find education space is your major problem, you might examine the following options:

1. *Remove adult education classes.* One idea already mentioned is to remove adult education classes that are held during the worship service. This provides more room for children and youth classes.
2. *Move offices off-site.* Many churches are moving their offices off-site and using what was formerly office space for education space. This is a rather simple alternative and does not seem to impact church life negatively.
3. *Rent additional facilities.* This has limited applicability, especially for younger children. Parents do not like the idea of dropping their children off in one place and then going to the church. It does work for some high school groups where many of the students have their own transportation.
4. *Add modular classroom space to your site.* This is perhaps the simplest solution. Modular classrooms are used in schools on a regular basis. Many companies are now producing these for schools, churches, and offices. In most cases this can be done quickly and provides immediate

space. Problems come into play only if you don't have the necessary land space to house the modular units, or if building or zoning codes make it prohibitive to use them. Because most schools are allowed to use modular class-rooms, churches usually are allowed the same flexibility. Normally these are only allowed as temporary facilities. That is, the city or county may require you to get rid of them after three to five years.

## Developing a Financial and Facility Game Plan

When planning for the future, you need to take into account not only the space you need but what financial resources you have to pay for the needed space. Usually you end up with some kind of a trade-off between finances and space. Most churches cannot build everything they want because they don't have the necessary resources.

### *Preliminary Considerations*

Some questions to consider include the following:

1. *What kind of growth rates are you anticipating?* Perhaps the first issue to settle is what growth rate you want to project for the church's future. Obviously the faster you grow, the more dollars you will have available for expansion. On the other hand, you don't want to depend on growth to finance all expansion, because if the growth doesn't take place, you'll find yourself in a difficult financial position.
2. *What is the church's position on debt?* It is wise for any church to have an official position regarding debt. Some churches have taken the position that any debt is nonbiblical. It is difficult to find any scriptural backing for this position, and Christian financial experts such as Larry Burkett and Ron Blue do not subscribe to it. Obviously the ideal scenario would be to build everything you need without having to borrow, but most churches, and particularly fast-growing churches, will probably have to use debt to finance a large portion of their facility needs.

While borrowing will be necessary in most cases, churches need to be careful about how much they borrow. The typical baby boomer notion of "borrow it now and figure out how to pay for it later" has meant trouble for a lot of churches. Here are some general guidelines that in most cases will keep your church out of trouble:

- Keep your debt servicing costs to no more than 25 percent of your income. Most lending institutions use this as their major criterion. Also, they look at what you brought in last year, not what you are projecting for the next several years. If you have an excellent relationship with a lending institution, the lender may be more generous than this, but it would be the exception rather than the rule.

- Borrow no more than $2,200 per attendee. This level of borrowing allows the church to pay off the loan in a relatively short period of time (less than ten years), but it requires some over-and-above giving campaigns to do it.

- Don't borrow more than the total of your last two years' income. This is similar to the $2,200-per-attendee rule.

- Churches that plan well ahead have found the best scenario to be what is called an "interest neutral" or "zero interest" plan. This plan has you raise approximately 65 percent of what is needed prior to any construction. The money that is raised or saved is put into some kind of account that draws interest. When the 65 percent threshold is reached the church begins the actual construction. They then take out a short-term loan to cover the remainder of the cost and pay the interest on that loan with the interest that was generated from the money raised earlier. This allows the church to say to potential donors that none of their contributions will go to pay interest costs. Every dollar will go to pay for actual building costs. This is a very popular option, but it requires substantial lead time. If you need the facilities immediately, this plan obviously won't work.

3. *What percentage of your operational budget do you want to allocate for facility expansion?* If you use 25 percent of your operating budget for debt servicing, this will negatively affect

some other budgeting areas. Normally there has to be a trade-off between the amount you budget for personnel and the amount you budget for debt. The norm for personnel is 46 percent of your operating budget. For fast-growing churches, it's more like 50 percent, but that is usually possible only if you are spending 15 percent or less for debt servicing out of the operating budget.

If you project using 25 percent of your operating budget for debt and you already are using 46 percent for personnel, you probably need to lower your personnel spending by 10 percent. This means you will be temporarily understaffed, but most churches find they have to do this during times of major facility expansion.

4. *How much over-and-above fundraising are you willing to do?* Most churches, particularly those that are fast growing, are unable to finance necessary facility expansion from only their operating budgets. They have to raise additional dollars through some type of stewardship campaign. Most churches spread this kind of campaign over three years. However, several rapidly growing churches have to do annual campaigns to keep up with their growth. To avoid creating false impressions, decide ahead of time which kind of campaign you are going to conduct.

  • Who is going to lead the over-and-above campaign? The basic choices are to do it yourself or hire an outside consulting firm to help you. Normally you'll raise significantly less funds (something like 33–50 percent less) if you do it exclusively by yourself. Therefore, you need to think hard and long before you decide to do it yourself. It has been suggested that self-led programs generate less income because:

    Most pastors are very poor fundraisers and do not do a good job of putting together a campaign.

    The time and effort it takes to do such a campaign often changes the focus of the church from ministry to fundraising. This is often confusing to the average person in the church and even causes some people to leave.

Outside consultants give you an "expert" to help formulate the campaign; they have a grasp of what does and doesn't work. They also address the congregation when necessary.

If you decide to use an outside consultant, make sure the firm understands your philosophy of ministry and will not violate the basic values of the church when leading the campaign.

5. *What length of time will you be in debt?* Long-term debt is a problem for most churches. So many things can happen over a twenty- to thirty-year period of time that it is usually unwise to be in debt for that length of time. Most lending institutions prefer fifteen- to twenty-year loan packages for churches, although a few will offer payoff terms of up to thirty years. Even if a church chooses the longer option to keep initial payments as low as possible, a plan should still be in place to pay off the loan in a much shorter period of time. To be fiscally safe, most churches devise a plan for paying off the loan in no more than ten years.

### *Developing Financial Need Projections*

The next step is to determine potential financial scenarios to see if you will be able to finance the facility expansion. You should include several variables as you develop your financial scenario. Again, these can be put into a spreadsheet so you can try various scenarios and come up with the best plan for your church. In Appendix D you will find a list of variables commonly included in a facility and financial plan.

## Summary

Churches face many problems related to facilities. The crucial thing to remember is that the purpose of facilities is to facilitate. And in this case they should facilitate the church's vision. That is why, while we can give some guidelines for how to determine the necessary facilities, each church must evaluate its own needs based on its own unique vision.

One of the biggest problems is accounting for the lag time necessary for facility development. Particularly in urban and suburban areas, it is not unusual for a building project to take four to five years from conception to completion. Not planning for this will have a negative effect on the health and effectiveness of the church.

Another problem is trying to plan for five to ten years into the future. While the average person in the congregation may not need to plan that far ahead, church leaders must have a financial and facility plan that provides for long-term needs. Anticipating future needs is difficult, but it is important to try.

Some churches focus on facilities without developing a ministry that will make full use of the facilities. Other churches focus on the ministry and wait until a crisis before dealing with facility issues. Both of these approaches are faulty and indicate poor stewardship on the part of the church.

The middle ground is a balanced approach to facilities that weighs all the necessary factors and comes up with a financial and facility game plan that will fulfill the vision and meet the projected needs of the church.

## Questions for Reflection

1. Have you done a site-development analysis? How long will your site be adequate? What's your plan after that?
2. What process are you using to project facility and financial needs?
   - Is your present process extensive enough to meet your needs?
   - If not, what is your plan to improve your process within the next year?
3. Using the questions in this chapter, what assumptions should you use in putting together your financial and facility projections?
4. Are your current facilities adequate for worship, education, parking, and office space? If not, when will you need additional space? How are you going to provide the needed space?

5. Will your facility and financial projections keep up with the anticipated growth? If not, what adjustments need to be made?
6. Do you have the financial resources necessary to sustain your projections? If not, what is your plan to get the necessary resources?

# NINE

# Developing a Game Plan (Part 3)

*Organizational Planning*

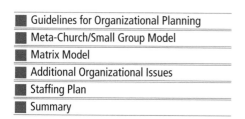

One of the most critical aspects of organizational planning is developing a maximally efficient design. Many times the organizational design prevents a church from fulfilling its mission and vision. Organizational designs are visual representations of how the people and tasks of a church are organized. These designs show the roles of people involved in the church as well as the relationships between these people.

## Guidelines for Organizational Planning

Churches are among the prime offenders in the Meeting Syndrome. Somehow we have confused two antithetical practices: ownership

227

of the decision-making process and pointless discussion. For good reason, we seek to get the laity involved in the process of ministry by having them reflect and decide upon the factors that shape ministry. Unfortunately, this focus on process often leads to a meandering series of interactions in which time is wasted, energy is squandered, excitement for ministry is minimized, and leaders are stretched thinner than the evidence used to challenge the Clarence Thomas nomination.[1]

George Barna

In several religious traditions, the most gifted and the most deeply committed volunteers are crammed off to serve on the governing board or to staff the finance committee or trustees. This reinforces the impression that governance, money, and real estate are the top priorities in congregational life.[2]

Lyle Schaller

While varieties of organizational structures are as numerous as churches, some guidelines can help you in designing an organizational system that will work for you.

- In some cases you will have preestablished entities to work around. These could be committees, boards, and other bodies that are required by your denomination or bylaws. If modifying or doing away with these entities is inconvenient or impossible, you will need to include them in your design.
- Design a system that will work for the church in the future, not just for today.
- Remember that every position, board, committee, and so on must be shown on your organizational chart.
- The idea is to design an organization that has as few levels as possible. The information should be as easily disseminated and collected as possible. The more layers you design into your organization, the slower the process and the less clear the information.
- Your organizational design should match your mission and vision as a church. Don't include committees and boards just because they are traditional or because somebody thinks they

are a good idea. Develop a functional organizational plan that reflects what it is you are trying to accomplish.

- Remember that ministry is accomplished by doing, not by meeting. If you create an organizational design that is overwhelmed with committees and boards, who have to meet all the time to discuss the ministry in the church, your best people will end up meeting rather than doing. Effective churches keep the number of meetings to a minimum and the amount of doing to a maximum.

- Show necessary lines of authority and reporting relationships in your design.

- As you compare your mission and vision with your current design, you're likely to find organizational units that should be eliminated. In other cases, new organizational units will need to be created. This is an ongoing process and should be viewed as positive, adaptive change. Effective churches are not afraid of change; they welcome it.

## Meta-Church/Small Group Model

The meta-church/small group model emphasizes the realities of church life from a relational perspective. Because organizations accomplish their mission and vision through people, it is important to understand not only reporting relationships but also how people will work together. In a sense the two models come together at this point with a focus on team building and teamwork.

To understand this model, we need to understand some of its fundamental assumptions, which are as follows:

- Large churches are a permanent feature of church life, particularly in urban areas. However, in order for a large church to survive, it must find a way to be large and small at the same time. The answer is the use of small groups in every aspect of the church's ministry.

- Without proper delegation, pastors of mega churches will not survive. The only way for churches to operate at maximum efficiency is for the pastor to do more leading and vision casting, while the congregation does more ministering. In order to get the congregation out of the stands and on to the playing field, it will be necessary to develop a structure of relationships that allows for maximum congregational development.

- Without maximum utilization of spiritual gifts, the church will not fulfill its mission. The church needs to be organized in such a way as to make full use of the spiritual gifts of the congregation. Ministry should not be viewed as a bunch of jobs to be done or positions to be filled but rather as a bunch of opportunities for spiritual gifts to be released.

- Without adequate pastoral care, large churches will not be able to survive. Pastoral touch is as important as ever. The difference is that pastoral care will have to be done through the ministry of the body of believers and not just the pastoral staff. Small groups provide the best opportunity for significant pastoral-care relationships.

- Group life should take multiple forms. No longer will Bible studies suffice to meet the diverse needs of our constituents. Churches ought to provide multiple opportunities for people to be involved in small group activities based on their own needs and interests.

- Leaders should be raised up and trained from within the church. The church will never be able to hire enough outside people to meet their staffing needs. Moreover, it is unwise to depend on outside hires for all staffing needs because understanding the church's philosophy of ministry and its culture takes time and is sometimes difficult.

  Instead, we need to recognize leaders within the church and develop them. As they prove themselves responsible with some tasks, they should be given additional responsibilities. Staffing becomes more of a natural recognition of what someone is already doing rather than placing a person into a position. Mentoring relationships will need to be developed at every level of church life. This will provide the needed systems for recruiting, training, deploying, and monitoring.

The meta-church model provides a good method for networking people throughout the church. It recognizes the need and provides a method for maximum congregational involvement.

# Matrix Model

> What are the two most significant changes in staffing churches in the new reformation? The first has been described earlier. That is the shift from the individual who will do it to the team and a greater emphasis on getting it done. . . .Teams are being evaluated in the new reformation on the basis of group performance, not on assigning credit or blame for who did what. This kind of evaluating continues to be an uphill struggle, but clearly teams are being recognized as the successors to solo performers.[3]
>
> Lyle Schaller

The matrix model emphasizes the realities of church life from an organizational perspective. The matrix model has several basic assumptions:

- The organizational design needs to remain the same regardless of whether the staff is paid or not. Some positions will be filled by full-time paid personnel, others by volunteers. The point is, all the positions need to be covered by someone. The decision as to which ones are paid and which ones aren't depends on the church's unique vision, its priorities, the gifts of the existing staff, and the financial resources available.

- The organizational design needs to remain the same regardless of the size of the church. The matrix model helps to decide the priorities for future hiring, and the new design does not need to change as new staff is added. At the same time there is great flexibility in designing the model itself.

- Churches today have two distinct types of ministry. The first is the people side of the ministry—the "who" or pastoral aspect of the ministry. Ministry staff involved in this area are generalists who are responsible for specific groups of people. The second is the task side of the ministry—the "what" or operational aspects of the ministry. Ministry staff in this area are specialists who are responsible for a specific area of ministry that deals with all ages and groups in the church.

- The basic format in which most staff workers will find themselves operating is a team environment. This means that depending on the assignment and task, the staff are likely to work with a variety of people on both the people and tasks sides of ministry. The arrangement of the teams will vary depending on the need. So, while a hierarchical sense to the structure emphasizes the vertical relationship of the levels, a horizontal aspect operates independent of these vertical relationships.

- Some churches choose to have ministry teams on only the people side (for example, a children's ministry team). Staff involved in task ministries are then viewed as resource specialists who assist the people-ministry teams.

- Some churches choose to have ministry teams on only the task side (for example, an evangelism ministry team). Staff involved in people ministries are then viewed as resource specialists who assist the task-ministry teams.

- Some churches choose to have ministry teams on both sides with individuals serving simultaneously on two teams, a people-ministry team and a task-ministry team.

The matrix is a grid with a vertical axis and a horizontal axis.[4] See Appendix E for an example. You might place the generalist ministries along the horizontal axis. These are the ministries that churches often group by age, sex, or social cluster. Along the vertical axis would be the *specialist* groups. These ministries are formed to achieve a specific task and generally represent the values or mission tasks of the church.

Each *generalist* ministry intersects with each *specialist* ministry creating a grid. As an example, let's look at worship on the *specialist* axis. The worship leader in most churches is primarily responsible for the thirty minutes of worship on Sunday morning. However, in the matrix model the worship leader is responsible to help develop worship in *each* generalist ministry in the church.

Here is how it would work. The worship specialist approaches the children's ministry generalist and together they work on developing a worship leader for the children's ministry. As a result the children's ministry now has its own worship band on Sunday mornings. In the same way the worship specialist also helps the youth ministry generalist to develop a worship leader in the high school. The worship specialist provides the training and mentoring, and the youth generalist provides pastoring and ministry opportunity.

Leaders are constantly on a talent search looking to train, equip, and release people into areas of ministry. This is also an important strategy for church growth. People want to belong and make a difference. People will make commitments to the church when they are in a position to make a difference. They don't want to be pew sitters; they want to be equipped for the work of the ministry!

Remember that the matrix system does not automatically determine which positions are paid and which are volunteer. Who is paid and who is not is determined by the size of the church, the resources available, and the mission and vision of the church.

### Overseeing Ministry Teams

Let's answer a logical question. Who is responsible for correction in the leadership team? For example, if the evangelism specialist for men's ministry is experiencing a problem, does the men's ministry leader or the evangelism leader bring direction or correction? This is where teamwork will really be tested. Both leaders are responsible but from different angles.

Remember that the generalists and specialists approach their ministries from different mindsets. The generalist will have a tendency to be more pastoral. He will tend to take the lead in issues relating to character. The specialists are going to be concerned if the issue has to do with performance. It is absolutely essential that the generalist leader and the specialist leader are real team players and communicating well.

The quality and quantity of ministry is directly related to the size and maturity of the church. Most churches have a tendency to establish generalist ministries before they think about specialists, with the exception of worship. In the early phase of building a church, everyone is trying to gather people and develop relationships. For this reason the church planter often values the generalists, who are good at gathering people and providing care, above the specialists. This is similar to having a football team with a great defensive team but little or no offensive team. Without an offense, it is pretty hard to advance the ball or score.

Just like the football's offensive and defensive teams need coaching, so do your specialist and generalist leadership teams. The senior pastor can do this, or a large church might assign a generalist and specialist coordinator or executive pastor.

The generalist coordinator oversees all of the generalist leaders. His or her job is to supervise, communicate, and train his or her generalist team. The coordinator is in contact with the senior pastor and the specialist coordinator, and assures them that the generalist leaders are connecting with specialist leaders as they select and manage their work force. The specialist coordinator does the same for his or her team and stays in contact with the senior pastor and the generalist coordinator.

As the church grows and becomes more fruitful, these coordinators are instrumental in developing new ministries in their areas. As new ministries develop, the net widens and is able to catch more people. This dynamic makes the matrix model very effective for continual church growth. The good news is that the church grows as a team instead of as a crowd.

The matrix and meta-church models are far from exclusive of one another. In fact, they overlap in several places. Most churches seem to prefer the organizational aspects of the matrix model, but the best of both could be incorporated into a single model.

## Additional Organizational Issues

It is no wonder that scholars have had trouble standardizing titles of church leadership in the New Testament. They were all different! Tasks, roles, offices, and leadership were different from place to place—and rightly so![5]

William Easum and Thomas Bandy

A common mistake made by many churches is to take their brightest and best people and turn them into bureaucrats by giving them more meetings to attend. You can drain the life out of people by scheduling a constant string of committee meetings. . . . We have imposed an American form of government on the church and, as a result, most churches are bogged down in bureaucracy as our government is. It takes forever to get anything done. Man-made organizational structures have prevented more churches from healthy growth than any of us could imagine.[6]

Rick Warren

You'll notice I haven't given definitions to the traditional roles of elder and deacon. I have a couple reasons for this.

- Churches are not at all unified when it comes to the roles of elders and deacons.
- Churches do not agree about the relationships between elders, deacons, and paid staff. In some cases they are the same people, in other cases they are totally different people. In many cases the roles of each overlap, but it varies from church to church.

For the above reasons it is much more difficult to factor in elders and deacons into the organizational design than generalists and specialists. Obviously, if your church has elders and deacons, the relationship between them and paid staff needs to be defined.

## *Role of Elders*

The elders' place in an organizational design usually falls within one of the following categories:

- They are totally separate from the staff with general oversight responsibilities (as with the board of directors of a corporation). They have little contact with the daily operation of the church
- They make up an elder board that is advisory only to the senior pastor.
- They consist of two types, ruling elders and other elders, making some staff members elders and others not.
- They are responsible for particular areas of ministry but not for others.
- They are responsible, either directly or in concert with staff members, for the people side of ministry.
- They are matched with staff, so they are totally involved and knowledgeable about every aspect of ministry.
- Elders and major staff members are one and the same.

## Role of Deacons

Deacons usually fall into one of the following descriptions:

- They are totally separate from the staff but are under the direction of staff, who are responsible for their area of ministry.
- They are the department heads (paid or unpaid).
- They are responsible, either directly or in concert with the staff members, for the task side of the ministry.
- They are the heads of ministries within the administrative area of church life (i.e., finances, benevolence, facilities, and so on).

## Role of Church Boards

To be effective, this means a change in the role for the traditional governing board. Instead of seeing itself primarily as a permission-granting and permission-withholding body, this model requires the governing board to fill five overlapping roles, (a) a long-range planning committee, (b) a support system for staff, (c) the hub of the internal communication system, (d) the blocking backs in leading proposals for change, and (e) a team of cheerleaders for a new tomorrow. . . . More and more governing boards are: (a) shrinking their size to be able to focus on performance rather than to emphasize their representative nature, (b) acting as long-range planning committees, (c) placing reaching new generations above perpetuating old traditions as a guideline in decision making, and (d) emphasizing innovation and performance above inputs and control as the primary goal in governance.[7]

Lyle Schaller

In most cases the church bylaws dictate the composition of the governing board. This does not mean the bylaws cannot be changed but doing so often requires a congregational vote.

The key is to make the governing board part of the organizational design in such a way as to maximize the effectiveness of the church. Oftentimes tradition dictates design whether the traditional design is best for the church or not.

Churches cannot afford to have inefficient or superfluous boards, nor can they afford to have a board that creates a *we-*

*they* relationship with the paid staff. The far-too-typical confrontational relationship between board and staff is counterproductive to the health and effectiveness of the church. While many churches claim to have the *biblical* design or the *New Testament* model, the differences between churches that make this claim demonstrate the impossibility of devising a single biblical or New Testament model. God has given us the freedom to organize ourselves, as long as we maintain certain principles. Interestingly, most of these principles refer to character and attitudes, not structure.

While it may be controversial, I strongly suggest that board members meet the following four criteria to be considered for board positions:

- They meet all the biblical qualifications of elders and deacons (Titus 1:5–9; 1 Tim. 3:1–13).
- They demonstrate true qualities of a servant.
- They are significant and regular givers.
- They are committed to the mission and vision of the church.

The last two seem to be the most controversial, but if you ask any parachurch ministry, they will tell you these are essential criteria for someone to be on their board. Why settle for any less with our church boards!

Some exciting new developments have taken place in regard to church and non-profit boards. John Carver's *Policy Governance* is one of the best models in use today for understanding how non-profit boards should operate. His book, *Boards That Make A Difference* (San Francisco: Jossey-Bass, 1997), provides some of the clearest thinking as well as specific recommendations for non-profit boards. Carver proposes that the primary responsibility of any board is to set policy and not get involved in the means or strategies to fulfill these policies. He suggests that boards establish clear policies in four areas.

1. *Organizational Outcomes.* The board defines which results are to be achieved, for whom, and at what cost.
2. *Executive Limitations.* The board establishes the boundaries of acceptability within which the CEO and staff can operate.

3. *Board-Executive Relationship.* The board clarifies the manner in which it delegates authority to staff, as well as how it evaluates senior personnel performance based on provisions of the organizational outcomes as well as the executive limitations policies.
4. *Board Process.* The board determines its philosophy, its accountability, and the specifics of its own job.

Carver points out that the most crucial function of the board is to establish a strategic plan in conjunction with the CEO (Carver writes from a business perspective).

While I would differ with Carver on the exact roles of the board and the CEO in the formulation of the strategic plan, I do believe he is on the right track in terms of how boards can and should operate.

## Staffing Plan

Once you have the basic organizational design in mind, you are ready to develop a staffing plan. Some basic guidelines you need to follow as you evaluate your staffing needs are as follows:

- An average range of expenses for personnel would be 40 to 55 percent of the total budget. Remember that this needs to include the benefits package and taxes you have to pay for all employees, which may add 10 to 15 percent above and beyond the actual salaries of the staff.
- You should have one paid ministry staff person for about every 150 people in attendance on Sunday including children.
- You should have one paid support staff person (e.g., custodial, secretarial) for about every 170 people in attendance on Sunday including children.

In thinking about your staffing needs for the immediate future (one to two years), be sure to take the following into account:

- The first ministry staff person hired after the senior pastor should be complementary in both personality style, gifts, talents, and abilities. In other words, you are trying to get as complete a team as possible when you add this person.

- Hire staff that are extremely capable and are committed to the vision of the church. Many churches hire people because they are available, or because they are willing to work for less, or because they pose no threat to the leadership. Actually, you probably want someone who does not meet any of these criteria. However, you also must make sure that anyone you hire understands and believes fully in the vision of the church.

- Interviewing should focus on what people have done rather than on what they think they would do. Any potential candidate can figure out what you want and sound good. What you really want is someone who has demonstrated the qualities you are looking for. Instead of asking them if they believe in team ministry, ask them to describe how they have developed and worked within a team ministry somewhere in their past. Pose similar questions for other key attributes for which you're looking.

- The particular emphasis of the vision statement of the church may dictate where major paid staff need to be allocated. Your budget and staffing need to reflect your priorities.

- Think carefully about who will be responsible for what. Obviously, if the church is smaller, the paid and unpaid staff must cover wider areas of responsibility. As the church grows, more positions can become full-time paid positions, and the jobs can be more specialized. The church should balance both the people and task sides of the ministry and provide the greatest coverage possible. In examining the present staff and future needs, where are the greatest needs?

- Hire staff who are recruiters and reproducers, not just specialists who prefer working alone. In today's church you will never have enough dollars to hire the staff you need if the staff members are not excellent trainers and equippers who enjoy implementing others into ministry.

## Summary

Organizational planning is a neglected aspect of most church planning efforts. However, the development of an organizational plan is just as critical as a ministry or facilities plan. Be sure to build in plenty of flexibility to your organizational plan, keeping in mind that each church must clearly define an organizational structure that will best facilitate its own vision. Simply allowing the organizational plan to develop by itself will mean plenty of confusion down the road.

Unfortunately, there is not a clear biblical design for church organizational planning. Churches should follow some key principles, but even the churches we read about in Acts and the Epistles varied widely in how they were organized. When it comes to elders and deacons, the Bible's emphasis is on their character much more than it is on their function and responsibilities. Thus, the implication of Scripture is that we can formulate our own organizational design while at the same time following biblical principles.

Many pastors and churches have a difficult time diagramming their organizational design in a traditional pyramid format. For many, the pyramid format implies a secular approach that is not acceptable. For others, the pyramid format implies a hierarchy of power that they do not wish to convey. For these reasons, you may want to consider using an alternative format, perhaps a bottom-up organization, a series of concentric circles, a hub design using circles, or a design that would look similar to an airline terminal.

## Questions for Reflection

1. How would you rate the effectiveness of your current organizational design?
2. To what degree does your organizational design match your mission and vision?
3. What aspects of the meta-church or matrix models might improve your organizational design?

4. If you currently have elders, how are they functioning? What do you see as the future role of elders in the church?
5. If you currently have deacons, how are they functioning? What do you see as the future role of deacons in the church?
6. What do you see as the future role of the church board in the church?

# TEN

# Developing a Game Plan (Part 4)

## *The Resourcing Phase*

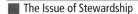

- The Issue of Stewardship
- Increasing the Volunteer Resource Base
- Increasing the Financial Resource Base
- Summary

Once the vision is in place along with the plans to get a church from where it is to where it wants to go, it is not unusual for the church to discover that it does not have the necessary resources to accomplish these plans. In fact, I have yet to work with a church where that was not the case. The inadequacy of resources is particularly noticeable in the areas of serving and giving. Until the church develops the necessary resources, it will be hamstrung as it attempts to implement its plans. In this chapter we will discuss how the church can increase its resource base.

## The Issue of Stewardship

Stewardship is the use of God-given resources for the accomplishment of God-given goals.[1]

Ron Blue

243

The stewardship process is more than simply fund raising; stewardship relates to the appropriate management of all personal resources in light of God's provision of those resources.[2]

George Barna

There is the inescapable conclusion that faith and wealth have not been considered theological issues because the church at large has avoided them.[3]

Justo Gonzalez

While almost all literature on church resources (usually categorized under "stewardship") focuses on finances, biblical principles regarding resources are much broader in scope and perspective. Stewardship is an essential part of Christian life as presented in the Scriptures. However, this is not necessarily true for the average church in America today. Let me share some of my assumptions and observations regarding stewardship in our churches:

- Average Christians misunderstand the concept of stewardship. The term itself is seldom used. Most Christians see little connection between what they do with their resources, their spiritual gifts, and their time on the one hand and being a disciple on the other. They tend to view giving, serving, and so on as a "have-to" rather than a "want-to." Despite the urges and pleas of church leaders, more and more jobs are left empty, while church attendance and financial giving is becoming increasingly irregular.
- The amount of pulpit teaching on stewardship has declined radically. As many churches have tried to make worship services more visitor-friendly, they are inclined to talk less about the biblical requirements regarding stewardship. Many pastors have done this because of research indicating that unchurched people believe all we talk about and all we are interested in is their money. Because financial giving is about the extent of most church's definition of stewardship, they have made the topic almost nonexistent in the life of the church.
- Many pastors are afraid to teach on stewardship because of the abusive practices and reputation of other pastors and

parachurch leaders. Trying to avoid being viewed as manipulative, they have chosen to remain relatively silent on the subject, leaving it up to the people themselves to determine what is or is not appropriate.

- The movement toward topical preaching has made it more difficult to know when and how often to introduce the concept of stewardship. As more and more pastors have gone away from traditional exegetical teaching and have made their sermons more topical, many feel guilty in introducing a sermon on stewardship because it doesn't seem natural. In the past, when pastors came to a scriptural passage on stewardship, they could teach it without apology because it was a part of the material they were covering and couldn't be ignored. However, now they have to insert a message, and it seems more awkward.

## Why Christians Are Not Giving and Serving As They Have in the Past

The average person has less than two hours a week to give to a volunteer organization. The competition for those hours is intense.[4]

Michael Slaughter

Before discussing the essential elements of stewardship and how we can increase the resources in our churches, we need to understand why these resources have continued to decline across the country. If we understand the changes that have taken place in the church in the United States, it helps us to understand the differences in the environment today versus several years ago. But it still doesn't answer the question of why people have become less engaged in their churches. The following is a discussion of some conclusions of those who have done research in this area.

### COMPASSION FATIGUE

Given the massive increase in communications today, people are much more aware of needs, not only in their own communities but also around the world. They are bombarded by appeals on TV as well as phone and mail solicitations. The net result for some is a feeling that even if they gave everything they had and volunteered full time, it still would not be enough. So they drop out. Some people have labeled this *compassion fatigue.* In a similar vein, many of the most faithful people in our churches are beginning to feel tired and discouraged. They see the shrinking number of donors and volunteers, and they begin to feel as if they are the only ones left who really care. As a result, many are decreasing their giving or withdrawing their involvement and participation.

### FEELING OF INSIGNIFICANCE

People want to direct their time and dollars toward making an impact; they want to accomplish something significant. This is especially true for baby boomers and baby busters. Along with these desires comes a general distrust of institutions. Younger generations have seen too many examples of people giving and serving only to find out that these same people were being manipulated or exploited. As a result they have developed a cynicism about life in general. In the area of giving, they would rather serve directly, so they can make sure people are really helped, instead of just donating money. However, most people feel like they can't serve the way they'd like to because they don't have the time.

When financial needs are expressed in thousands or millions of dollars, or when serving needs are shown as requiring long-term commitments, people feel overwhelmed. They feel like the little they have to offer, be it financial resources or time, is not sufficient to meet the need. They feel if they don't participate, it will not make a big difference because they would not have added much anyway.

### LACK OF CLARITY OR VISION REGARDING THE NEED

It is true that most Christians over fifty-five give and serve because God said so, or the church leaders said so. Those under fifty-five are much more cautious and reluctant to serve and give, because they are not sure the church really needs the money or will do anything significant with their resources.

It is interesting to note that in the area of giving, many of those fifty-five and older are stuck on the concept of a tithe and have never increased their giving beyond the 10-percent level, while many of those under fifty-five never give more than token dollars.

Most Christians do not know what financial resources it takes to run a church. The typical budget information does not compute with personal giving in the minds of most church constituents.

For example, if you calculate how much it costs per person including children and convey it to average churchgoers, they are amazed. When a family of four who have been giving $10 a week suddenly realizes that the average cost per person may be more like $15–$20, it doesn't take them long to realize that in order for them to attend and take advantage of the many ministries the church has to offer, another family of four must be putting in their own $60–$80 plus another $50–$70 for them as well.

### LACK OF ACCOUNTABILITY

One of the sad characteristics of many churches today is a genuine lack of accountability. Many Christians think they can be true disciples yet not participate regularly in any church. Unfortunately, that is a lie of the enemy that is designed to defeat Christians. Christianity has always been a community-operated faith. Only when people are in genuine fellowship and relationship can they grow and be cared for.

How many churches really know how people in their congregations are doing in the areas of giving and serving? And even if they know how they are doing, what are they doing to challenge each other to grow in the stewardship dimension of their spiritual lives?

On the other hand, it is not unusual today for people to attend more than one church at a time, or to attend once every third week, but believe they are regular and committed participants. All of these factors indicate a lack of sincere commitment to other believers. Obviously what follows is a lack of commitment and accountability in every area of their lives. What they don't realize is that their lack of commitment may be a veiled attempt to make themselves unaccountable to anyone. While this may seem like freedom, it is usually very unhealthy unless it is for only a short period of time. It is easy for people in most churches to withdraw their participation gradually without anyone knowing about it. Usually they feel they have a good reason for this disengagement, but very few do. Many signal they are in the process of leaving by withdrawing or significantly reducing their participation in serving and giving.

## Essential Biblical Principles of Stewardship

We would be wrong to try to increase resources in the church without first coming to a clear understanding of what the Scriptures have to say about stewardship. Until and unless we really believe that improving stewardship and increasing service is good for people and essential to their personal growth as disciples, we will be unable to approach them with the necessary teaching and challenge.

The following principles appear to be foundational to biblical stewardship.

### EVERYTHING WE HAVE COMES FROM GOD AND BELONGS TO HIM—NOT US

As Christians we have to decide whether we really believe that everything we have belongs to God and we get to choose what we keep, or if everything really belongs to us and we are forced to decide what we can give up for God (see Luke 16:13; Acts 5:1–11).

### WE ARE TO BE GOOD STEWARDS OF OUR RESOURCES

Freely you have received, freely give.

Matthew 10:8

So, then, each of us will give an account of himself to God.

Romans 14:12

Now it is required that those who have been given a trust must prove faithful.

1 Corinthians 4:2

From everyone who has been given much, much will be demanded; and from the one who has been entrusted with much, much more will be asked.

Luke 12:48

God entrusts to us everything we have, and he expects us to do something of eternal value with what we have. God wants us to learn how to manage money and things and not let them manage us. He wants to teach us how to live disciplined lives, so we can not only take care of ourselves but be a blessing to others.

In the example from the parable of talents (Luke 19:12–27; Matt. 25:14–30), the manager commended servants who took what they had been given and figured out ways to make it increase. He made an example of the one who simply held on to what he had been entrusted. The manager took what was given him and gave it to the servant who had already increased the money given to him. This only makes sense; God is not going to waste his resources on us if he knows we will use them foolishly or, worse, not use them at all.

Research shows us that as people come to Christ and begin following his principles for their lives, they normally improve their economic situation.

### Proper Stewardship Demonstrates the Nature, Heart, and Passion of God

For God so loved the world that he gave his one and only Son, that whoever believes in him shall not perish but have eternal life. For God did not send his Son into the world to condemn the world, but to save the world through him.

John 3:16–17

Giving and serving are the very nature of God. Jesus Christ demonstrated these principles during his life on earth. The Bible teaches us that God did not give because he had to but because he wanted to. He gave not after deciding whether or not he wanted to be inconvenienced, but because of his love and compassion for his creation.

### Proper Stewardship Is an Act of Worship

"But you ask, 'How have we shown contempt for your name?' . . . By saying that the Lord's table is contemptible. When you bring blind animals for sacrifice, is that not wrong? When you sacrifice crippled or diseased animals, is that not wrong? Try offering them to your governor! Would he be pleased with you? Would he accept you?" says the Lord Almighty.

Malachi 1:6–8

When we are good stewards, we are demonstrating our love for God. We are presenting to him those things that are precious to us. We are placing him first in our lives. The stewardship of our time, talents, and resources is an act of worship. In order for that worship to be acceptable to God, it must meet the true tests of both Old and New Testament Christianity:

- It must be from our first and best, not from what is left over or what we don't want (Prov. 3:9; Mal. 1:6–14).
- It must be given freely, willingly, and joyfully (2 Cor. 9:5, 7).

Given these guidelines, it is sad that what many Christians see as an offering or sacrifice of their time, talent, and resources is really unacceptable to God because of the wrong attitudes that are associated with it.

### Proper Stewardship Teaches Us to Make Christ Lord of Our Lives

No servant can serve two masters. Either he will hate the one and love the other, or he will be devoted to the one and despise the other. You cannot serve both God and money.

Luke 16:13

When observing children as they first begin to deal with the issue of possessions, one of the first words out of their mouths is "mine." It continues in a more sophisticated form as we get older. We are always going to wrestle with the issue of self. Before we were Christians, we were the center of life. Now God wants us to learn how to make him that center and remove ourselves. This is a process that takes time, and we are likely to struggle with it all of our lifetimes.

### Proper Stewardship Helps Us Overcome the Fear That We Will Not Have Enough

"So do not worry, saying, 'What shall we eat?' or 'What shall we drink?' or 'What shall we wear?' For the pagans run after these things, and your heavenly Father knows that you need them."

Matthew 6:32–33

When we think we will not have enough, we end up making money and things the center of our concerns. Learning to give and serve releases something inside us that resists the enemy. Something about the sinful nature says we will never have enough. The inner voice of the enemy always says we need to fear. It attacks us in every area of our lives, not just finances. Often our response is to hoard, to demand of others, to try to fill up the emptiness, but it is still there.

If we examine the testimony of many who have had an abundance of riches or fame, in most cases they say they were just as empty with the abundance as they were when they had nothing. The lesson of such testimony is that true wealth isn't about money; it's about being in a close relationship with the Father.

### PROPER STEWARDSHIP TESTS OUR OBEDIENCE AND OUR FAITH

But just as you excel in everything . . . see that you also excel in this grace of giving. I am not commanding you, but I want to test the sincerity of your love by comparing it with the earnestness of others.

2 Corinthians 8:7–8

It's easy to talk about our faith and our obedience, it's another thing to live it. When we are faced with the tests of stewardship, it helps us discover whether our commitment goes any further than our heads.

### PROPER STEWARDSHIP HELPS US FOCUS ON ETERNAL THINGS, NOT JUST THE THINGS OF THIS WORLD

Do not store up for yourselves treasures on earth, where moth and rust destroy, and where thieves break in and steal. But store up for yourselves treasures in heaven, where moth and rust do not destroy, and where thieves do not break in and steal. For where your treasure is, there your heart will be also.

Matthew 6:19–21

The principle of the above passage is that you can tell what people treasure by their focus—what occupies their thinking, attitudes, and actions. If they are constantly concerned about their earthly possessions—thinking about them, worrying about them, demonstrating jealousy and greed, mistreating others to gain more—their treasures will be on this earth and nowhere else. This is where their heart is. Conversely, if they are consistently thinking in terms of how they can use their time, talents, and material possessions to glorify God—how they can meet others' needs, how they can further God's work, how they can invest in eternal purposes—their treasure is in heaven. Scripture's admonition is to remember the temporary nature of earthly treasures and the eternal nature of heavenly treasures.

## Increasing the Volunteer Resource Base

Then he said to his disciples, "The harvest is plentiful but the workers are few. Ask the Lord of the harvest, therefore, to send out workers into his harvest field."

Matthew 9:37–38

The chief contribution of lay people to the growth of the church can be summed up in one word: ministry. . . . Every church member is supposed to be an active minister . . . biblically we should not think of a church as a group with one or two ministers, but rather as a group in which every one is a minister.[5]

Peter Wagner

The mission has to be clear and simple. It has to be bigger than any one person's capacity. It has to lift up people's vision. It has to be something that makes each person feel that he or she can make a difference—that each one can say, I have not lived in vain.[6]

Peter Drucker

Volunteer involvement is a very important part of the life of any church. A variety of jobs need to be done to meet not only the needs of the members but to reach out to the community as well. One of the unwritten criteria people use when evaluating a church is the quality of the ministry offered. This often includes the quality of worship, the friendliness of greeters and ushers, the care and concern shown by children's workers, and so on. Volunteers do almost all of these jobs. In some churches these jobs seem to be filled by enthusiastic and fulfilled church members. In other churches these jobs are often not filled, and the people who are serving do so because they feel forced to or because they did not know how to say no.

Unless the leadership of the church really believes that serving in various volunteer roles of the church is both necessary and profitable for people's spiritual health, lay people are right to wonder why the leadership recruits volunteers. Few pastors have developed a theology of service or participation; this may be one reason why appeals for volunteers go unanswered.

Max DePree summed up his perspective on why people want to serve with the word "opportunity"—opportunity "for self-realization, for being part of a social body that is attractive and rewarding. Opportunity for doing work which will help me to reach my potential. Opportunity to be involved with something that's meaningful. Opportunity to be an integral part of something. We do not develop vital surviving organizations unless we take into account these needs for meaningful work."[7]

So what are some of the ideas that have proven effective in increasing the level of volunteer service in our churches?

1. Change recruiting strategies from mass appeals to more personal approaches.
   - Recruiting should be done, whenever possible, on a one-to-one basis and preferably by someone who knows the prospective volunteer.
   - Recruiting should be done, whenever possible, by someone who is already doing the work—someone in the trenches.
   - Communicate clearly the vision and purpose of the ministry opportunity.
   - Communicate clearly what support systems are in place.
   - Communicate clearly the expectations regarding time and duration.
2. Develop a theology regarding spiritual gifts along with a plan to help people discover, develop, and use their gifts.
3. Help people understand the role of false assumptions and expectations as they serve. Examples include:

- The church and staff exist to make my area of ministry succeed.
- Deep personal relationships with staff and fellow leaders will result from my personal involvement and ministry within the church.
- Everyone realizes the amount of time and energy I have put in and fully appreciates my contribution.
- Most other people in the church are as excited about my area of ministry as I am.
- Successful ministry implies no conflict.
- Once I get through with this project, this job, this situation, my life will plateau and I can rest and enjoy my walk with God.
- The present strategies and methods that I am using will probably not have to be changed in the future.

4. Do an annual survey of where people are serving in your congregation. This serves several functions.
   - It shows people the multiplicity of ministry opportunities that are available in the church.
   - It identifies where and how many people are already serving.
   - It gives people an opportunity to identify areas of ministry in which they would like to be trained and equipped.
   - It gives people an opportunity to sign up to serve in a particular area.
   - It gives you insight into the attitudes and opinions of people in the church regarding serving.

5. Develop mission or ministry teams as part of the small group ministry.

6. Provide clear and definitive job descriptions and expectations for all ministry positions, as follows:
   - An explanation of how this particular ministry helps fulfill the unique mission and vision of the church
   - An explanation of the time requirements and duration of the ministry
   - An explanation of the expectations of the position

- An explanation of the resources available to help them in this task
7. Develop a staff or ministry leader position in the area of volunteer involvement.
8. Help ministry leaders develop a recruiting plan that's all year long, not just once a year.
9. Develop different degrees of commitment for volunteer involvement.
10. Celebrate more often!

## Increasing the Financial Resource Base

The first (challenge) is to convert donors into contributors. . . .We know that we can no longer hope to get money from "donors"; they have to become "contributors." . . . To make contributors out of donors means that the American people can see what they want to see—or should want to see—when each of us looks at himself or herself in the mirror in the morning: someone who as a citizen takes responsibility. Someone who as a neighbor cares.[8]

Peter Drucker

If we believe stewardship of financial resources is critical not just to the life of the church but to the life of the believer, we need to have a plan to develop this area of their lives. Most churches hope that it happens but have no particular plan to see that it happens. That's a big mistake.

Moreover, churches cannot afford to make mistakes about finances because if resources are allocated improperly, ministry is compromised. The concept of Christian stewardship includes the implication that the church is careful and strategic about what it does with the tithes, gifts, and offerings it receives from its members. While the church is not a business, every church should have significant objectives it is trying to accomplish and standards for assessing progress on these objectives. In other words, we need to be serious about our mission and vision, and we need to make sure we are using the resources we have in the most effective manner possible. Unfortunately, churches in the United States spend an incredible amount merely to maintain the status quo.

Oftentimes churches discover they don't have enough money to fund some really outstanding projects or ideas. What can they do? Visionary and innovative churches often examine income-acquisition ideas to see what they might do to increase income. Here are some possibilities:

1. Increase involvement in other activities in the church.
2. Improve communication with donors.
   • Report ministry opportunities and needs rather than just how much came in and its relationship to the annual budget.
   • Increase your reporting to people in the church on how they are doing in their giving.
   • Increase your reporting to people in the church on what their giving is accomplishing.
3. Be more professional in the use of contributions.
   • Make the church books open to anyone at any time.
   • Go to a zero-based budgeting process.
   • Allow for more interactive opportunities when you communicate with your congregation.
4. Categorize contributors and provide different types of communication based on:
   • Level of involvement
   • Area(s) of interest
   • Level of giving
   • Demographic criteria
   • Combinations of the above

Don't try to reach different market segments with the same message. . . .We were crystal-clear on the goal; but we did not really spend enough time thinking through the market segments. We tried to sell the program to everybody the same way. After six or seven years of working very hard and not getting very far, we sat down and said, Look, we really have three quite separate markets. They may all belong in the same program, but they are coming for different reasons.[9]

Peter Drucker

5. Develop large-gift donors.

Large-gift donors . . . are more likely to view a relationship as personal involvement in operational activities. . . . Having the ear of the decision-makers facilitates the feeling that the individual is in on the inner workings of the operation—and thus raises the perception that they, personally, are a meaningful player in the organization.[10]

George Barna

6. Provide teaching and training opportunities in the area of financial stewardship, including:
   - Special classes or seminars on financial issues
   - Small group emphasis on stewardship
   - Financial counseling
   - Special sermon series on stewardship at regular intervals
7. Give people creative ideas for how they can increase their giving.
8. Increase giving opportunities by developing
   - a separate facilities fund
   - a separate missions fund
   - ministry modules as focal points for contributions
9. Make stewardship vision driven.
10. Develop planned giving or creative giving opportunities.
11. Break special giving projects into bite-size pieces.
12. Celebrate more often!

Research reminds us that it is important to reinforce people's decisions to donate by enabling them to feel good about themselves.[11]

George Barna

### *Biblical Examples of Giving*

Because of all the current concerns about giving, it is good to review key examples in Scripture where giving was the primary focus. Three examples come immediately to mind.

## THE BUILDING OF THE TABERNACLE (EXODUS 35–36)

The first major example of raising resources to build facilities was when Moses built the Tabernacle according to his instructions from God. Moses asked the people to give to the project, and

> All the Israelite men and women who were willing brought to the LORD freewill offerings for all the work the LORD through Moses had commanded them to do.
>
> Exodus 35:29

The people were so willing that quickly Moses had more materials than he needed. In fact he had to instruct the people not to bring any more offerings:

> Then Moses gave an order and they sent this word throughout the camp: "No man or woman is to make anything else as an offering for the sanctuary." And so the people were restrained from bringing more, because what they already had was more than enough to do all the work.
>
> Exodus 36:6–7

Wouldn't churches today love to have the problem Moses did with this building project?

## THE BUILDING OF THE TEMPLE (1 CHRONICLES 29)

When David decided to build the Temple to honor God, he was told that his son Solomon was the one who would supervise the actual building of the Temple. However, in 1 Chronicles 29 we see the strategy and results of David's efforts to raise the resources necessary for the building project.

> Then King David said to the whole assembly: "My son Solomon, the one whom God has chosen, is young and inexperienced. The task is great, because this palatial structure is not for man but for the LORD God."
>
> 1 Chronicles 29:1

David then went on to define what he personally would give to the project. He then challenged the leaders of the people of Israel for their response.

"Now, who is willing to consecrate himself today to the LORD?" Then the leaders of families, the officers of the tribes of Israel, the commanders of thousands and commanders of hundreds, and the officials in charge of the king's work gave willingly. . . . The people rejoiced at the willing response of their leaders, for they had given freely and wholeheartedly to the LORD. David the king also rejoiced greatly.

1 Chronicles 29:5–6, 9

The people followed their leaders and gave willingly to the Temple project. David then prayed and praised God for the faithfulness of the people and their leaders.

"But who am I, and who are my people, that we should be able to give as generously as this? Everything comes from you, and we have given you only what comes from your hand. . . . O LORD our God, as for all this abundance that we have provided for building you a temple for your Holy Name, it comes from your hand, and all of it belongs to you. I know, my God, that you test the heart and are pleased with integrity. All these things have I given willingly and with honest intent. And now I have seen with joy how willingly your people who are here have given to you. O LORD, God of our fathers Abraham, Isaac and Israel, keep this desire in the hearts of your people forever, and keep their hearts loyal to you."

1 Chronicles 29:14, 16–18

### THE APOSTLE PAUL RAISING FUNDS FOR THE CHRISTIANS IN JERUSALEM (2 CORINTHIANS 8–9)

The apostle Paul gives a New Testament approach to giving as he raised funds to help the believers in Jerusalem. Paul used the opportunity to teach the Corinthian church the principles and practices of New Testament giving.

First he told the Corinthian church of the generosity of the Macedonian churches as they personally supported his apostolic ministry. Then he went on to present his appeal for the church in Jerusalem.

"I am not commanding you, but I want to test the sincerity of your love by comparing it with the earnestness of others. For you know the grace of our Lord Jesus Christ, that though he was rich, yet for your sakes he became poor, so that you through his poverty might become rich. And here is my advice about what is best for you in this matter: Last year you were the first not only to give but also to have the desire to do so. Now finish the work, so that your eager willingness to do it may be matched by your completion of it, according to your means. For if the willingness is there, the gift is acceptable according to what one has, not according to what he does not have."

2 Corinthians 8:8–12

Later Paul wrote:

"Remember this: Whoever sows sparingly will also reap sparingly, and whoever sows generously will also reap generously. Each man should give what he has decided in his heart to give, not reluctantly or under compulsion, for God loves a cheerful giver. And God is able to make all grace abound to you, so that in all things at all times, having all that you need, you will abound in every good work."

2 Corinthians 9:6–8

The result was a large offering that was taken to minister to the needs of the Christians in Jerusalem.

We can see that the principles and practices of stewardship are the same in the Old and New Testaments. Stewardship is a natural part of the behavior of God's people, and they are expected to give on a regular basis as well as for special projects.

## Summary

Developing the resources necessary to accomplish the mission and vision of the church is essential. Churches are going to have to learn to think more like parachurch ministries. Parachurch ministries understand that if they don't develop the necessary donors and volunteers, they will fail. They plan and work hard to ensure that they have the necessary resources. Churches often act like they have a captive audience and that both participation and financial resources are automatic. Today they aren't. Because giving directly benefits the church and everyone in the church, it makes sense for churches to emphasize the importance of good stewardship.

## Questions for Reflection

1. How would you rate the present level of stewardship in your church? What about volunteer involvement? What about financial involvement?
2. What factors or influences are limiting your stewardship efforts? Which ones can you address? Which ones should you address?
3. What biblical principles would you add or subtract from the list given in this chapter?
4. Which ideas listed for increasing the volunteer resource base could help your church? What's your plan for implementing them?
5. Which ideas listed for increasing the financial resource base could help your church? What's your plan for implementing them?

# ELEVEN

# Playing the Game
## *The Implementation Phase*

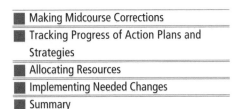

- Making Midcourse Corrections
- Tracking Progress of Action Plans and Strategies
- Allocating Resources
- Implementing Needed Changes
- Summary

The implementation phase is where the real work takes place. Although it may seem difficult for most churches to define their mission, vision, objectives, and standards, the real test is when they implement their action plans and strategies.

It's much like a football team that plans and practices all week in preparation for a big game. What they have done up to kickoff is strategic thinking. They have analyzed what they think their opponents will do. They have assessed what they think they can do. And they have come up with a game plan that they believe has the best chance for success. This is similar to what the church does in the discovery, pre-visioning, visioning, and planning phases. Most of the work has been theoretical. We believe this, we assume this, therefore we should do this.

The implementation phase is similar to what happens after the kickoff in a football game. All the theory and strategy that have been developed during the week gets tested in the reality of a game. The focus shifts from *strategy* to *tactics*. The term "tactics" refers to the give and take that happens during the game. What if the opponent does something different than what we expected? What if some of our key players are unable to play? How does this change our strategy? What if our strategy isn't working? What adjustments are needed along the way?

## Making Midcourse Corrections

> We live by the motto, "Do it. Fix it. Try it." If you try something and it works, you keep it, if it doesn't work, you fix it or try something else.[1]
>
> Wal-Mart Executive

Let's face it, nothing ever goes exactly as we plan. There are always things that surprise us—some of them good, some of them bad. Yet churches often operate as if this tactical side of the process doesn't exist. How often have we seen a ministry outlive its usefulness? How often have we seen major changes in the composition or needs of the community or the congregation, and yet the church operates as if nothing has changed? Change is a reality that churches must deal with. It was a problem for the first-century church, and it will continue to be a problem until the Lord comes. We are called to face it, not ignore it.

The church today cannot afford to say, "We never did it that way before" or "We've always done it that way." It must be very serious about the Great Commission and the other assignments given to it by Christ. The church must do everything in its power to make sure dreams become realities. This requires both a willingness and a commitment to change along the way.

Churches must agree to measure and assess their progress on the established objectives and standards on a regular basis. As this evaluation takes place, adjustments or midcourse corrections will need to be made. These are normal.

Churches fail to evaluate for two major reasons:

- Fear of finding out that they are not achieving what they set out to do
- Fear of an evaluation process that becomes interrogative and punitive

Evaluation does not have to be a negative process. It is necessary for every area of our lives. Because people have had negative experiences with evaluation in school or on the job, they shy away from any type of evaluation in the church. Good evaluations simply tell you how you're doing and how you can improve to achieve better results. Also, good evaluations involve a team approach whereby the evaluator(s) and those being evaluated join together to ask hard questions about how they are progressing.

The solution when things are off-track is to make adjustments. Maybe the action plan or strategy needs additional resources to succeed. If that is the case, the leadership team will have to decide if they can allocate the needed resources. If they can't, obviously the expectations for the action plan or strategy need to be lowered. In fact, the action plan or strategy may have to be scrapped if the necessary resources are not available. This does not imply that those attempting to carry out the action plan or strategy were at fault, but it does force both the leaders and the implementers to take a hard look at what they are doing and decide what adjustments need to be made.

Remember that action plans and strategies are the easiest things to change in the future. If the ones you select do not work as well as you want, you can change them as you go, or identify completely new plans that you think have a better chance of doing the job. Implementation demands flexibility and above all a results-oriented focus. The purpose of all of our planning is to accomplish the objectives and meet the standards. Whatever plans or strategies best meet this test are the ones we're looking for. We don't have to worry about failure. Failure simply tells us one more plan or strategy that doesn't work. By constantly modifying and adapting our plans or strategies, we will get closer and closer to what it is we set out to accomplish. In the long run we will get closer and closer to accomplishing the vision of the church, which is the ultimate purpose of the whole planning effort.

## Tracking Progress of Action Plans and Strategies

There are a lot of ways you can track your progress as you implement your action plans and strategies. Because you have developed objectives and standards, you have an automatic system for measuring your progress.

One possible method is to make a large chart, listing all the objectives and standards down the left side and the time periods you are measuring across the top. I suggest you track your progress on a monthly or quarterly basis. However, you may find quarterly or even semiannual evaluations more realistic.

At the end of the first assessment period, evaluate as many of your objectives and standards as you can. Some churches have used stick-on dots that are colored as follows:

- Red: At this point we are below the minimum for our standard
- Yellow: At this point we are above the minimum and below the acceptable success level for our standard
- Green: At this point we are above the acceptable success level for our standard
- White: At this point we cannot measure progress on our standard

If you use this type of measuring system it will give you a visual picture of your progress to date. A visual reminder seems to motivate people as well as tell you where you may have to increase your efforts.

Also, if you frequently measure your progress, you can make more timely adjustments where you are falling behind your intended standards.

## Allocating Resources

It is not unusual for the budgeting process to lag behind the planning process. This means, particularly in the early phases, the budget categories, priorities, and dollar amounts may not align perfectly with the revised ministry plans.

Each church handles this somewhat differently, but some possible guidelines include the following:

- Most churches allow ministries to trade apples for oranges. They are allowed to change spending priorities within their ministry area as long as they do not go over the total amount allocated for that ministry.
- If a department needs additional funds, it has to submit a request to those in charge of the budget. The request is considered according to the present level of income in the church and whether or not dollars from other areas of ministry could be redirected to meet this request.
- During the next budgeting phase, each ministry is required to submit a budget that reflects its new plans and priorities. It is particularly important that the budgeted items are prioritized so in case there are inadequate resources available to fund the whole list, the highest-priority items are funded first.
- After a couple of years of working the process, the budget should accurately reflect the priorities and plans established by the various ministries.

## Implementing Needed Changes

Another question that is frequently asked is, "What is the process or procedure for ministries to change their plans or programs?" Again, there is no simple answer because every church does it somewhat differently. However, the following guidelines may help:

- Every ministry should go through a planning process each year to review, clarify, or change objectives, standards, and benchmarks. These plans should be reviewed by those responsible for the oversight of the ministry and approved or renegotiated until the responsible parties are in agreement about how to move forward.
- Most churches allow departments to change specific action plans or strategies as necessary without approval from any governing body. However, this is not true for every church.

The leadership of the church needs to be clear about what departments are required to do to change an action plan. If there are budget implications for any of the changes, these need to be communicated through the proper channels. Normally changes are a consequence of the evaluation process. Because we are committed to accomplishing the objectives, meeting our standards, and fulfilling our vision, not to specific programs, action plans, or strategies, we will make whatever changes are necessary to move us closer to our vision.

The ministry of the apostle Paul should be encouraging to church planners. You can see a definite plan to his missionary efforts. However, you can also see that he continually made adjustments and changes along the way (see Acts 16:7–10; 17:19–34). The fear that planning forces churches into a rigid format is simply not based on reality. The willingness to make changes when they are necessary must be a natural part of the implementation process of any strategic plan.

## Summary

The implementation phase is the true test of the strategic planning process. The intention of strategic planning is to do the work of ministry, not just talk about it. The goal is to be more focused and proactive so that the church can more powerfully represent Jesus Christ. The goal is not to be successful in a worldly sense, nor to boast about our individual accomplishments, but simply to be good stewards of everything God has entrusted to us.

Leading churches is an awesome responsibility. We are held accountable for what we do with all that we have been given. The sad state of many of our churches does not reflect the power of the gospel or our Lord and Savior Jesus Christ; it reflects our apathy. Now is a time of incredible opportunity to increase and to strengthen the people of God, and to have a lasting impact on the world around us. We must not shrink from the task.

> Let us not become weary in doing good, for at the proper time we will reap a harvest if we do not give up.
>
> Galatians 6:9

May he give you the desire of your heart and make all your plans succeed.

Psalm 20:4

We pray for you constantly, that God will count you worthy of his calling, and by his power may fulfill all your good intentions and every effort of faith.

2 Thessalonians 1:11 PHILLIPS

## Questions for Reflection

1. What is the process for making midcourse corrections in the various ministries of the church?
2. To what degree do ministries seriously measure progress on their plans and strategies? How often do they measure progress?
3. How close is the relationship between the church budget and the mission and vision of the church? How closely are they aligned?
4. What freedom do ministries have to change ministry dollars or re-allocate funds? What freedom should they have?
5. How open and accepting are the ministry leaders to change?
6. Now that you've read through the entire strategic planning process, how would you rate your church's planning efforts?
   - What modifications need to take place in your planning process?
   - Where's the best place to start?
   - What time frame should be used? What information do church leaders need to improve their planning efforts? What's the best way to get this information to them?

# Developing a Vision Statement

## Step 1—Identifying Ministry Styles and Strategic Choices

The following are common ministry styles that represent the main philosophies of churches today. Underneath each of the styles, you will find a list of *strategic choices* that a church might make as it applies the style to its unique context. Read through each ministry style and its list of strategic choices. First eliminate or change any wording that you think is inaccurate to your situation. Also, feel free to use a separate sheet of paper and add other choices.

Specifically, think about your own church situation and make sure that any strategic choice that your church might make is listed under at least one of the ministry styles. If you think of a strategic choice that is not included, add it. You can even add a new ministry style if that makes sense to you, along with its accompanying strategic choices.

### 1. Target Market-Driven Church
   A. Responds to the needs of young families
   B. Responds to the needs of baby boomers
   C. Responds to the needs of Generation X
   D. Responds to the needs of unchurched people who are not Christians

    E. Responds to the needs of unchurched people who are Christians

    F. Responds to the needs of Hispanics

## 2. Technology-Driven Church

    A. Extensive use of technology in services including video, Power Point, multimedia, etc.

    B. Extensive use of computer databases for segmented mailings, surveys, tracking of involvement, analyzing giving patterns, etc.

    C. Extensive use of computer software for generating communication pieces including brochures, bulletins, mailings, etc.

    D. Extensive use of web site for providing contact and interaction with constituents

    E. Extensive use of computer software for surveying constituents, decision making, etc.

## 3. Spiritual-Growth-Driven Church

    A. Emphasis on quality, not quantity

    B. Focus on spiritual growth, nurturing, spiritual maturity, discipleship, spiritual disciplines including prayer, holiness, and personal devotion

    C. Sermons focus on an in-depth expository study of God's Word with note taking common and a focus on becoming like Christ

    D. Small groups focus on Bible study, learning God's Word, and developing quality and character through personal accountability

    E. Design church services with believers in mind

    F. Design extensive programs and ministries aimed at meeting the needs of members

    G. Extensive adult classes

    H. Senior pastor's primary role is teacher

## 4. Outreach-Driven Church

    A. Focus on evangelism, outreach, and impacting the local community with the gospel message

    B. Sermons focus on what God can do for those who are willing to follow after him and how a personal commitment to him can radically change lives

C. Designs church services with unchurched, non-Christians in mind

D. Designs decision-oriented services or emphasizes lifestyle evangelism of members

E. Small group ministry focuses on praying for unsaved people, encouraging one another to reach out in natural networks, and using small groups as entry vehicle for unchurched people

F. Programs and ministries aimed at meeting the needs of unchurched non-Christians

## 5. Political-Action-Driven Church

A. Focus is on involvement in Christian political activities (political action groups, marches, protests, demonstrations, etc.) to promote Christian values

B. Develop own Christian school or strongly support home schooling

C. Sermons focus on role of Christians as source of light and truth in a troubled world

D. Small group ministry focuses on how to live authentic Christian lives in the world today including being involved in politics and community activities to represent Christian worldview

## 6. Caring Church

A. Sermons focus on a message of hope in the midst of stressful Christian life

B. Focus is on developing relationships

C. Designs extensive pastoral care opportunities, counseling resources, twelve-step programs, etc.

D. Sermons focus on message of hope in the midst of stressful Christian life

E. Small group ministry is extensive and focuses on fellowship and developing significant networks of relationships inside the church, reaching out to unchurched Christians in the community, and helping people with dysfunctional or addictive life patterns

## 7. Celebration Church

A. Focus is on contemporary worship, drama, celebrative arts, practical sermons

B. Extensive large-group events such as concerts, musicals, plays, vacation Bible school, etc.

C. Sermons focus on practicality of God's Word including application for today's world

D. Small group ministry has variety of formats and focus (love groups, learn groups, task groups, mission groups, support groups)

E. Excellence in presentation and communication is stressed

F. Services feature a powerful time of worship including contemporary music

G. Senior pastor's primary role is vision caster

## 8. Signs and Wonders Church

A. Focus on spiritual gifts, particularly tongues, interpretation of tongues, healing, miracles, and prophecy

B. Extensive time of ministry during or after service to meet personal prayer and healing needs

C. Sermons focus on power of God and role of Holy Spirit in the lives of Christians

D. Small group ministry focuses on exercise of spiritual gifts

## 9. Training and Equipping Church

A. Focus is on training and equipping Christians for service inside and outside the church

B. Programs and ministries provide extensive opportunities for discovering and using spiritual gifts, how-to classes, parenting classes, marriage classes, etc.

C. Sermons focus on responsibility of Christians to be ministers, actively using their spiritual gifts to glorify God

D. Small group ministry focuses on specific ministry tasks and missions work

E. Extensive training seminars and leadership training, equipping members to use all types of personal evangelism methods

F. Senior pastor's primary role is trainer and equipper

## 10. Missions Church

A. Focus is on role of Christians in serving/impacting their community and world, demonstrating the love of Christ in practical and personal ways in the community

B. Extensive opportunities for being involved in social action projects in the community and demonstrating the love of Christ in practical ways or short-term mission projects

C. Sermons focus on a message of hope in the midst of a troubled and confused world with particular emphasis on Christians being active in touching and reaching their community; a focus on the role of Christians as change agents in the world

D. Small group ministry focuses on meeting significant needs in the community and world

E. Extensive programs and ministries outside the church to meet needs of community/world (food, benevolence, clothing, ministry projects, church planting, etc.)

## Step 2—Analyzing the Ministry Styles and Strategic Choices from Four Perspectives

Now look at the four ways strategic choices can be categorized:

1. **Personal Definition of Success**—Strategic choices that emphasize the characteristics most important to you personally and that you believe best reflect the unique call of God for your church in its context.
2. **Ministry Forecast**—Strategic choices that are emphasized by effective churches across the country.
3. **Congregational Capabilities/Distinctives**—Strategic choices that are effective in your church and somewhat unique when compared to other churches in the area. It might be that other churches are emphasizing similar choices, but you feel you are doing an exceptional job in one particular area.
4. **Ministry Area Demographics**—Strategic choices that would be of most interest to the people who are in your ministry area (within twenty minutes of your church), given the demographic and psychographic characteristics of that population.

### Step 2A

Look at the four perspectives listed below. Rate how important you believe each of them should be to you as you define the future vision of the church. Assign somewhere between 1–100 points for each perspective, with the total of all four perspectives equaling 100 points.

_____ Personal Definition of Success (PDS)
_____ Ministry Forecast (MF)
_____ Congregational Capabilities/Distinctives (CC/D)
_____ Ministry Area Demographics (MAD)
_____ (Total: 100 points)

## Step 2B

Start with the first perspective—Personal Definition of Success. Read through each of the ministry styles and their accompanying strategic choices. Choose ten strategic choices that best fit your personal definition of success. List them below in order of importance, your most important choice first, your second choice second, etc. You can simply list them using the number and letter of your choice (for example, 2B, 4D, etc.).

1. _____ (10 points)
2. _____ (9 points)
3. _____ (8 points)
4. _____ (7 points)
5. _____ (6 points)
6. _____ (5 points)
7. _____ (4 points)
8. _____ (3 points)
9. _____ (2 points)
10. _____ (1 point)

## Step 2C

Move to the second perspective—Ministry Forecast. Read through each of the ministry styles and their accompanying strategic choices. Choose ten strategic choices that best fit those being used by effective churches that you personally know or have heard about. List them below in order of importance.

1. _____ (10 points)
2. _____ (9 points)
3. _____ (8 points)
4. _____ (7 points)
5. _____ (6 points)
6. _____ (5 points)
7. _____ (4 points)
8. _____ (3 points)
9. _____ (2 points)
10. _____ (1 point)

## Step 2D

Move to the third perspective—Congregational Capabilities/ Distinctives. Read through each of the ministry styles and their accompanying strategic choices. Choose the ten strategic choices that best describe what is working best in your church today and is somewhat different or unique compared to other churches in the area. List them below in order of importance.

1. _____ (10 points)
2. _____ (9 points)
3. _____ (8 points)
4. _____ (7 points)
5. _____ (6 points)
6. _____ (5 points)
7. _____ (4 points)
8. _____ (3 points)
9. _____ (2 points)
10. _____ (1 point)

## Step 2E

Move to the fourth perspective—Ministry Area Demographics. Read through each of the ministry styles and their accompanying strategic choices. Choose the ten strategic choices that best describe what you believe would be most effective given the demographic and psychographic characteristics of the people in your ministry area. List them below in order of importance.

1. _____ (10 points)
2. _____ (9 points)
3. _____ (8 points)
4. _____ (7 points)
5. _____ (6 points)
6. _____ (5 points)
7. _____ (4 points)
8. _____ (3 points)
9. _____ (2 points)
10. _____ (1 point)

## Step 3—Determining the Relative Value of the Strategic Choices

In step 2A you awarded points to each of the different perspectives. In steps 2B, 2C, 2D, and 2E you rated the top ten strategic choices. Now fill in the chart below (e.g., if you awarded "Personal Definition of Success" 50 points and your first strategic choice under step 2B was 3B, then it gets 10 points and the result in the last column would be 500 points).

| Perspective | A Perspective Points | Strategic Choice | B Strategic Choice Points | Total Points Multiply A times B |
|---|---|---|---|---|
| Example—PDS | 50 | 3B | 10 | 500 |
| PDS | | | | |
| PDS | | | | |
| PDS | | | | |
| PDS | | | | |
| PDS | | | | |
| PDS | | | | |
| PDS | | | | |
| PDS | | | | |
| PDS | | | | |
| MF | | | | |
| MF | | | | |
| MF | | | | |
| MF | | | | |
| MF | | | | |
| MF | | | | |
| MF | | | | |
| MF | | | | |

| | | | | |
|---|---|---|---|---|
| MF | | | | |
| MF | | | | |
| CC/D | | | | |
| CC/D | | | | |
| CC/D | | | | |
| CC/D | | | | |
| CC/D | | | | |
| CC/D | | | | |
| CC/D | | | | |
| CC/D | | | | |
| CC/D | | | | |
| CC/D | | | | |
| MAD | | | | |
| MAD | | | | |
| MAD | | | | |
| MAD | | | | |
| MAD | | | | |
| MAD | | | | |
| MAD | | | | |
| MAD | | | | |
| MAD | | | | |
| MAD | | | | |

## Step 4—Determining the Strategic Choices That Are Most Critical for Your Vision

Now we want to find the strategic choices that received the most points. Make a list of the ten strategic choices that received the most total points using the table below. Be sure to include points from choices picked more than once.

| Strategic Choice) (Number and Letter | Points | Strategic Choice |
|---|---|---|
| Example—3B | 750 | Focus on spiritual growth, nurturing, spiritual maturity, discipleship, spiritual disciplines including prayer, holiness, and personal devotion |
| | | |
| | | |
| | | |
| | | |

| Strategic Choice) (Number and Letter | Points | Strategic Choice |
|---|---|---|
|  |  |  |
|  |  |  |
|  |  |  |
|  |  |  |
|  |  |  |
|  |  |  |

## Step 5—Writing Visioning Scenarios

Now we want to put together the results of our exercise and come up with some possible vision statements.

### Step 5A—Scenario 1

Start by listing the five strategic choices that received the most points. It is usually wise, though not essential, to include at least one strategic choice from each of the four perspectives. If your first five strategic choices did not include any items from one of the perspectives, you may want to include the highest rated item from that perspective in your list of the top five choices.

| Strategic Choice (Number and Letter) | Perspective | Strategic Choice |
|---|---|---|
| Example—3B | PDS | Focus on spiritual growth, nurturing, spiritual maturity, discipleship, spiritual disciplines including prayer, holiness, and personal devotion |
|  |  |  |
|  |  |  |

| | | |
|---|---|---|
| | | |
| | | |
| | | |
| | | |

Now, assuming these were in fact your top five strategic choices, write a one-paragraph scenario describing how these choices would be emphasized in your church. It is usually best to describe the five choices starting with the most important and working your way to the least. An alternative would be to write a brief (one- to two-sentence) introduction and then list five objectives (ministry targets) for the church during the next one to two years that reflect each of the top five strategic choices. See the examples below.

### EXAMPLE 1

We believe God has called us to focus on reaching those in Cedar Hill and the surrounding areas that do not regularly attend any church. As a result, the Cedar Hill area will be different in ten to fifteen years with the Christian influence being increasingly felt in homes, businesses, education, and politics. We further intend to multiply our worldwide ministry by planting churches, by preparing our people for leadership roles in vocational ministry and parachurch groups, by sending out missionaries, and by becoming a resource center and model for Texas and the nation.

### EXAMPLE 2

We are mercifully loved by the Awesome Living God. Therefore, we extend the contagious atmosphere of God's kingdom to every person in Cincinnati—to see our community enveloped in Christ's love, acceptance, and forgiveness.

- We generously bring God's love in practical ways to all kinds of people.

- We celebrate God's presence in fun, culture-current biblical models.
- We grow together and experience healing as we are touched by God's Spirit.
- We empower one another toward service to God.
- Small things done with great love will change the world.

Now try writing your own scenario.

### *Step 5B—Alternative Scenarios*

Now try a couple other combinations of strategic choices, probably keeping your top two to three but adding a couple of others that scored significantly in the evaluation process. Write scenarios for each of these combinations just as you did above. Before finalizing your vision statement it is a good idea to create and envision several alternative scenarios to get a feel for how a reshuffling of your strategic choices can result in a very different vision. Play with various combinations until you come up with one that simply feels right.

#### SCENARIO #2

| Strategic Choice (Number and Letter) | Perspective | Strategic Choice—Written Out |
|---|---|---|
| Example—3B | PDS | Focus on spiritual growth, nurturing, spiritual maturity, discipleship, spiritual disciplines including prayer, holiness, and personal devotion |
| | | |
| | | |
| | | |
| | | |
| | | |

## Scenario #3

| Strategic Choice (Number and Letter) | Perspective | Strategic Choice—Written Out |
|---|---|---|
|  |  |  |
|  |  |  |
|  |  |  |
|  |  |  |
|  |  |  |
|  |  |  |

## Scenario #4

| Strategic Choice (Number and Letter) | Perspective | Strategic Choice—Written Out |
|---|---|---|
|  |  |  |
|  |  |  |
|  |  |  |
|  |  |  |
|  |  |  |
|  |  |  |

## Step 6—Writing Final Vision Statement

Finally, put together the best of your scenario efforts into one last version. Try to use wording that is particularly compelling and attractive. If you find this kind of writing difficult, you might want to bring in someone who has specific writing skills and work with them to craft your final version. You now have the first and major piece of the strategic plan—a clear and compelling vision statement.

# Collecting Data on Past History

■■■

Develop a database that includes categories similar to those listed below. If you can gather this information for the last two to three years, it will increase the reliability of your data. However, if that's impossible, at least use data from the last few months, so you have information you can use for future planning.

- **Average total attendance for all services**—This should include everyone that attends the worship services, Sunday school classes, and adult education classes. If you run Friday or Saturday night services that are duplicates of the Sunday morning service, count these numbers also. However, you will want to make sure you do not count any individuals twice. For example, if adults attend service one hour and Sunday school the second hour, you do not want to count their attendance during the second hour. The same would be true for children who are there more than one hour. You may have to estimate the final number but try to be as accurate as possible.
- **Average total Christian education attendance**—Most churches keep a weekly count of those who attend Christian education (Sunday school) classes. If you do, simply enter the average for each Sunday. Include all adults and children. If possible, try to eliminate counting the same children twice if they attend more than one service. If this is not possible, simply list the total C.E. attendance for all services and all Sunday school hours.

- **Average total adult worship attendance**—Most churches keep a weekly count of attendance in each worship service. If you do, simply enter the average number of adults for each Sunday. If children are in with their parents for a portion of the worship service, it will be necessary to subtract the number of children from the adults to get an accurate count of just the adults. In projecting the maximum capacity of the facility, we usually assume that the children will not be in the services. If you do plan on keeping the children in the services, you should write down the number that includes them.

- **Average total Christian education attendance during services**—If you hold any C.E. classes simultaneous with your worship services, list the average total C.E. attendance during this period of time. If you have a separate Sunday school hour, do not include this figure.

- **Average largest service worship attendance**—List the average worship attendance for your largest service.

- **Average largest Christian education attendance**—List the average C.E. attendance for the period of time in which you have the greatest attendance.

- **Average largest service total attendance**—Simply add the last two numbers together.

- **Average second largest service total attendance**—If you hold multiple services, determine the average total attendance at the second largest service (both worship and C.E.).

- **Average third largest service total attendance**—If you have three services, determine the average total attendance at the third largest service (both worship and C.E.).

- **Average largest Christian education hour**—If you have Sunday school simultaneous with the worship services, or if you have a separate Sunday school hour, determine the hour with the largest C.E. attendance.

- **Average nursery attendance largest service**—Determine the number of children ages two and under who are in C.E. during the largest C.E. hour.

- **Average preschool attendance largest service**—Determine the number of children three to five years old (those not yet in grade school) who are in C.E. during the largest C.E. hour.
- **Average grade school attendance largest service**—Determine the number of children in first to sixth grade who are in C.E. during the largest C.E. hour.
- **Average Jr./Sr. High attendance largest service**—Determine the number of youth in Jr. High/Sr. High classes during the largest C.E. hour.
- **Average adult education attendance largest service**—Determine the number of adults in classes during the largest C.E. hour.

# Developing Future Projections

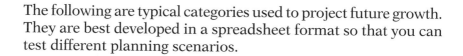

The following are typical categories used to project future growth. They are best developed in a spreadsheet format so that you can test different planning scenarios.

- **Projected growth rate**—This is the percentage of growth you decided upon for each of the next ten years.
- **Projected total attendance**—You take the total attendance from the previous year and multiply it by the projected total attendance for the next year, factoring in your growth rate (e.g., if you projected a 10-percent growth rate, you would multiply the previous year's total attendance by 1.1 to get the new projected total attendance).
- **Average giving**—You take the average giving per person (including children) from the previous year and multiply it by some factor that takes into account inflation (e.g., if you believe inflation will be 4 percent a year, you would multiply the previous year's average giving times 1.04 to get the new projected average giving). Do not assume that average giving per person will go up on its own (not including inflation) unless you have a specific strategy that will be implemented to increase giving.
- **Number of ministry staff needed**—Divide the projected total attendance by the denominator of the ratio of staff to lay people  you want to have for your ministry staff (e.g., if

you want a ratio of 1 staff person per 150 lay people, divide the projected total attendance by 150). You can round the number up or down, or leave it as a decimal and assume some part-time staff.

- **Number of support staff needed**—Divide the projected total attendance by the denominator of the ratio of support staff to lay people you want for your ministry (e.g., if you want a ratio of 1 support staff person per 170 lay people, divide the projected total attendance by 170). You can round the number up or down or leave it as a decimal and assume some part-time staff.

- **Projected total worship attendance**—Take a look at the data you collected from your past history. Find out what percentage of the total attendance was worship attendance. Multiply that percentage by the projected total attendance (e.g., if your worship attendance was 65 percent of your total attendance, multiply the projected total attendance by .65).

- **Projected total Christian education attendance**—Take a look at the data you collected from your past history. Find out what percentage of the total attendance was Christian education attendance. Multiply that percentage by the projected total attendance (e.g., if your Christian education attendance was 35 percent of your total attendance, multiply the projected total attendance by .35).

- **Number of services needed**—It's a good idea to wait until you've seen the results of the rest of your calculations to decide how many services you will need. It will be based on your projections as well as on how much space you have available. Remember that you should not allow the worship, education, or parking space to exceed 90 percent of capacity. If you do, you should plan on lowering your growth rate, as the lack of facilities will keep you from growing at your maximum rate.

- **One-service format with a separate Sunday school hour**— Use the calculations below to determine your needs.

  **Projected total service attendance**—This would be the same as your projected total attendance above.

**Number of off-street parking spaces**—Divide the projected total service attendance by 2.2. This will give you the necessary parking spaces for all the people attending the service. Then multiply the result by 1.1 to determine how many spaces (10 percent of the total) should be open.

**Projected worship attendance**—Look at your past history and determine what percentage of people attend worship services. Multiply that percentage by your projected total service attendance above.

**Worship seating space needed**—Multiply the projected worship attendance in the last item by the number of square feet you need per person (eleven in a normal situation). Then multiply the result by 1.1 to find out how many square feet (10 percent of the total worship space) should remain open.

**Projected total C.E. attendance**—Look at your past history and determine what percentage of people will attend Christian education. Multiply that percentage by your projected total service attendance above. Remember, with this format you're likely to have people staying for both the worship service and the Christian education hour. This means the total of your projected worship attendance and the total C.E. attendance could be more than your projected largest service total attendance.

**Total C.E. space needed**—Multiply the projected total C.E. attendance from the last item by twenty-five square feet per person. Then multiply the result by 1.1 to find out how many square feet (10 percent of total C.E. space) should remain open.

- **Two-service format with a separate Sunday school hour**—Most of your calculations will be similar to those above, except for your projected largest service total attendance. If you have run multiple services before, figure out what percentage your largest service was of the total service attendance. If you have not run multiple services before, multiply the projected total attendance by .55. What this means is you are predicting 55 percent of those attending services will be in the largest service.

- **One-service format with a simultaneous Sunday school hour**—Start by determining your projected total service attendance. Then calculate the rest of the needs as you did above. Use your past history to determine what percentage of your total service attendance will be in the worship space and what percentage will be in the Christian education space. The total of those two percentages must equal 100 percent.

- **Two-service format with a simultaneous Sunday school hour**—Start by determining your projected total service attendance. If you have run two services before, figure out what percentage your largest service was of the total service attendance. If you have not run two services before, multiply the projected total attendance by .55. What this means is you are predicting 55 percent of those attending services will be in the largest service.

- **Three-service format with a simultaneous Sunday school hour**—Start by determining your projected total service attendance. If you have run three services before, figure out what percentage your largest service was of the total service attendance. If you have not run three services before, multiply the projected total attendance by .45. What this means is you are predicting 45 percent of those attending services will be in the largest service.

- **Four-service format with a simultaneous Sunday school hour**—Start by determining your projected total service attendance. If you have run four services before, figure out what percentage your largest service was of the total service attendance. If you have not run four services before, multiply the projected total attendance by .35. What this means is you are predicting 35 percent of those attending services will be in the largest service.

# APPENDIX D

# Developing a Financial and Facility Game Plan

Use categories such as the following to develop spreadsheets for projecting financial and facility scenarios.

- **Average attendance**—Use the projected average total attendance from the projections you made earlier.
- **Projected growth rate**—Use the projected growth rate from the projections you made earlier.
- **Average giving**—Use the projected average giving per person from the projections you made earlier.
- **Projected annual giving**—Multiply the average giving per person times the average total attendance and then multiply the result by fifty-two.
- **Debt level**—Calculate the amount of debt at the end of each year. Take the previous year's debt and subtract the principal payments from the ensuing year. If you intend to retire the debt faster than the amortization period, simply add in the amount by which you intend to reduce the principal each year. If it will be necessary to add debt, take the previous year's debt and add to it the new debt.
- **Average annual interest expense**—Calculate the projected interest expense for the year. If you intend to borrow new

dollars, estimate the interest rate for those dollars and add it to the interest expense from existing loans. It is better to project the interest rates a little higher than you actually expect them to be, so you are on the safe side in your projections. You can try different scenarios based on fifteen-, twenty-, twenty-five-, or thirty-year mortgages.

- **Average annual principal expense**—Calculate the projected principal payments for the year the same way you calculated the interest expense.

- **Average annual mortgage payments**—Simply total the last two items to determine the total annual mortgage payments.

- **Projected largest worship service**—Using your previous projections and based on the number of services you intend to have, determine the projected largest worship service attendance.

- **Percent of capacity for largest service**—Take the projected largest worship service attendance from the last item. Multiply it by eleven (or whatever number you are using for square feet per person), then multiply the result by 1.1 (to allow for 10-percent open space). Divide the result by the number of square feet you actually have or will have for worship space. This is your percent of capacity for the largest service.

- **Projected nursery space needed**—From your previous projections take the projected total Christian education attendance (be careful to use the correct figure based on the number of services and service format you intend to use). Multiply that number by the percentage of C.E. that is devoted to nursery-age children (two years old and younger). Multiply the result by 1.3 (to allow for open space and various class sizes).

- **Percent of nursery-space capacity during largest service**—Take the projected nursery space needed from the last item and divide it by the actual space you have or will have available for nursery-age children.

- **Projected preschool space needed**—From your previous projections take the projected total Christian education attendance. Multiply that number by the percentage of C.E. participants who are preschool age. Multiply the result by 1.3 (to allow for open space and various class sizes).

- **Percent of preschool-space capacity during largest service**—Take the projected preschool space needed from the last item and divide it by the actual space you have or will have available for preschool-age children.

- **Projected grade school space needed**—From your previous projections take the projected total Christian education attendance. Multiply that number by the percentage of C.E. that is grade-school age. Multiply the result by 1.3 (to allow for open space and various class sizes).

- **Percent of grade school space capacity during largest service**—Take the projected grade school space needed from the last item and divide it by the actual space you have or will have available for grade school age children.

- **Projected Jr./Sr. high school space needed**—From your previous projections take the projected total Christian education attendance. Multiply that number by the percentage of C.E. that is made up of Jr./Sr. high school age participants. Multiply the result by 1.3 (to allow for open space and various class sizes).

- **Percent of Jr./Sr. high school space capacity during largest service**—Take the projected Jr./Sr. high school space needed from the last item and divide it by the actual space you have or will have available for Jr./Sr. high school C.E. classes.

- **Projected adult space needed**—From your previous projections take the projected total Christian Education attendance. Multiply that number times the percentage of C.E. that is adults. Multiply the result times 1.3 (to provide for open space and various class sizes).

- **Percent of adult-space capacity during largest service**—Take the projected adult space needed from the last item and divide it by the actual space you have or will have available for adults.

- **Number of parking spaces needed**—From your previous projections take the number of parking spaces needed (be careful to use the correct figure based on the number of services and service format you intend to use). Multiply the result times 1.1 (to allow for 10 percent open space).

- **Percent of parking capacity used during largest service**— Take the number of parking spaces needed from the last item and divide it by the actual number of parking spaces you have or will have available.

- **Office space needed**—Calculate the amount of office space needed as follows. Multiply the number of ministry staff members by 250. Multiply the number of support staff members by 150. Add the two products together along with whatever space you deem necessary for reception space, conference space, and work space.

- **Percent of office-space capacity being utilized**—Take the office space needed from the last item and divide it by the actual space you have available or will have for office space.

- **Money available from operating budget**—Based on your decisions earlier about what percentage you are willing to allocate from your operating budget for facility needs, multiply that percentage times the projected annual giving.

- **Money available from over-and-above giving**—If you are planning on doing an over-and-above giving campaign, use one of the following calculations. If you are doing a self-led campaign, multiply the projected annual giving times 15 to 20 percent. If you are using an outside consultant, multiply the projected annual giving times 30 to 40 percent.

- **Cumulative available for proposed projects**—Add the last two items together to determine what dollars you have available for facility needs.

- **Proposed projects**—Remember that when any space is 90-percent full, you need to have additional new space available. The decision of how much new space to build depends on how many dollars you have available, how much you are willing to borrow, and how long you want the new facilities to last. You will need to do some additional calculations to determine the actual amount of new space needed as follows:

  **Worship space**—Take the amount of new worship space needed and multiply it by 1.4 (this provides the space you will need for an appropriately sized foyer). Then multiply the result times 1.25 (this allows for the space necessary for hall-ways, storage, rest rooms, etc.).

**Education space**—Take the amount of new education space needed and multiply it by 1.3 (this allows for the space nec-essary for hallways, storage, rest rooms, etc.).

**Office space**—Take the amount of new office space needed and multiply it by 1.3 (this allows for the space necessary for hallways, storage, rest rooms, etc.).

- **Proposed project costs**—To determine the projected costs for new construction, use the following estimates, which are averages from across the country. To get more specific num-bers for your geographical area, I would suggest you contact a few commercial contractors and get comparative infor-mation from them. When your project is actually designed, a detailed cost estimate should be provided as part of the architectural services.

  **Worship space, education space, office space**—Multiply the number of square feet needed for new worship space (including foyer, hallways, etc.) by $140 (this includes the actual construction cost plus the cost of architects, con-sultants, etc., plus some protection for cost overruns). You will want to multiply the result of any project costs by the same inflation figures you used before, so your projections will be accurate for future years. If you want to factor in furnishings, you will need to add $15 to $30 per square foot depending on the quality and amount of furnishings desired.

  **Parking space**—Multiply the number of parking spaces you need by $1,100 (assuming you are building normal parking spaces, not a parking garage).

- **Excess money to pay down the mortgage**—If the total pro-jected costs are more than the projected income to be used for building projects, you will have to borrow the needed amount. If the cumulative available for proposed projects is greater than what is needed for any project costs, it is assumed you will use those dollars for increased debt ser-vicing payments, so you can eliminate the mortgage as soon as possible.

By combining the results of your facility scenario with the financial scenario, you can project what needs to be spent and when. By adjusting the numbers you should be able to determine what is the best plan for your church. You may have to delay facility projects because you don't have the necessary resources. Also, be sure to revise your facility and financial scenarios each year to take into account any changes in numbers or assumptions that you want to make.

# Sample Matrix Grid

| Sr. Pastor | | | Executive Pastor Generalist Ministries | | | | | | | | | | | | | |
| --- | --- | --- | --- | --- | --- | --- | --- | --- | --- | --- | --- | --- | --- | --- | --- | --- |
| Administration | Associate Pastors Directors | | Children's Ministries | | | Student Ministries | | | Adult Ministries | | | | Specialized Ministries | | | |
| Associate Pastors | | | Nursery | Pre-school | Grade School | Jr. High | Sr. High | College | | | | | | | | |
| Assimilation | Small Group Ministry | | | | | | | | | | | | | | | |
| | Visitor Follow-up | | | | | | | | | | | | | | | |
| | New Member Classes | | | | | | | | | | | | | | | |
| Discipleship | Christian Education Classes | | | | | | | | | | | | | | | |
| | Spiritual Disciplines | | | | | | | | | | | | | | | |
| | Mentoring | | | | | | | | | | | | | | | |
| Evangelism | Evangelism Training | | | | | | | | | | | | | | | |
| | Evangelistic Events | | | | | | | | | | | | | | | |
| | | | | | | | | | | | | | | | | |
| Missions | Local, National & International Missions | | | | | | | | | | | | | | | |
| | Community Outreach | | | | | | | | | | | | | | | |
| | Church Planting | | | | | | | | | | | | | | | |
| Pastoral Care | Short-term Counseling | | | | | | | | | | | | | | | |
| | Crisis Care | | | | | | | | | | | | | | | |
| | Benevolence | | | | | | | | | | | | | | | |
| Prayer | Corporate Prayer Events | | | | | | | | | | | | | | | |
| | Prayer Team | | | | | | | | | | | | | | | |
| | | | | | | | | | | | | | | | | |
| Training and Equipment | Spiritual Gift Discovery | | | | | | | | | | | | | | | |
| | Volunteer Involvement | | | | | | | | | | | | | | | |
| | Ministry Training | | | | | | | | | | | | | | | |
| Worship | Drama | | | | | | | | | | | | | | | |
| | Music | | | | | | | | | | | | | | | |
| | Celebrative Arts | | | | | | | | | | | | | | | |

# Notes

## Introduction

1. George Barna, *The Barna Report—1992–1993* (Ventura, Calif.: Regal Books), 72.
2. Rick Warren, *The Purpose Driven Church* (Grand Rapids: Zondervan, 1995), 14, 16.
3. Joel A. Barker, *Paradigms: The Business of Discovering the Future* (New York: Harper-Collins, 1992), 37.
4. Alvin J. Lindgren and Norman Shawchuck, *Management for Your Church* (Nashville: Abingdon, 1977), 14.

## Chapter 1—Preparation: the Necessity of Proper Planning

1. Vance Havner, in William Pannell, *Evangelism from the Bottom Up* (Grand Rapids: Zondervan, 1991), 20.
2. John Maxwell, *Failing Forward* (Nashville: Thomas Nelson, 2000), 42.
3. John and Sylvia Ronsvalle, *Behind the Stained Glass Window* (Grand Rapids: Baker, 1996), 298.
4. Michael Slaughter, *Out on the Edge* (Nashville: Abingdon Press, 1998), 35.
5. Peter Drucker, *Managing the Nonprofit Organization* (New York: HarperCollins, 1990), xiv–xv.
6. Ronsvalle, *Behind the Stained Glass Window*, 156.
7. George Barna, *The Second Coming of the Church* (Nashville: Word, 1998), 1.
8. Leonard Sweet, *Faithquakes* (Nashville: Abingdon, 1994), 45.
9. Lenny Bruce, in Os Guinness, *The Call* (Nashville: Word, 1998), 108.
10. Lindgren and Shawchuck, *Management for Your Church*, 45.
11. Henry Mintzberg, *The Rise and Fall of Strategic Planning* (New York: Macmillan, 1994), 114.
12. Barna, *Second Coming*, 95.
13. Marc Spiegler, "Scouting for Souls," *American Demographics*, March 1996, 49.
14. Gary Hamel and C. K. Prahalid, *Competing for the Future* (Boston: Harvard Business School Press, 1994), 308.
15. Dallas Willard, *The Divine Conspiracy* (San Francisco: HarperCollins, 1998), 308.
16. Robert E. Coleman, *The Master Plan of Evangelism* (Old Tappan, N.J.: Fleming H. Revell, 1963), 18.
17. Maxwell, *Failing Forward*, 48.

## Chapter 2—The Playing Field: Challenges Facing the Church

1. Princeton Religious Research Center, *Emerging Trends* 15, no. 6: 4.

2. Princeton Religion Research Center, *Emerging Trends* 15, no. 6: 2.

3. *Newsweek*, 23 June 1997, 23.

4. Guinness, *The Call*, 99.

5. George Gallup Jr., *The Next American Spirituality* (Colorado Springs: Victor, 2000), 143.

6. Sweet, *Faithquakes*, 163.

7. *Newsweek*, 23 June 1997, 23.

8. International Mass Retail Association/Age Wave, quoted in *USA Today*, 22 July 1994.

9. Leith Anderson, *A Church for the 21st Century* (Minneapolis: Bethany, 1992), 41.

10. Wade Clark Roof, *A Generation of Seekers* (San Francisco: HarperCollins, 1993), 54.

11. George Barna, *The Index of Leading Spiritual Indicators* (Dallas: Word, 1993), 54.

12. Barna, *Second Coming*, 4.

13. Ibid., 58.

14. Anderson, *Church for the 21st Century*, 48–49.

15. Roof, *A Generation of Seekers*, 41.

16. Mike Regele, *Death of the Church* (Grand Rapids: Zondervan, 1995), 121.

17. William M. Easum and Thomas G. Bandy, *Growing Spiritual Redwoods* (Nashville: Abingdon, 1997), 179–80.

18. Warren, *Purpose Driven Church*, 241.

19. Anderson, *Church for the 21st Century*, 152.

20. Easum and Bandy, *Growing Spiritual Redwoods*, 187.

21. Sweet, *Faithquakes*, 17–18.

22. Ibid.

23. Peter Wagner, *Churchquake* (Ventura, Calif.: Regal, 1999), 23.

24. Sweet, *Faithquakes*, 104.

25. Ronsvalle, *Behind the Stained Glass Window*, 49.

26. Regele, *Death of the Church*, 221.

27. Slaughter, *Out on the Edge*, 55.

28. Ronsvalle, *Behind the Stained Glass Window*, 29.

29. John and Sylvia Ronsvalle, *The State of Giving through 1995* (Champaign, Ill.: Empty Tomb, 1997), 92.

30. Caryn A. Spain and Ron Wishnoff, *Strategic Insights* (Grants Pass, Ore.: The Oasis, 2000), 5.

31. Easum and Bandy, *Growing Spiritual Redwoods*, 183.

32. George Barna, *Ten Years Later* (Glendale, Calif.: Barna Research Group, 1992), 26.

33. Sweet, *Faithquakes*, 27.

34. Barna, *Leading Spiritual Indicators*, 36.

35. Slaughter, *Out on the Edge*, 45.

36. Sweet, *Faithquakes*, 28.

37. George Gallup Jr., in Barna, *Leading Spiritual Indicators*, 104.

38. Willard, *The Divine Conspiracy*, xiv.

39. George Gallup Jr., *The Next American Spirituality*, 32.

40. Ronsvalle, *Behind the Stained Glass Window*, 75.

41. Regele, *Death of the Church*, 238.

42. Slaughter, *Out on the Edge*, 25.

43. Slaughter, *Out on the Edge*, 107.

44. Bob Buford, *Halftime* (Grand Rapids: Zondervan, 1994), 131.

45. Barna, *Leading Spiritual Indicators*, 58.

46. Clyde Reid, in Willard, *The Divine Conspiracy*, 201.

47. Wagner, *Churchquake*, 12.

## Chapter 3—Team Psychology: Understanding How Organizations Work

1. Noel Tichy and Stratford Sherman, *Control Your Destiny or Someone Else Will* (New York: Doubleday, 1993), 31.

2. James C. Collins and Jerry I. Porras, *Built to Last* (New York: Harper Collins, 1994), 127.

3. Ibid., 71.

4. Anderson, *Church for the 21st Century*, 121.

5. Alvin Toffler, *Future Shock* (New York: Bantam Doubleday Dell, 1971), 1.

6. Noel M. Tichy and Mary Anne Devanna, *The Transformational Leader* (New York: John Wiley and Sons, 1990), 31–32.

7. Maxwell, *Failing Forward*, 2.

8. Donald Miller, in Wagner, *Churchquake*, 18.

9. Tichy and Sherman, *Control Your Destiny*, 85.

10. Wagner, *Churchquake*, 19.

11. George Barna, *Without a Vision the People Perish* (Glendale, Calif.: Barna Research Group, 1991), 138.

12. John Kotter and James L. Heskett, *Corporate Culture and Performance* (New York: Macmillan, 1992), 146.

13. Warren Bennis and Burt Nanus, *Leaders: The Strategies for Taking Charge* (New York: Harper and Row, 1985), 107.

14. Easum and Bandy, *Growing Spiritual Redwoods*, 177.

15. Grace Murray Hopper, in Pat Riley, *Winner Within* (New York: G. P. Putnam's Sons, 1993), 161.

16. Tichy and Sherman, *Control Your Destiny*, 151.

17. Bill Parcells, *Finding a Way to Win* (New York: Doubleday, 1995), 97.

18. Tichy and Sherman, *Control Your Destiny*, 132.

19. Jack Balswick and Walter Wright, "A Complementary-Empowering Model of Ministerial Leadership," *Pastoral Psychology* 37, no. 1 (Fall 1988): 8.

20. Bill Hamon, in Wagner, *Churchquake*, 214.

21. Greg Ogden, in Wagner, *Churchquake*, 214.

22. Bill Walsh, *Building a Champion* (New York: St. Martin's Press, 1990), 60–61.

23. Tichy and Sherman, *Control Your Destiny*, 151.

24. Willard, *The Divine Conspiracy*, 15.

## Chapter 4—The Scouting Report: Discovery Phase

1. Jack Heacock, in Spiegler, "Scouting for Souls," 46.

2. Wagner, *Churchquake*, 93.

## Chapter 5—Team Philosophy (Part 1): The Pre-Visioning Phase

1. Regele, *Death of the Church*, 229.

2. Burt Nanus, *Visionary Leadership* (San Francisco: Jossey-Bass, 1992), xv.

3. Parcells, *Finding a Way to Win*, 12.

4. J. Oswald Sanders, *Spiritual Leadership* (Chicago: Moody Press, 1967), 91.

5. Warren, *The Purpose Driven Church*, 82.

6. Drucker, *Managing the Nonprofit Organization*, 149.

7. Bennis, *On Becoming a Leader*, 178.

8. George Barna, *Without a Vision the People Perish*, 36.

9. Bennis, *On Becoming a Leader*, 111–12.

10. Joe Paterno, in Howard E. Ferguson, *The Edge* (Cleveland: Getting the Edge, 1991), 1–17.

11. Henri Frederic Amiel, in Ferguson, *The Edge*, 1–19.

12. Harry Truman, in Ferguson, *The Edge*, 2–31.

13. Parcells, *Finding a Way to Win*, 84.

14. Sanders, *Spiritual Leadership*, 89.

15. Joe S. Ellis, *The Church on Purpose* (Cincinnati: Standard, 1982), 131.

16. Lyle Schaller, in Wagner, *Churchquake*, 74.

17. F. F. Bruce, *The Spreading Flame* (Grand Rapids: William B. Eerdmans, 1958), 189.

18. Ralph Burnett, "Sold on Risk Taking," *World Traveler*, March 1996, 48.

19. Rick Warren, in Wagner, *Churchquake* , 89–90.

20. Peter Wagner, *Your Church Can Grow* (Glendale, Calif.: Regal, 1976), 61.

21. Barna, *Leading Spiritual Indicators*, 118.

22. Warren, *The Purpose Driven Church*, 31.

23. Carl F. George and Robert E. Logan, *Leading and Managing Your Church* (Old Tappan, N.J.: Fleming H. Revell, 1987), 148.

24. Regele, *Death of the Church*, 222.

25. Nanus, *Visionary Leadership*, 3.

26. Hamel and Prahalid, *Competing for the Future*, x.

27. Larry Wilson, in Bennis, *On Becoming a Leader*, 99.

28. Walt Disney, in Riley, *Winner Within*, 181.

29. Charles Chaney and Ron Lewis, *Design for Church Growth* (Nashville: Broadman, 1977), 78–79.

30. Parcells, *Finding a Way to Win*, 15.

31. Hamel and Prahalid, *Competing for the Future*, 142.

32. Aubrey Malphurs, *Ministry Nuts and Bolts* (Grand Rapids: Kregel, 1997), 42.

33. Collins and Porras, *Built to Last*, 222.

34. Spain and Wishnoff, *Strategic Insights*, 34.

35. Barna, *Ten Years Later*, 92.

## Chapter 6—Team Philosophy (Part 2): The Visioning Phase

1. Ellis, *The Church on Purpose*, 21.

2. Shearson Lehman/American Express, "Vision" *Business Week*, 4 June 1984, 42–43.

3. Jim Dethmer, "How to Communicate Vision" (audio cassette, *Pastor's Update*, Fuller Institute, Pasadena, California, September 1990).

4. Bennis and Nanus, *Leaders*, 89.

5. Barna, *Without a Vision the People Perish*, 28.

6. James M. Kouzes and Barry Z. Posner, *The Leadership Challenge* (San Francisco: Jossey-Bass, 1987), 89.

7. John Kotter, *A Force for Change* (New York: Macmillan, 1990), 36.

8. Malphurs, *Ministry Nuts and Bolts*, 10.

9. Markus Pfieffer (seminar, *Christian International Business Network*, Santa Rosa Beach, Fla., 1997).

10. Gary Hamel and C. K. Prahilid, "Competing for the Future," *Hemispheres*, October, 1994, 40.

11. Quoted in *Ministry Advantage* 5, no. 6 (July/Aug. 1994): 3.

12. Kouzes and Posner, *The Leadership Challenge*, 86–87.

13. Malphurs, *Ministry Nuts and Bolts*, 116.

14. Hamel and Prahalid, "Competing for the Future," 109.

15. Norman Lear, in Bennis, *On Becoming a Leader*, 35–36.

16. Søren Kierkegaard, in Guinness, *The Call*, 3.

17. Guinness, *The Call*, 46.

18. Wagner, *Churchquake*, 194.

19. Spain and Wishnoff, *Strategic Insights*, 35.

20. This list was provided courtesy of Bethlehem Baptist Church, Minneapolis.

21. Parcells, *Finding a Way to Win*, 12.

22. Barna, *Without a Vision the People Perish*, 138.

23. Bennis and Nanus, *Leaders*, 223–24.

24. Collins and Porras, *Built to Last*, 33.

25. Barna, *Without a Vision the People Perish*, 50.

26. Kouzes and Posner, 1987, 113.

27. Jim Dethmer, *Ministry Advantage* 5, No. 6 (July/Aug. 1994): 4.

28. Bennis, *On Becoming a Leader*, 146.

29. Norman Lear, in Bennis, *On Becoming a Leader*, 148–49.

30. Malcom Muggeridge, in Guinness, *The Call*, 186.

31. The character of Jean Valjean in Victor Hugo, *Les Misérables*, in Maxwell, *Failing Forward*, 92.

## Chapter 7—Developing a Game Plan (Part 1): Ministry Planning

1. Lew Richfield, in Riley, *Winner Within*, 211.

2. Spain and Wishnoff, *Strategic Insights*, 48.

3. Collins and Porras, *Built to Last*, 89.

4. Drucker, *Managing the Nonprofit Organization*, 117.

5. Barna, *Ten Years Later*, 141.

6. Collins and Porras, *Built to Last*, 188.

7. Hamel and Prahalid, "Competing for the Future," 152.

8. Tom Landry, in *The Edge*, 3–13.

## Chapter 8—Developing a Game Plan (Part 2): Facility and Financial Planning

1. Peter Wagner, *Your Church Can be Healthy* (Nashville: Abingdon, 1979), 88–89.

## Chapter 9—Developing a Game Plan (Part 3): Organizational Planning

1. Barna, *Ten Years Later*, 97–98.

2. Lyle Schaller, *The New Reformation* (Nashville: Abingdon Press, 1996), 84.

3. Schaller, *The New Reformation*, 87.

4. Tri Robinson, *Matrix Manual: Building Teamwork in the Vineyard* (Boise, Idaho: Vineyard Christian Fellowship, 1995).

5. Easum and Bandy, *Growing Spiritual Redwoods*, 110.

6. Warren, *The Purpose Driven Church*, 376.

7. Schaller, *The New Reformation*, 86–87.

## Chapter 10—Developing a Game Plan (Part 4): The Resourcing Phase

1. Ron Blue, *Master Your Money* (Nashville: Thomas Nelson, 1991), 23.

2. George Barna, *Raising Money for Your Church* (Glendale, Calif.: Barna Research Group, 1994), 80.

3. Justo L. Gonzalez, *Faith and Wealth: A History of Early Christian Ideas on the Origin, Significance and Use of Money* (San Francisco: Harper and Row, 1990), 230.

4. Slaughter, *Out on the Edge*, 107.

5. Wagner, *Your Church Can Grow*, 131.

6. Drucker, *Managing the Nonprofit Organization*, 149.

7. Max DePree in Drucker, *Managing the Nonprofit Organization*, 41.

8. Drucker, *Managing the Nonprofit Organization*, xvii.

9. Ibid., 66.

10. George Barna, *The Heart of the Donor* (Glendale, Calif.: Barna Research Group, 1995), 1.

11. Barna, *Raising Money for Your Church*, 51.

## Chapter 11—Playing the Game: the Implementation Phase

1. Collins and Porras, *Built to Last*, 148.

---

**Henry Klopp** is president of the International Graduate School of Ministry (www.igsmin.com), a training institute for church leaders. He holds a Doctor of Ministry degree in the field of church growth and has done graduate work at both Fuller Theological Seminary and the California Graduate School of Theology. Klopp speaks at conferences across the country and resides in Bellevue, Washington. He can be reached by email at <hklopp@igsmin.com>.